Fitz William Thomas Pollok

Fifty Years' Reminiscences of India

a retrospect of travel, adventure and shikar

Fitz William Thomas Pollok

Fifty Years' Reminiscences of India
a retrospect of travel, adventure and shikar

ISBN/EAN: 9783337078621

Printed in Europe, USA, Canada, Australia, Japan

Cover: Foto ©Andreas Hilbeck / pixelio.de

More available books at **www.hansebooks.com**

FIFTY YEARS' REMINISCENCES OF INDIA

A Retrospect of Travel, Adventure and Shikar

BY

COLONEL POLLOK
Madras Staff Corps
AUTHOR OF 'SPORT IN BURMAH,' ETC.

ILLUSTRATED

EDWARD ARNOLD
Publisher to the India Office

LONDON
37 BEDFORD STREET

NEW YORK
70 FIFTH AVENUE

1896

PREFACE.

The only apology the author has to offer for the publication of these reminiscences is the hope of amusing and instructing those who may be thinking of taking to sport in earnest.

The love of hunting is stronger in Englishmen than in any other nation in the world, our cousins in America perhaps excepted. Our large possessions give us opportunities which are denied to other people, and, as Thackeray wrote, 'The jungle is the battle-field of play-hours; it leads straight to the Red Ribbon and the Victoria Cross. Subject your young hopeful to the discipline of the saddle; put him on pony-back almost as soon as he can walk; do not check the instinctive longings of boyhood after the workmanship of Purdey and Manton. For a soldier there is rough work before him, for which he will need a true eye and a steady hand—a strong nerve not to be acquired in the schoolroom and the cramming-shop. Do not fret yourselves if you find that he takes more kindly to the stable and the rabbit-warren than to Euclid and Eutropius. When the struggle comes, as come some day it will, for dear life, what will avail him that he can demonstrate the Pons Asinorum or recount the labours of Hercules? But that true eye, that steady hand, that firm seat in the saddle, with all the cool courage of the hunting-field, these are the aids which will find him out in the hour of trial, and help him to the front in the grand Indian career.'

The above was written of James Outram, the Bayard of India, than whom there was not a more accomplished shikarie, sportsman, and legislator to be found in our annals, rich as they are with the names of distinguished men. The author, when he went out to India, had the privilege of coming across such good sportsmen as Shakespear, Nightingale, the Orrs, and many others, and has recorded some of his reminiscences connected with them, and of sport in various parts of the world, in which either he or those well known to him had a part.

CONTENTS.

CHAPTER I.

EARLY RECOLLECTIONS.

Scottish descent—My great-grandfather—Settles in Wiltshire—My grandfather is disinherited, and enters the service of the East India Company—My father embarks in the *Kent*, which is burnt in the Bay of Biscay—He is again wrecked, and finally, after two years, reaches India—Is appointed to an irregular regiment in the Nizam's contingent—My childhood and early recollections—My initiation in wild sports—Love of the sepoys of that day for their officers—What led to the Mutiny of 1857—The old officers compared with the new—Dangers of travelling in India from 1830 to 1840—Our detachment attacked by Rohillas—At attempt at dacoity—Result of kicking over an idol—A tiger chase in the Caves of Ellora—A happy childhood—Death of our parents—Sent to Madras to embark for England—Consigned to an officer of the Veteran Battalion—Our treatment by him—Our voyage home—Cape girls—Cape horses—Arrive in England—Am sent to school—A mean guardian—School life—A Chinese school-mate—Get a nomination for Woolwich—Our crammer—The two Gordons, Chinese and Adam Lindsay—Lose my nomination for Woolwich—Am offered appointments to Sandhurst and Addiscombe—Choose the latter—Death of my grandfather—Get a direct cadetship—Embark for India -   -   -   -   1—24

CHAPTER II.

CADET DAYS.

Sail from Southampton—Egypt and the desert—Disastrous news from India—Aden—Adventures on shore—The prettiest girl on board—Her sad fate—Madras—Our messmates—Horses purchased—The Veteran officer attempts extortion—Sad accident—Two of us tried for our lives and acquitted—My first experience of Bangalore—A runaway horse and a smash—A swearing General—Permanently posted—Ordered to Secunderabad—Generous behaviour of our brother officers—Our Commandant—Hospitably entertained at Kurnool—An eccentric officer and his pranks—Secunderabad—A boyish-looking Adjutant - 25—42

CHAPTER III.

SECUNDERABAD.

Secunderabad in 1849—Nightingale—'Master not fight fair'—An obstreperous Captain—How to manage natives—Sad death of an Adjutant—Mole Alley races—Amusements—Gambling—Regiment ordered to Samulcottah—My stud—Am appointed to the sappers and miners—Difficulty of getting to Burma—Rangoon—Employed on field-service—Miraculous escape of two drunken gunners - 43—62

CHAPTER IV.

BURMA FORTY YEARS AGO.

Rangoon in 1853—Voyage up the Irrawadie—Prome—Famine—Sad sights—Death of Maddigan and Latter—Cruelty of Burmese—Construct a stockade—Officers, gallant and otherwise—Carpet knights on service—Burmese tactics—Ramghur Irregular Cavalry—Dacoits—A girl outraged and murdered—Lord Dalhousie—Gallantry of Engineer officers—Loot—Bengal troops compared with those of Madras—Red-tape in Madras—The Sappers—Am transferred to the Engineer department—A boxing-match—A British soldier hanged—Attempts to proselytize sepoys—Injudicious officers - 63—91

CHAPTER V.

BURMESE LIFE.

Failure of missionaries among the Burmese—Their success among the Karens—Matrimony in Burma—Relation of the sexes—Origin of the Burmese—Their freedom from caste—Their manners, customs, and characteristics—A romp in the river—Burmese fondness for children—Their courtship—Their priests—Roman Catholic nuns—The Buddhist religion—Karens—Burmese theatricals and dancing girls—The Assamese—Half-breeds—The Kachens—Fires in Burma—An affray—A soldier punished for doing his duty—Sir A. Phayre—'Dismal Jemmy'—His treatment of me—A gallant Brigadier—One of another kind—Anecdotes—How the two Brigadiers left Tongo—Our chief engineer—Roguery of subordinates—Public works—Abandonment of Namyan—Sir Trevor Wheler astonishes a Burman—Gallantry of 'the Sweep'—A mad doctor - - 92—125

CHAPTER VI.

PIG-STICKING.

The first sport in the world—My first hunt—Hunting over an enclosed country—Extraordinary speed and endurance of wild-boar—How to ride a pig—Chased—A fall—Thirty-five minutes from start to finish—Another chase—Struggle for first spear—Not always to the fastest—A fighting boar—Narrow escape of a horse—Particulars of my first hunt—My comrade falls into a *dul-dul*—Kill the boar—A hunt near Guntoor—A good thrust—How to meet a charging boar—Spearing under difficulties—A horse killed - 126—141

CHAPTER VII.

ELEPHANTS.

Two varieties of Indian elephants—How to kill them—Game in the Prome district—Purchase of two rifles—Burmese shikaries—Their dislike of Europeans—Mosquitoes—How to circumvent them—My first elephant hunt—Tree-leeches

—Native cookery dying out—Bag my first elephant—A sad disappointment—D'Oyly and Moung Goung Gye's state elephant—Gallantry of a young sowar—Habits of elephants—Anecdotes—Elephants do not breed in captivity—Difficulty of finding a good shikar elephant—Mahouts—Their duties—Death of Wedderburn—Necessity of elephants for shooting tigers—Their furniture—Battery for sport—How to manage elephants—A pitched battle   142—182

CHAPTER VIII.

BUFFALOES.

Wild buffaloes more dangerous than tigers—Very difficult to kill—Plentiful in Burma and Assam—How wild bulls appropriate herds—D'Oyly and his pony tossed—Archie Campbell's elephant overthrown—His critical position—I am called to his rescue—A savage encounter—A runaway elephant—Meet a tiger—Encounter with a bull which fights desperately—A pugnacious herd—Charged by a couple of bulls   -   -   -   -   -   183—192

CHAPTER IX.

INDIAN RHINOCEROS.

Erroneous ideas as to the impenetrability of a rhinoceros' hide—Generally harmless, but dangerous when wounded—Herd with elephant and buffalo—Meet them first in Burma, then in Assam—Elephants indispensable—Difficulty of obtaining them—My first Indian rhinoceros—Make a sad mess of others—Rhinoceros-shooting in cold weather—Size of horns—Their value—A savage charge—Just in time—Charged by two rhinoceroses-   -   193—199

CHAPTER X.

SPORT IN THE NORTHERN DISTRICTS, MADRAS PRESIDENCY.

Discovery of the Bison Hill—The islands of the Godavery—Abundance of feathered game—Linga Reddie, the freebooter—A stiff climb—Lovely scenery—Abundance of game—Dreary life at a single station—Tatapoodi—Cossipooram—Ascend the ghauts—Change of flora and climate—Galicondah—Heavy rain—Go after gaur—Go to a distant jungle—Disgraceful shooting—Indian and Burmese gaur compared—Kill a tiger - - - - 200—217

CHAPTER XI.

SPORT IN THE HILLY DISTRICTS, NORTHERN CIRCAS, MADRAS PRESIDENCY.

Start for Daraconda—Brinjarie hunters—Salt-licks—Scene at daylight—Variety and abundance of game—Bear-shooting—A hunting chita—Porcupines—Firing the grass—On the table-land—Tigers, bears, and deer—Buffaloes and swamp deer—Four tigers—A mixed bag on Christmas Day—Camp in the forest—Twenty-one days' sport—Return to the coast - - - - - - 218—247

CHAPTER XII.

MAN-EATERS AND BUFFALOES.

Go to Bustar—How to live well in the jungles—Bengal humps—My shikaries—Toddy—Escape of the man-eater—Nine people killed—Move camp—Sand-grouse—Miseries of night-watching—Shoot a tiger—Another beat—A woman killed—The man-eater killed by buffaloes—Spotted deer—A panther—Bears—Fail to bag one out of eight—Jungle fowl—Dummape—Abandon carts—Share ponies—A hunt with dogs described—A tigress—Teak forests—Mahseer-fishing in the Godavery—Sironcha—Large game in Bustar—Vicious charge of buffaloes—Shots at a sambur and tiger—Encounter between buffalo and tiger—Salt-licks—A mad gaur converted into beef—Send for camp—Two bears with sore heads—Brinjari dogs—Four-horned antelope—Camp at last—Cause of delay—A bullock killed—I am tossed—Carried to the coast - - - - 248—303

CHAPTER XIII.

ADVICE TO SPORTSMEN GOING ABROAD.

Advantages of medical knowledge—Native idea of Europeans—Precautions against the sun—What to wear—Underclothes—Clothes—Boots—Socks, etc.—Shoes for stalking—Waterproofs—Sleeping on the ground—Fever—Trestle-cots—Mosquito-curtains—A list of articles to take—Tents—Natives—Men and women—Tree-leeches—What to wear to keep them out—Buying a gun—Selling it again—Gunpowder—To harden bullets—Best bullets for different game—What size shot to choose—How to keep your health—Total abstinence—Stimulants—Night-shooting—How to make the foresight visible—How to obtain fire—How to make soap—Sanitary precautions and cleanliness - 304—320

APPENDIX.

SIMPLE RECIPES FOR USE IN TRAVELLING - - 321—341

FIFTY YEARS' REMINISCENCES OF INDIA

CHAPTER I.

EARLY RECOLLECTIONS.

Scottish descent—My great-grandfather—Settles in Wiltshire—My grandfather is disinherited, and enters the service of the East India Company—My father embarks in the *Kent*, which is burnt in the Bay of Biscay—He is again wrecked, and finally, after two years, reaches India—Is appointed to an irregular regiment in the Nizam's contingent—My childhood and early recollections—My initiation in wild sports—Love of the sepoys of that day for their officers—What led to the Mutiny of 1857—The old officers compared with the new—Dangers of travelling in India from 1830 to 1840—Our detachment attacked by Rohillas—An attempt at dacoity—Result of kicking over an idol—A tiger chase in the Caves of Ellora—A happy childhood—Death of our parents—Sent to Madras to embark for England—Consigned to an officer of the Veteran Battalion—Our treatment by him—Our voyage home—Cape girls—Cape horses—Arrive in England—Am sent to school—A mean guardian—School life—A Chinese school-mate—Get a nomination for Woolwich—Our crammer—The two Gordons, Chinese and Adam Lindsay—Lose my nomination for Woolwich—Am offered appointments to Sandhurst and Addiscombe—Choose the latter—Death of my grandfather—Get a direct cadetship—Embark for India.

My great-grandfather was the scion of an old Scottish family, an ancestor having been created a Baronet in

1634. He settled in England about 1760, and married the daughter and sole heiress of the then Postmaster-General, purchased a living in Wiltshire, and resided at a place called Girdlestone Hall. He had a family of two sons and seven daughters. The eldest lad entered as a cornet in the Scots Greys, rose to be a Major in that distinguished corps, and died unmarried of wounds received at the Battle of Waterloo.

The second son, Tom, was educated at Winchester and Oxford, and it was intended that he should take Holy Orders, and succeed his father in the living, which was worth some £1,500 a year; but prior to ordination, as was the custom in those days, he made the Grand Tour, resided for two years in Germany, learned several languages, became a proficient in music, and imbibed latitudinarian ideas; on returning home he refused to enter the Church, left his home disinherited, after a stormy interview with his father, and never saw him again.

He was just twenty-two, stood six feet in his socks, had received a first-rate education, and was well connected, so when he presented himself before the Chairman of the Court of Directors of the Honourable the East India Company, and offered himself as a volunteer for service in India, he was at once accepted, and joined the Cadets' Company in Madras in 1790. He saw much active service in those troublesome times, was at the taking of Seringapatam, served under Wellington at Assaye, accompanied the gallant Gillespie to the relief of Vellore, and had risen to the rank of a field-officer when the officers' mutiny broke out. His superior education (for officers in the East in those days were not noted for their attainments) and commanding position led to his being one of the ringleaders, and one day he and some dozen other officers were summarily dismissed the service. They appealed to Parliament, and after three years' struggle he and several others were reinstated.

In the Mahratta and Pindarie war of 1816-18, he commanded a brigade under his old friend Doveton, and he, his leader and a few other officers were created C.B.'s in 1823, being among the first of the Company's officers to receive a decoration from their Sovereign.

He married a lady who was related to our great national hero, Lord Nelson, and by her he had two sons and one daughter. The elder son died of cholera soon after joining his regiment in India. My father, the second son, held for a short while a commission in the Austrian Army, but at his father's urgent request he resigned it for a cadetship in the East.

He embarked in the East Indiaman *Kent*, which was burned in the Bay of Biscay. The directors gave him a fresh outfit and a free passage in one of their vessels, but ill-luck again attended him, as the day before the fleet was to sail a terrific storm wrecked nearly every vessel in Plymouth Sound, and the cadet lost again everything but his life. His masters again provided him with a new kit, and this time, there being luck in odd numbers, he arrived in Madras in the *Undaunted*, Captain Coffin commander, in 1827, just two years after his first attempt to leave old England.

Through the interest of my grandfather, who was then commanding the Hyderabad Subsidiary Force, my father, after passing in the native languages, which he had never quite forgotten, was appointed Adjutant of an irregular corps. He married early, and of his three children I am the only son and second child. How distinctly I remember my childhood! Pay was good and living cheap in those days; my father had also inherited some considerable property from one of his aunts. His only sister had married the leading merchant in Madeira, and used to send him out a butt or two of madeira and malmsey wines every year, and he and his brother officers kept open house and lived luxuriously.

We had a large retinue of servants, a couple of elephants, a dozen or more horses, ponies, dogs, hunting chitas, etc. In the days I am writing of I may say that every officer in the Nizam's service was a sportsman. The country swarmed with game. Hog-hunting and tiger-shooting parties were of frequent occurrence. We often accompanied our father into camp; I had seen many a tiger bowled over, and seven or eight boars laid out in a row before the mess tent, before I was six years of age.

I lived in the open air, and there was not a *tat*, vicious or otherwise (and most of these Mahratta ponies had tempers of their own), that I could not ride. I was allowed to enter into all the sports and games with the lads belonging to the regiment. India, in the days I allude to, was a very different place to what it is at present. There was more *camaraderie* between the European officers and their men. The native officers and sepoys loved their commanders, and it was not thought *infra dig.* for the English lads to compete with the sons of the commissioned, non-commissioned officers, and privates belonging to the native regiment. The Europeans and natives also met in friendly rivalry in tent-pegging and other games requiring skill, a correct eye, and considerable strength. There was not a man in the corps who would not have laid down his life for his sahib or any of his family. Alas, what a difference twenty years made! Very many of the descendants of those faithful men lost confidence in their British officers, joined the mutineers of 1857, and helped to kill the very men, women, and children their fathers would have died to save!

When India was closed to all Europeans save the servants of the Company or those holding permits, the natives believed in us. But when the country was gradually thrown open, and the stringent and wholesome orders of the Company were relaxed, loafers, demagogues and missionaries flocked into India, and the natives, coming into contact with an altogether different class to what they had been accustomed to, began to lose faith in us, until distrust culminated in the terrible events of 1857-58.

Our old masters used their patronage judiciously. The greater part of the civilians and cadets were the sons or near relations of either themselves or of those who had served in their employ in Hindoostan. Thus, the history of nearly all who went to the East was known, not only to their brother officers and civilians, but also to the natives, and all old names were welcomed. Since the Company ceased to exist the changes have not been for the better. Anyone can now enter the Indian service, provided his people can afford to have him crammed to pass the competitive examinations. More than half the men who thus get employment are not what they ought to be. Book-learning by rote does not turn out efficient officers.

Whilst of the men who formerly entered the service, either through Addiscombe or by direct commissions, very many rose to eminence, such, for instance, as Malcolm, the Lawrences, Edwardes, Broadfoots, Nicholson, Neil, and many others too numerous to name, who has come to the front under the new regulations? Men have doubtless done their duty, but none have distinguished themselves like the despised nominees of the old John Company. Moreover, it is a mistake admitting men into the service in India whose parents have not occupied any social position. I don't mean to say that, because a man is the son of people in trade, he is therefore an inefficient officer, but send as few of this class as possible to India; the natives are great judges of what constitutes a gentleman, and if they perceive that a man appointed to command them comes short of what they have been accustomed to, they will not hold him in the same respect as they did those of the old régime.

India should be ruled by a department independent of Parliamentary control, and the appointments should be given principally to the sons and relations of those who have served, and perhaps died, in that country, provided, of course, that the applicants have been properly educated and are physically fit.

Although slavery had been abolished in our territories, it still existed in my childhood in the independent native States, and our ayahs and most of the domestics were all slaves, though not treated as such, and there was not one, from the highest to the lowest, who was not proud to belong to a sahib's household.

The country was then and for many years afterwards in a very disturbed state; gangs of Rohillas and Arabs, Dacoits and Thugs, wandered over central India, where, sheltered by the interminable forests, they bided their time, sallying forth now and then to pounce down, not only on travellers, but even on small detachments of soldiers.

I remember once our camp was pitched in a tope of trees. Our detachment consisted of a company of infantry and a troop of cavalry, escorting treasure, and we were something like halfway between Hingolie and Jaulnah. An hour or two before daybreak a band of Rohillas fell upon us. The ropes were cut, and the tents fell upon their inmates. Dire was the confusion. We were asleep in palanquins, ready for a start at daylight, and were awakened by the frightful yells and screams of the combatants, and more than half smothered by the fallen canvas. When Greek meets Greek, then comes the tug of war! Our cavalry consisted then, as it does even now, of a large admixture of Pathans, Rohillas and Arabs, closely allied in blood to our assailants. The infantry consisted principally of sturdy Mahrattas. The first surprise over, our men rallied; a stubborn fight took place, and discipline told. After considerable slaughter on both sides the marauders were driven off and the treasure saved. In the melée my father received a severe sabre-cut across the forehead, the mark of which he carried to the grave.

A year or so afterwards our regiment was quartered at Aurungabad, a large struggling cantonment. Our bungalow was on the very outskirts. It had an upper story, very unusual at any time in Indian houses in the Mofussil, and quite unique in those days. Our compound was an extensive one, surrounded by a mud wall some four feet high. A spy brought intelligence to our Commandant that our house, containing as it did the regimental treasure-chest, would be attacked on a certain night, after the receipt of pay, by a band of robbers. Our usual guard consisted of a naigue and three sepoys. We were quietly reinforced after dark by some of the irregular cavalry, who were hidden away in the outhouses.

About two in the morning the Dacoits, some fifteen in number, well mounted and well armed, came on the scene. Some dismounted to force an entrance, when the gates were thrown open, and my father and his men fell upon them. The thieves were taken by surprise, and at first ran for their lives, but on being overtaken turned to bay. The moon was at its full; we children hurried into the veranda of the upper story and watched the struggle. It did not last long. Eight of the robbers were killed, and the remainder captured. On our side we had two killed and three wounded.

So in my very young days I had not only seen much sport, but had witnessed two free fights. Whilst at Jaulnah a picnic was got up, and a large party of ladies and gentlemen visited some native temples.

My father very thoughtlessly and very foolishly spurned an out-lying idol with his foot, and upset it. The priest looked daggers, but said nothing. Those present chid my father for committing such a reprehensible act, and bid him beware of the vengeance of the priests, who, they said, would probably do something in retaliation. The culprit was very sorry for what he had done, picked up the idol, replaced it, and expressed his great regret to the priest for his thoughtless act, and thought no more of it, never thinking for a moment that the mild Hindoo would do anything in revenge. But he was mistaken, for within a few days three of our best horses died, and several others were very ill. Leaves of the *Nux vomica* were found in their fodder, placed there doubtless by the agency or instigation of the priest, or some of his followers.

On another occasion we were visiting the famous caves of Ellora. My sister and I, with our attendants, somehow got separated from the rest of our party, in some of the many intricate passages which intersect these wonderful subterranean shrines, which, excavated out of solid rock, are sacred to the Hindoo deities. Our torch-bearer suddenly threw down his flambeau and fled, crying 'Bagh, Bagh!' (Tiger!). We and our two ayahs, both young girls, ran hither and thither for our lives, not knowing which way to turn, and expecting every moment to have the brute pounce upon us. Our cries attracted the attention of the remainder of our party, who were not far off, and who hurried to our assistance. We were sent back to camp, rifles and guns were procured, a novel tiger-chase by torchlight took place, and although the beast's pugs were visible here and there, the passages were so numerous and intricate that the animal escaped.

On our birthdays we were decorated by the natives with wreaths of jasmine and other flowers. The amount of cakes and sweetmeats given us would have stocked a pastrycook's shop; if we had eaten a tenth part of the good things thus lavished upon us we should have been no doubt seriously ill, so all the elephants belonging to the officers and regiment were collected and regaled on the surplus of our goodies. At other times the chitas would be taken out after antelope, but even as a child I thought it rather a tame sport.

Our childhood was a happy one, but we were early deprived of our parents. In 1838 our father, whilst hog-hunting—a sport in which he excelled, and to which he was devotedly attached—lost his helmet, but continued the chase bareheaded. It was a frightfully hot day. He killed his boar, but received a sunstroke, and was found lying on the plain insensible by a brother officer, who had been following a pig in another direction. He was taken home in a dhooly, but never recovered consciousness, and died during the night.

The events that followed are as vivid as if they had occurred but yesterday. The room in which our father's remains lay was thronged by sepoys crying and lamenting the death of one who had endeared himself to them by many acts of kindness, and he was followed to the grave by not only every European, but by every native in the place.

Misfortunes never come singly. To add to our misery, our mother followed her husband to the grave very shortly, and we were left orphans indeed, and at that time we had not a single relation in the country.

A brother officer, Captain J., took charge of us, and, indeed, was as good as a second father to us. Telegraphs and steamers were unknown then. Communications were few and far between England and her great dependency, and it was nearly a year before a reply came as to our disposal.

We were five or six hundred miles from Madras, and had to get there the best way we could. I need not describe how sorrowful we were when we left our kind friends, especially Captain J., and the rank and file of our regiment.

We were sent in charge of a pensioned havildar, who had been our grandfather's orderly during the Mahratta war, and three ayahs and two girls who were but little older than ourselves, and had been playmates since we could remember. We travelled in native carts fitted up for our accommodation. It took us some three months to reach our destination. On the way we put up in dâk bungalows, where such existed, otherwise in choultries, built more for the use of native travellers than for Europeans; but go wherever we might, our name was well known, and we met with the greatest kindness, especially from the pensioned sepoys in charge of the bungalows, and from natives of all creeds and conditions.

We were consigned to the care of an officer of the Veteran Battalion, to whom considerable sums had been remitted on our behalf. In his younger days he had received much kindness from our grandparents, and he had been at one time a most promising officer, but whilst on furlough he had contracted a most unfortunate marriage with the daughter of a lodging-house-keeper.

Hitherto we had met with nothing but kindness from friends and strangers alike, but we now learned what unkindness and neglect could be meted out to us by those who ought to have been the most friendly, as they had been most liberally paid to look after us. We were put into a dilapidated bungalow, little better than a *godown*. We were all but half starved; indeed, had it not been for the kindness of a few Europeans and many natives—many of the latter very poor themselves—who, hearing of our treatment from our attendants, gave food and even money to our ayahs for our use, we should have been in a sad plight.

Vessels left India at fixed dates and at long intervals, and generally formed a convoy. I do not remember how long we were in Madras; it seemed to us an age. But for the parting with our two sable attendants, I think we would have welcomed even death itself.

Our grandmother, who had made all the arrangements, had directed that a stern cabin of an East Indiaman should be secured for us, and that two of our ayahs should accompany us home; but at the last moment the wretched Veteran and his wife pocketed the passage-money for one of the natives, sending only one on board to look after three children, the youngest only two years of age, pretending that the other had run away at the last moment, thus leaving us in a great measure to the tender mercies of perfect strangers.

A day before we sailed a young and attractive widow, who had lost her husband but a few days before of cholera, appeared on the scene, and we were placed nominally under her charge. When she came on board she was apparently heart-broken, but before she had been a fortnight at sea her grief had evaporated; she became the gayest of the gay, and flirted with the male passengers in a manner that drew unfavourable comment from the other lady passengers. Before the month the widow turned us out of our cabin, appropriating it for herself, while we were bundled into a miserable side-cabin. The stewardess was a kind-hearted soul, and did all she could to help our ayah to make us comfortable and happy. A clergyman on board took charge of the boy passengers, of whom there were several beside myself, and taught us to read and write. We touched at the Cape, and a resident, who had known our people when they spent a couple of years there on furlough, took us on shore and bought us a lot of toys and playthings.

In the early part of this century, the Court of Directors discouraged their officers from taking furlough to England, but allowed them instead two years' leave either to the Cape or to its east, on full pay and allowances, of which indulgence very many officers availed themselves. Those were the halcyon days of the Cape. The officers spent their money freely; many brought back, as wives, pretty Cape girls who were half English and half Dutch. These girls were a decided acquisition to Indian society, for they were not only young and pretty, but most of them could ride like Centaurs, dance and flirt; they were not so strait-laced, but quite as virtuous as their English cousins. Great attention was paid to horse-breeding at the Cape, and the nags were in great demand in India for hunting, and as remounts and chargers. Australian horses were all but unknown in those days. Few Indian officers go to the Cape now; the Cape horse is all but unknown in the Presidencies. More's the pity, for its substitute, the waler, is but a poor beast compared to the other.

A few days after leaving the Cape, a storm scattered the fleet; several vessels sank; we escaped with the loss of various spars and sails. After a voyage of little more than three months, considered very speedy then, we arrived at Plymouth, and were met by our dear old grandmother. A kindlier and nobler soul never breathed. We journeyed with her by coach to London, and until her death we lived within sight of Lord's cricket-ground. The locality was then almost in the country, and not surrounded, as it is now, by streets. Our grandfather was abroad, and beleaguered, I believe, in Antwerp during the siege of that town, and we did not see him for two years. His wife died in December, 1842, and we children were at once sent off to school. By that time I had forgotten the native dialects, and, strange to say, when I returned to India they never became as familiar to me as they had been in my childhood.

Our grandfather was seldom in England, and as we inherited some property under the will of our grandmother, she appointed three guardians to look after our interests. One was a cousin, Mr. A.; another, Sir George S., Governor of Sandhurst, an old Peninsular and Waterloo veteran; and the third General B., a retired Indian officer.

Our guardians left Mr. A. to look after us. He was very well off, but very close-fisted. Money was his god. He certainly took care of our money, but never spent a farthing of his own on us, although he owed his success in life entirely to his aunt, our grandmother. When he resigned his trust, years afterwards, I was greatly amused by coming across such items as the following: 'Gave W. half a crown pocket-money;' 'Paid sixpence for a chop for W.,' etc., and he actually charged us for board and lodgings the few times he ever asked us to his house! His wealth did him little good; he quarrelled with his only son, as fine a fellow as ever lived, and I believe I might have had the greater part of his money, had I fallen in with his views and married a girl I had never seen. But I was an independent fool in those days; I wrote back that he ought to leave his money to his son, and not dower a girl in no way connected with him. This gave him dire offence. When he died, he left his son only £2,000, to us not a penny, and the rest of his large fortune he left to strangers who had toadied to him in his old age.

Sir George S. came to see us now and then, and tipped us freely, and when he died left us legacies, in return, as he said, for kindnesses shown to him in his youth by my people.

Of General B. I remember very little. We saw him occasionally, but that was all.

On a cold raw day in January, 1843, I was taken to Hanwell, and deposited at Dr. Emerton's collegiate school. It was during the vacation, but I found myself one of six youths who, having no parents in England, had to reside at school all the year round. What this means only the initiated can tell; can there be a greater cruelty than leaving a boy at school when all his mates are going to kind homes and friends and relations? But I must say that at Hanwell we were treated more as members of the family than as pupils; it was the nearest approach to home, though not a home. At that time Dr. Emerton's eldest sister superintended her brother's house; he was then a widower with three little girls. He married soon afterwards a lady related to a distinguished officer, still living and occupying a very high position.

The academy consisted of a junior and senior department; the former was presided over by Miss Emerton and Mr. Burton. I entered in the lower form, but soon passed into the senior. The house was very large; it had been built expressly for academic purposes, and stood in its own most extensive grounds. We had a gravelled yard for use in winter; a large covered-in shed for play during inclement weather; we had extensive fields for cricket and football, and the meadows were bounded by a rivulet, in which during the summer months we were allowed to bathe. We were taught fencing, boxing and single-stick. We had also the finest gymnasium I have ever seen, and one of Angelo's assistants came every Saturday to drill and instruct us in all manly exercises. Our food was ample and good. The principal, his sister and the masters, sat down at the same tables, and partook of the same food as was served out to us. We were instructed in Latin, Greek, French and German, drawing, mathematics, history, geography and chemistry; a wholesome spirit of emulation was kept up amongst the scholars by pitting the two ablest in a class, and by giving numerous prizes half-yearly to those who proved themselves the most proficient in the different subjects taught. There was no cramming; the education imparted was thorough. We were well grounded in everything. I had a good memory, could learn rapidly, and remember afterwards. I was generally first in history and geography, forward in mathematics, but failed in all languages; but as I was never ill and most of my class-mates suffered one quarter, to my own amazement I figured first in Latin, French and Greek, whereas my knowledge in those subjects was inferior to that of many other boys. I had been first in Divinity, and, never doubting the result, one term examination I sat between two lads and helped them both considerably. When the prize was called out, I was getting up to receive it, when I heard the names of the boys I had assisted called out as first and second, whilst I was only third! After that I took good care to keep my knowledge to myself.

We had to pay a medical fee of a guinea a quarter whether well or ill, and as I invariably enjoyed robust health, I did not see why I should not get something out of the medico in return. So periodically I presented myself for vaccination, though lymph in those days was somewhat expensive, and after this operation we were excused lessons for some days. As a child I had had small-pox severely, but not a single mark was visible. The doctor was ignorant of this, of course, and wondered why the vaccination had no effect on me; I took good care not to enlighten him till I was leaving, when I told him. He was very angry, and used bad language. I was and am fond of reading, and used to read up history, etc., of an evening; but if wet during our play-hours I used to practise single-stick, fencing, and boxing, and I may say that in the first no one in the school could touch me. When fine I was always running, jumping, or at gymnastics; there was no boy anywhere near my age who had a chance with me in running from a hundred yards to three miles. I never lost but one race, and that to a boy I had often beaten, but I was suffering from chilblains at the time of my defeat, and held my adversary too cheap. During the holidays we were allowed considerable liberty; we used to play at hare-and-hounds, and I have often run from morn till dusk with but a short rest during the heat of the day. I fancy the out-door life I had led in India conduced to give me a good constitution, and constant practice in all school games helped to consolidate and strengthen my spare but wiry form, and enabled me to exist in deadly climates for over forty years without any very serious illness. I have to thank that school for a fair education and for pleasant memories of my school-days. The greater part of my school-fellows were the sons of gentlemen; we had others of a lower grade, but these were in no way inferior either in sports, intellect, or conduct to those born socially above them.

One of the pupils was a Chinese. The story ran that he was a protégé of our Queen, that during one of our wars with China this lad was the sole survivor in a city taken by us by storm, and that, although almost a child at the time, he had informed our General that, before evacuating the place, the Chinese had poisoned all the wells. Anyhow, he was sent to the school by the Government of the day. He dressed on weekdays like the other pupils, the only difference being his long pig-tail; but on Sundays he appeared in full mandarin costume, and was placed in a most conspicuous position in church. He was a passionate lad, and had to stand a good deal of chaff from his playmates, but on the whole he was liked. After leaving Hanwell I lost sight of him for three years; but just before leaving England for India, I was walking down Baker Street, not far from Madame Tussaud's, when I saw my Chinese friend driving down towards me. He was evidently a swell, as he had a page or tiger behind him, but he had not discarded his pigtail. Directly he saw me he pulled up sharp, jumped off, and ran up to me with open arms. I must own I should have preferred our meeting to have taken place in a more secluded spot. In such a thoroughfare we were soon surrounded by a crowd, who chaffed and laughed at us good-naturedly, asking if my friend was the Emperor of China, and so on. My friend took it as a matter of course, for he, poor fellow! was used to such mobbing; but I was cad enough to wish myself far away, and was not sorry when Johnny wished me good-bye, remounted his trap, and was off. I do not know what became of him, but I think I did hear that he had been admitted to our navy as a midshipman. He was not half a bad fellow.

Occasionally I was asked to spend a holiday at the home of some boy; at other times I was left at school, or I visited my grandfather, but as he was a martyr to gout, and was very irritable, I was not sorry to get away.

Early in 1846 the Master-General of the Ordnance gave me a nomination to Woolwich. I was then removed from Hanwell, and sent to a crammer's at Shooters Hill, who had undoubtedly the best repute for successfully passing his pupils into the Academy. How such a man got together such a school is a puzzle to me. He had been, it was rumoured, originally a carpenter, and was self-educated and a good mathematician. Many of the older boys were very unruly, and there used to be frequent rows between him and them, after which he used to retire to his bed and not appear for two or three days, for which we were duly thankful. Although his fees were double what I had to pay at Hanwell, we were not half as well fed. Our lives were a burden to us during our meals, as he used to catechize us the whole time, asking us questions out of Euclid, geometry, etc. But he thoroughly understood the art of cramming, and his boys all passed well.

He cared little for general education; all he thought of was that we should learn enough of such subjects as were required to pass into the three military colleges of Woolwich, Sandhurst, and Addiscombe. When I went there first, he examined me and told me I knew enough history and geography, that I need not study them longer, but devote myself to mathematics, plan-drawing, fortification, surveying, and civil and military engineering. He had the examination papers of the three colleges for the past ten or twelve years, and used to make us go through them time after time, 'For,' said he, 'many of these questions are sure to be set again.' It would have been odd if the boys from our school had failed to pass into Woolwich, for three or four of our tutors were the examining masters at the Academy, and they were not likely to 'spin' their own pupils. In those days a lad was only allowed one chance; if he failed, he could not go up again.

Many of my schoolfellows from that school have risen to eminence, but the most distinguished were the two Gordons—Charles, better known as Chinese Gordon, and Adam Lindsay, commonly called the Australian poet. Charles was a quiet, chubby-faced boy that everybody liked. As a lad he did not give one the idea that he would become the hero he did. He was not a brilliant boy in any way, and he did not excel either in the schoolroom or in the play-ground. He was more plodding than studious. After entering the Academy, most of his class-mates got their commissions in two years, but Gordon studied on for four years until he was pronounced qualified for the Engineers, on which he had set his heart. Knowing him as I did intimately for three years, I can only say he differed but little from the other boys. We corresponded off and on at long intervals, and the last time I heard from him was when he was to succeed Stanley on the Congo, where I was then serving; he then expressed the great pleasure he should have in meeting me again after all the years that had passed, but at the last moment he accepted the fatal mission to Khartoum.

Adam Lindsay Gordon, no relation of his distinguished namesake, was also the son of an officer. When he came to us he was a little over twelve; he had outgrown his strength, and was a long, lanky, narrow-chested, short-sighted lad. He was not clever in the general acceptation of the word, but as a romancer, and more particularly as a poet, he excelled. Give him a theme, and he would write page upon page. Many of his tales written before he was twelve were as thrilling and exciting, and much on the same lines, as 'The Mysteries of Udolpho' or 'The Castle of Otranto.' But the difficulty was to induce him to stick to any one thing long. He would begin a dozen tales and poems, and leave them all unfinished. I was somewhat older, and had some influence over him, and tried to induce him to finish a poem he called 'The Disinherited'; he had completed some ten cantos when I left, but I fear that he never got further, for it is not amongst his published works. It commenced:

> 'On Royston stood the Castle fair;
> Its banners floated in the air.'

I had quite a collection of his tales and poems for years, but lost them in Burma, with the greater part of my kit.

Hunt, our classical tutor, was madly fond of poetry, and used to walk about tossing his arms, spouting Tasso and other Italian poets, quite oblivious that twice thirty-five eyes were watching his antics. He would spin round and catch us grinning at him, and try to look as unconcerned as possible. It was as good as a play to watch, first, his disgust as the greater part of us stumbled through our portion of Virgil, and then his delight as Gordon would spout his in classical verse, of which neither Dryden nor Pope need have been ashamed. We fully expected that Adam would fail to pass the medical examination for entrance into the Academy owing to his defective eyesight; but he was equal to the occasion, and, when asked what he saw on the road near the Rotunda, replied, 'A cart and horse.' The medico looked, but could see nothing; but Adam, no way abashed, said, 'Oh, they were close to the corner, and must have turned it.' The surgeon, not knowing his defect, and suspecting nothing, passed him. I have read in an illustrated sporting paper of the wonderful feats of strength performed by the poet, and of his excelling in boxing and in athletic exercises; all I can say is, that up to the end of 1848 he was weakly for his size, and did not shine then in any sports, and as for boxing, he had not an idea of how to use his fists.

Soon after going to Shooters Hill my nomination to the Academy lapsed through the death of the Master-General of the Ordnance. Sir George S. then offered me an appointment to Sandhurst, but my grandfather preferred that I should go to India. Sir James Lushington, the Chairman of the Court of Directors, first gave me a nomination for Addiscombe, but after the death of my grandfather, in February, 1848, he very kindly gave me, at my request, a direct cadetship. My cramming was not altogether thrown away, because, before I had forgotten what I had learned, I passed in surveying, and civil and military engineering, and was pronounced qualified to serve in the Department of Public Works.

Before leaving England, my guardian, Mr. A., gave me a bundle of papers containing receipts for remittances to Madras on our behalf when children, and correspondence between our grandmother and the Veteran to whom we had been sent, telling me to be careful not to lose it, as several demands had been made after the old lady's death by those unscrupulous people to extort money under various pretexts. But he said that of late years he had heard nothing further, as he had threatened to proceed against them for attempting to levy blackmail; adding, however, that he fully expected other endeavours would be made by them after my arrival in India, which proved to be correct, as I shall relate hereafter.

CHAPTER II.

CADET DAYS.

> Sail from Southampton—Egypt and the desert—Disastrous news from India—Aden—Adventures on shore—The prettiest girl on board—Her sad fate—Madras—Our messmates—Horses purchased—The Veteran officer attempts extortion—Sad accident—Two of us tried for our lives and acquitted—My first experience of Bangalore—A runaway horse and a smash—A swearing General—Permanently posted—Ordered to Secunderabad—Generous behaviour of our brother officers—Our Commandant—Hospitably entertained at Kurnool—An eccentric officer and his pranks—Secunderabad—A boyish looking Adjutant.

I WAS just sixteen years and two months old when I left Southampton in a Peninsular and Oriental Company's steamer. How different a passage was in those days compared to what it is at present! We had 120 passengers, many of them officers hurrying to join their regiments, then engaged in the Punjaub with the gallant Sikhs, who, not content with their defeat in 1845-46, again tried the arbitrament of war.

There were a great many cadets for the three Presidencies—thirteen for Madras alone. The passage-money cost £120, against £60 as at present, but then wine, beer, and all liquids were supplied gratis Even champagne was served out twice a week, and an excellent table was kept. When the weather permitted, the band played of an evening, while those who pleased danced to their hearts' content; and during the day there were all kinds of games.

We had a rough time of it in the Bay of Biscay. We did not see much of Gibraltar, but spent a day at Malta, and went back laden with sacks full of oranges. On arriving at Alexandria we had half a day to see the sights, being obliged to mount donkeys bearing the most aristocratic and distinguished names. There were Palmerstons, Johnny Russells, Wellingtons, Bluchers, Brights, Cobdens, etc. Indeed, there was scarcely a man of note in Europe who had not an asinine representative—at all events in name. We visited Cleopatra's Needles—one is now on the Thames Embankment, and the other in the United States—and also Pompey's Pillar; and we also had our first experience of a Turkish bath. We then embarked on large barges, and were towed up the Mahmoodie Canal until the Nile was reached, when we were transferred to a small steamer which took us up to Cairo. There our stay was just long enough to enable us to visit the Pyramids, to have a chat with the homeward-bound passengers who had just arrived, and to hear of the disastrous battles of Ramnugger and Chillianwallah, where two schoolfellows of mine were killed, one over the dead body of his father. One of our cadets was looking forward to meeting his father, the Adjutant-General of the Bengal Army, but the first news he received after landing at Calcutta was that his father had been killed at the crowning victory of Goojerat.

Our journey across the desert commenced at dusk.

There was a bright moon. Each van held six passengers, which was rather a close fit in such a conveyance for such a long, tedious trip; but I know that I for one thoroughly enjoyed myself. I was seldom inside; I either ran alongside or mounted on a small step outside and did 'conductor,' leaving more room for the others. We saw a few gazelles and sand-grouse, and visions of future sport flitted before our eyes. Even at that time of the year the sun was very powerful, and at some of the halting-places it was no uncommon sight to see a fowl spin round and round, and then drop down dead, to be speedily converted into 'spatch-cock,' which in the East is generally termed 'sudden death.'

We had many spinsters on board. We cadets saw very little of them, as they were monopolized by our seniors, but of course we came to know most of them. There was a pretty little girl, Miss G., bound for Aden to join her sister, who was married to a doctor on the Bombay side, attached to the European regiment then quartered there. We reached the port rather late at night, so late that passengers were forbidden to land until next morning, as the captain, an officer of the Indian Navy, said it was not safe to venture on shore during the dark, as there were many bad characters about.

But Miss G. wanted a letter taken to her sister, so I volunteered, and with another cadet slipped into a boat that came alongside. We were not seen, and got ashore all right. We did not know a word of Arabic or Hindoostani, or anything of the place, but we simply trusted to luck. We found a few donkeys ready saddled, mounted a couple, and rode along a road which we presumed led to the cantonment. We found it much further than we had bargained for, and it was past midnight when we reached the main guard, and how the sentries permitted us to pass I do not know, for we knew neither parole nor countersign; but we got in somehow, and commenced to inquire where Dr. D. lived. To do this, we had to knock up several individuals, who, not pleased at being disturbed at that time of night, told us to go to a place even hotter than Aden. What to do we did not know. It must have been close on 3 a.m. We began to despair, and thought of dismounting and lying down somewhere, but determined as a last forlorn hope to try once more. We went boldly up to a small house, and there we found a sapper officer, P., who good-naturedly sent his servant with us to point out the medico's domicile.

Dr. D.'s astonishment may be imagined when we presented him with a letter at 3.30 a.m. But he was hospitality itself. We were pressed to eat and drink; beds were improvised for us, on which we threw ourselves, and were fast asleep in a few minutes. At daylight, after a refreshing bath, we accompanied the doctor to the steamer, and returned again to his house with the fair spinster. The captain pitched into us for disobeying orders, but all's well that ends well; we had had our spree, and were none the worse either for our journey or his jobation. We spent a very pleasant day with Dr. D. and his family, and my comrade was so smitten with the charms of the young lady that he confided to me his intention of returning and marrying her. There were fifty-two regiments in Madras then, only one of which was stationed at Aden, so the chances were greatly against his returning there—and he was of the mature age of sixteen! Strange to say, he was posted to that very regiment, the 3rd Native Infantry; but when he reached that Gibraltar of the East, he found his fair one already the bride of the very man who had assisted us to find Dr. D.'s house the night of our adventure.

Amongst the young ladies there were two sisters, bound to Madras. They were both very good-looking, but the younger was almost beautiful, decidedly the belle of the ship, and of course received a great deal of attention. A certain officer won her affections, and on our arrival at Madras there was a very painful scene. The poor girl lost all control over herself, and lay fainting in his arms, for he was bound for Calcutta. He tried to soothe her, and swore he would return and marry her. The elder sister married very soon, and well. The younger remained a spinster, refusing many offers which she received. For ten years nothing was heard of her lover, beyond that he was transferred from one staff appointment to another. But on being promoted to a field-officer he was ordered to rejoin his regiment, then stationed at one of our frontier stations in Burma, where the poor girl, still unmarried, and worn to a mere shadow of her former self, was living. He got as far as Rangoon, and then, hearing whom he was likely to meet on joining, took leave on urgent private affairs, and exchanged into another regiment; and thus was sacrificed the life and happiness of as pretty and as good a girl as ever lived, through board-ship flirtation.

It was almost dusk when we anchored off Madras. A sergeant came on board for the cadets. We were put into palanquin coaches for conveyance to Palaveram, the cadets' headquarters. These wretched traps are called *shigram poes* (go quickly), for the reason that they crawl along. It must have been close on midnight when we arrived, wild with delight at getting on shore again. We were hungry, and clamoured for food, and fortunately there were the remains of a repast provided for another party, which the native servants soon prepared and placed before us.

There were but seven cots for thirteen of us, but by putting them alongside of one another we found we could manage till next day. While these arrangements were being carried out, one of the cadets began dancing on a bedstead, and in fun kicked off the butler's turban—an insult so flagrant as to astonish even that ancient official! He, however, gave a reproachful glance at his assailant, picked up his head-gear, and said quietly: 'Master young gentleman not know better.'

The matey* was a character. He had been many years there, and had been taught by various cadets to sing English songs, most of them of a very questionable character, without understanding a word of them. He would repeat them like a parrot, amidst the laughter of his audience.

Next morning we were inspected by Wilder, our Superintendent. There could not have been a fitter man for the post. He knew how to combine *fortiter in re* with *suaviter in modo*. He belonged to the

* A subordinate native servant.

mounted branch of the service, and had been a noted pig-sticker and an all-round sportsman, and though no longer young, he had not forgotten his youth, or what boys are made of. He put no undue restrictions upon us, but in the most gentlemanly way told us what we could and what we must not do, and he was thoroughly obeyed. We not only liked but respected him. The Quartermaster-General of the Army, had known my people, and he was most kind to us all, inviting us to dine with him at his bungalow, situated on a high pinnacle at Palaveram, near our quarters.

It is time I said a few words of our messmates. One of them, B., was a fine-looking, manly, powerful fellow, very good company, who could sing a good song, and spin yarns of sport which made our mouths water. Unfortunately he was *mauvais sujet*, but not to us. He never did us out of a penny, or allowed us to be imposed upon in his presence. He had at one time been orderly officer at Addiscombe, but getting into money difficulties, he had retired to France for a while, where he had picked up a pretty little girl with a moderate *dot*, which cleared him of his difficulties for the time, and enabled him to return to India. She was really very nice and lady-like, but she knew little or no English, and only one of us 'griffs' could converse with her in her own language, so I am afraid she led rather a humdrum life.

There was also a subaltern officer in command of a detachment of Native Infantry. He was married, and had a sister-in-law to dispose of, whom he would not have objected to hand over to any of the griffins, had anyone shown the least inclination that way. He was not a nice character. He had a broken-kneed horse, which he swore was a first-rate pig-sticker; but I strongly suspect he was some cast horse from either the Cavalry or Horse Artillery, which had been bought for a rupee or two. He was generous enough to offer each of us an old worn-out rifle, which he declared had slain numerous tigers. These estimable goods were to be disposed of for the ridiculous sum of 400 rupees each.

He was also kind enough to take off our hands as gifts certain under-clothing and knick-knacks, for which he assured us we should have no use. In appearance, ways, and means, he reminded one greatly of Soapy Sponge, without the manliness of that character. If B. was present, this gentleman was mute; but in his absence he used to brag greatly of what he had done. Wilder knew his man, and cautioned us to have nothing to do with him or the goods he wished to dispose of, but more particularly to avoid any entanglement with the 'spin.' Wilder was reputed to be the best judge of a horse in the Presidency, and the stable-keepers in Madras were only too glad to receive an order from him to send up some forty or fifty horses for his inspection. Each nag was critically examined and ridden, and he purchased for each of us a fair one, which cost us about 250 rupees. We had nothing to do, so spent our time in shooting and riding. I had numerous letters of introduction, but did not use one of them, as they were generally termed tickets for soup—that is, when you presented one, you were asked to dinner, and there the acquaintance probably ceased.

I had been in India only some ten days or a fortnight, when I received a letter from the wife of the Veteran I have before mentioned. She commenced by recalling herself and her husband to my recollection, enumerated the many acts of kindness lavished upon us by them, mentioning that they were heavily out of pocket owing to the inadequate remittances sent to them from England, and that she felt confident she had only to mention the amount due to them for me either to pay it at once, or, if I was unable to do so, to make arrangements for its liquidation—she could introduce me to a sowcar, who would advance me the money; and wound up by saying that she would not have pressed for payment, but that they were so hard up.

She little guessed that I had documents proving that not only had every farthing due to them been paid, but that they had failed to account for nearly £300 out of the money received by them.

I replied that I considered her and her husband a couple of swindlers, and that I would not only not pay them a pice, but would take legal proceedings to recover the amounts embezzled by them. To do the Veteran justice, I believe he had no hand in the attempted extortion. What she told him I do not know, but she worked him up to forward my letter to the Commander-in-Chief. I got a letter through Wilder from the Adjutant-General, calling for an immediate retraction and apology for the strong language I had used, and stating that but for my youth and experience his Excellency would have brought me to a court-martial. Wilder asked me what it was all about. I laid all the papers in my possession before him, and explained the treatment my sister and I had received at their hands when we were children.

That evening Wilder and I dined with the Quartermaster-General, and we told him the whole story. He told me I should have consulted Wilder before sending such a reply, as its tone was unjustifiable when addressed to a senior officer; but he asked me to leave the papers with him and he would lay them before his Excellency. I heard nothing more officially on the subject, but the Quartermaster-General told me the Chief had ordered the Veteran up to the Adjutant-General's office, and had walked into him handsomely, and that but for the abject apologies he made, laying the whole blame on his wife, and pleading his ignorance of the attempted blackmail, he would have been placed under arrest and probably tried.

C. told me it was not likely that I should be annoyed or molested again, but advised me to lay all the correspondence before the leading solicitor in Madras, who told me any claim I might have had was barred by the law of limitation, which also applied to the Veteran as well, and that from the papers I had given him there was no doubt they had no claim on me, but if they ever wrote to me again I was to refer them to him. I never heard anything more from them, nor did I meet them in any society.

I have now to relate a sad accident. Word was brought one day that a couple of hyænas had been marked down on some rocky hills about two miles distant. I went after them in company with a fellow-cadet. We beat all the likely places, but not finding them, commenced to fire at a small earthenware pot suspended on a stalk of a Palmyra palm for the purpose of collecting the juice, which is commonly called by Europeans toddy.

Beyond this tree, which was one of many forming a tope, there were visible only boulders of rocks and hills seemingly uninhabited, and we never dreamt that there could be the least danger to anybody from a stray shot. We had each fired several times, when there arose suddenly a great outcry, and the men with us declared someone had been shot. In a few minutes hundreds of excited natives turned up as if by magic, armed with *latties* (formidable staves), threatening us with blows, and attempting to disarm us. It was I who had fired the last shot. We discharged our remaining barrels into the air, and on a peon appearing, we surrendered our weapons to him and were marched back to Palaveram, taken before Wilder and charged with wilful murder. Wilder at once assembled a court of inquiry, took down the evidence, and ordered us to our quarters under arrest. The proceedings were sent to army headquarters, and by the verdict we were acquitted and released. But the newspapers, more especially the native ones, were very bitter against us, and kept showering accusations upon us. So Wilder received orders to take us before the sessions judge, that the case might be thoroughly investigated in court. So on the appointed day Wilder drove us to the residence of the judge (who, by-the-by, bore an extraordinary likeness to the Great Duke). We breakfasted with him, and then were marched off to the court, tried for our lives and honourably acquitted.

It was proved that the fatal shot had glanced off the stalk of the palm, struck a stone a hundred and fifty yards away, and, ricocheting, had hit a man stooping down planting out paddy, and caused almost instantaneous death. As the shot immediately before the accident was mine, I accepted the blame, and by Wilder's advice I paid the widow 300 rupees, and allowed her 7 rupees a month for life. Directly this was known, women sprung up by the dozen, all claiming to be the real widow, and all with innumerable children, and I believe nine-tenths of the married women would have consented to become widows on the same terms. But Wilder arranged everything; the pension was paid for about two years, and then lapsed, for the claimant ceased to appear. Whether she had died, or remarried and gone far away, I never knew.

After a short residence at the cadets' quarters, we were appointed to do duty with various regiments, and the greater part of us were sent to Bangalore under charge of an officer of the Madras Fusiliers, who had been a fellow-passenger with us. We had a delightful march. The stages were easy. The cold season was not quite over, and as duck, teal, and snipe abounded, we expended much ammunition, and if we did not slay much, we enjoyed ourselves greatly. The regiment I was sent to was the 14th Madras Native Infantry, commanded by a certain Major who had come out in the same steamer with us. One of the officers of the corps was also a brother of him who had taken charge of myself and my sisters on our father's death, and all the officers were a particularly nice set, and showed us much kindness.

I shall not forget my first drive in Bangalore. After reporting my arrival at the brigade office, I was hunting about for a suitable house to live in. My conveyance was the usual *shigram po*. The horse took fright and ran away; charged a high mud wall, and was killed on the spot; the driver was sent sprawling over the wall, and I was left deposited without a bruise amidst the débris of the carriage, which was completely smashed. The 14th were armed with the flint musket, and I learned my musketry exercise with that ancient weapon. Our Brigadier was very unpopular; he was a great martinet, and frightfully given to cursing and swearing at officers and men on parade. Some years ago the Gilbert court-martial caused a great sensation. Something very similar occurred in Bangalore when I was there. The General was swearing at and abusing an officer of H.M.'s 51st King's Own Light Infantry, who stepped out of the ranks, sheathed his sword, saying, 'Sir, I did not enter H.M.'s service to be sworn at by you,' and walked off the ground. Of course he was put under arrest, but was never tried. He went home on furlough and the thing blew over, but I believe the General caught it well from the Commander-in-Chief; and afterwards, whenever he wanted to vent his spleen, he used to swear frightfully at his horse, and add, 'Captain (or Mr.) So-and-so, you know what I mean.'

The late Sir Thomas Peyton was our Adjutant, and a right good officer he was, too; like the rest of his family, he excelled as a whip, and used to drive four-in-hand. Bangalore was a very pleasant station, but not a very moral place for a lot of youngsters to be sent to.

We soon passed our drill, and made some little progress in Hindoostani. At last we were posted permanently to native regiments. Mine was at Secunderabad, some three hundred miles distant. Our Colonel told us never to borrow money from native sowcars, but if ever we were hard up for a few rupees to go to him. We received our marching orders, although the monsoon had not quite ceased. After all our liabilities had been paid, it was a toss-up which of us was in the most impecunious state. I know I had only 7 or 8 rupees left. I did not like to ask the kind old Major for help, so I was all but a beggar when I left.

We had reached our first stage, and were wondering how we should manage, when an orderly arrived with a note from one of the senior Captains of the regiment, saying he had heard of the state of poverty we were in, and sent 200 rupees to be repaid when quite convenient, as they were in no hurry for it, it being a joint contribution of himself and brother officers. Here was a godsend! What an act of consideration and kindness! Very few would think of doing such an act nowadays, but the old Indians were very different then to what they are now. I was able to repay the amount within three months, as I wrote to my guardian for some funds, which he remitted with many a grumble.

As two of us were going to Secunderabad, we kept 150 rupees, and gave 50 rupees to one who was only going to Bellary, but he grumbled and growled at my not giving him more.

An officer of the 5th, who had charge of us, was a

big, strong fellow, under thirty, who had some time before been badly mauled by a bear, but was then sound and well. We had a very pleasant march. The rivers were in flood, and we had great trouble in crossing some of them, especially the Toomboodra. On arrival at Kurnool, we were the guests of the mess of the 5th Native Infantry. The rains recommenced, and Armstrong, a Captain in the corps, persuaded the Commandant to detain us until there was a lull. We had no officer going on with us. We knew nothing of the country or of the languages, so as the roads were nearly impassable, the difficulties forward were very great. The officers would not permit us to become honorary members; they insisted on our being their guests, so we lived in clover for a fortnight or more without being put to any expense.

Armstrong was a noted character. He played more practical jokes on his seniors than any other man would have dared to do, but he was known to be a first-rate officer, and was allowed great latitude. On one occasion he was ordered to take up six or seven griffins, and leave them at a station commanded by an old enemy of his. The Brigadier was as bald as a vulture, and very touchy. Armstrong provided himself with a wig. On nearing the station, on some pretence, he left the carts containing the ensigns' uniforms, etc., behind, but took good care to have his own kit handy. He had written to friends to lay out a dâk for him. Directly he reached the headquarters of the brigade, he reported his arrival and departure at the office. He then returned to the dâk bungalow, sent for a barber, and in front of his protégés had his head shaved, and told them it was by order of the General, and that they too must undergo the same operation. They, thinking it was a bonâ-fide order, and trusting to the example set them, submitted to the operation. Armstrong departed with his bald head to call upon the General, but took care of course to put on his wig before he got there. In a brief interview, he explained that the young gentlemen would pay their respects next day, as the carts with their uniforms had not arrived. He then took his leave, returned to the bungalow without his wig, and, alleging that he had received orders to leave at once, bade the griffs adieu, warned them to be at the General's at 11 a.m. on the morrow, got on his horse, and, picking up his relays, was far beyond the General's jurisdiction before daybreak. At the appointed time the seven griffs called and were shown up to the reception-room, the General then being busy in his office. There they sat in a row facing the door. When the mighty official entered, he saw before him seven scalps more bald than his own! He swore, he raved; would listen to no excuses, banged the door to, rushed to the Brigade Major, and bade him confine the cadets to their quarters under close arrest. That official went off to execute his unpleasant task, wondering what in the world was the matter; but when he saw the lads with their shaven crowns he went into roars of laughter, and asked them what they meant by appearing in such a guise. They explained matters, and were told to go home and not to show themselves to the General until their crops had grown again. When the right version was told to the General, he was doubly furious, and sent off an orderly to bring back Armstrong; but that astute individual was beyond recall. The General then complained to the Commander-in-Chief, who only laughed when he heard the story; but Armstrong was admonished not to play such pranks again.

I duly reached Secunderabad. It was a holiday, and very early in the morning. I was directed to the Adjutant's quarters, and I found he was in bed, so I sat down in the veranda to await his appearance. All the Adjutants I had seen had been fine, big men. Ours had passed as interpreter in some four languages, and somehow I pictured him to myself as of the same build as the others; but my amazement may be imagined when a boyish-looking, small-built individual appeared on the scene. Poor Mac! He was a good fellow; he had not sought the appointment, for which he was quite unfit. His ambition was to get into the commissariat, and having no interest, he kept passing in language after language till the authorities were forced to give him what he required, and he was the commissariat officer in after-years in Tongho whilst I was executive engineer. He was afterwards drowned in the Bay of Bengal in the *Persia*, which was never heard of after leaving Rangoon.

He and the Major were living together, and they very kindly put me up until I found quarters for myself.

I was introduced to my brother officers, who individually were nice enough, but collectively did not get on well together. There had been rows in the regiment, and one of the senior officers had been tried by a court-martial and suspended for six months. He was the cause of all the squabbles. The immediate cause of his suspension was egging on two young officers to fight a duel, which had then been strictly forbidden. It is true that a few duels occurred in the army after I joined, but they were known only to the combatants and their seconds. That duelling was occasionally abused there is no doubt. Still, it had a deterrent effect, and for some injuries was the only mode of obtaining satisfaction, and it is a pity that it was altogether abolished.

CHAPTER III.

SECUNDERABAD.

Secunderabad in 1849—Nightingale—' Master not fight fair '—An obstreperous Captain—How to manage natives—Sad death of an Adjutant—Mole Alley races—Amusements—Gambling—Regiment ordered to Samulcottah—My stud—Am appointed to the sappers and miners—Difficulty of getting to Burma—Rangoon—Employed on field-service—Miraculous escape of two drunken gunners.

IN 1849 Secunderabad was a jolly place. We had a large force, and each regiment had its band, billiard-table, and its swimming-bath, and we were all on the most friendly terms. Some of the native regiments had good elevens, and in the cold weather cricket was frequently played. The 40th Native Infantry, commonly called the 'Forty Thieves,' could hold their own at our national game against most European corps. The artillery gloried in a lot of reckless riders, and in one steeplechase four of the officers were lying in a ditch, and the others jumping over them and over the obstacle, a strong four-foot fence. They were a capital set of fellows, but regular madcaps. There were many officers who had known me as a child, and I received the greatest kindness from them all. We had many famous soldiers and shekaries—Shakspear,

Nightingale, the two Orrs, Wedderburn, Wyatt, Clougstoun, and many others. Frank Vardon, one of the early pioneers in South Africa, who had been a friend of my father's, asked me to visit him, and showed me much sport.

I had been a short while in Secunderabad, when there was a grand field-day. As a griff I was a mere looker-on. Standing near the flag-staff, I noticed a particularly handsome man in a gorgeous native costume talking to the Brigadier, James. He was fair, with blue eyes, jet black hair, whiskers and beard parted at the chin, and brushed up towards the ears, with a long drooping moustache; I don't think I ever saw a finer or a handsomer man. He was superbly mounted. From his dress, I thought he was some great man from the city, and was astonished at his talking in fluent English; so I asked a bystander who was the native who was conversing with the General. He replied, 'What native?' I said, 'The one in the gorgeous costume, with blue eyes and black beard.' He burst out laughing, and said: 'Why, don't you know who that is? Why, it is Shakspear, of the Nizam Irregular Cavalry.' I was astonished. Familiar as must have been the uniform to me in my younger days, I had quite forgotten it, and had not, since my joining my regiment, met any of the Bolarum men. His cousin, H. W. Blake, was very like him, and both were first-rate shekaries.

Nightingale was not a handsome man; he had high cheek-bones and a ragged, nondescript beard. He was a splendid horseman, and had probably no equal, unless it was Frank Simson, as a hog-hunter. When he was mounted he invariably carried a hog-spear, and would prod a leaf here and a twig there, and seldom missed his mark. He had means of his own, and good pay from Government. He had seldom less than a dozen horses in his stable. He obtained them from Bombay with the remounts for his regiment, made thorough hunters of them, and by the sale of two or three paid for the rest. He could sing a capital song and accompany himself on the piano. He was also a bit of a poet in his way, and wrote some good hog-hunting songs. He was undoubtedly a great sportsman, but was not a pleasant companion in the field, as he was inclined to be jealous. He had great influence with his sowars, and they would have obeyed him to the death.

He and the Orrs constantly hunted together, and had frequent rows, and the wonder is they did not come to blows, for the Orrs were probably the most passionate men in India, and 'Bulbul' used certainly to try their temper. I heard the following story: There had been a hard fight for first spear, which, as usual, fell to Nightingale. His opponent rode up to him, boiling with rage, and said: 'Sir, I think during the run you called me a ——' 'Well, that is odd!' replied Bulbul, as cool as a cucumber; 'I never opened my lips during the run, and how you have divined my thoughts I do not know; but although I said nothing, I have often thought you one!' The audacity of the reply tickled the other's fancy to such an extent that he burst out laughing, and for the time being they were on speaking terms again, which did not happen often.

Nightingale had a lot of very savage Polygar dogs; they had got used to one particular boy, and he and he only could manage them; a stranger they would have torn to pieces. This lad was absolutely necessary to Nightingale, yet he often maltreated him. The poor wretch stood it as long as he could, and then asked for his discharge, which Nightingale refused with a kick. The native, driven wild, appealed to his brother, a cook-boy in H.M.'s 84th Regiment, to help him. Now, very many of these low-caste Madrassies are very powerfully built, and only require tuition and training to become nasty customers in a row. European soldiers were hard pushed for amusement in those days, so the Tommy Atkinses, to pass away the time, used not only to pit these cook-boys against each other, but would take a turn with them themselves, until the Peramootoos, or whatever their names might be, learned not only to use their fists, but to stand a good deal of punishment; and as they were kept constantly in training they got as hard as nails and as strong as brewers' carmen, and became no mean proficients in the art of self-defence and attack. The brother came to Nightingale's quarters and asked very respectfully for his brother's discharge. Nightingale, astounded at the man's impudence in daring to interfere, gave him a clout on the head and told him to go about his business, and that if he dared to show his face again he would thrash him within an inch of his life. The native took the cuff without flinching, and coolly saying, 'Master do that business, I do same,' commenced to strip. Nightingale saw at once he had caught a tartar. The man's muscles stood out like balls of whipcord, and the way he held up his maulies proclaimed that he was no novice at the game of fisticuffs. A terrific fight took place. Nightingale was severely punished, and, but for his extraordinary length of arm and always being in good fettle, would probably have had the worst of it; but finding the native too strong and skilful for him, he trusted to his great reach, and hit out whenever he saw a blow coming, and countered without receiving much punishment after the first few rounds, during which the native had had a long way the best of it. I heard Nightingale describe it as the hardest fight he had ever had in his life. At last English pluck and endurance, aided by length of arm, won the day, and Nightingale knocked his opponent down senseless; when he recovered, I am sorry to say, Nightingale was in such a rage that he gave the man an unmerciful thrashing, and feared he had almost overdone it, so he sent the cook-boy to the Brigade Major, with the following letter:

'My dear A.,
　　'This nigger has been most insolent. Please punish him.'

A. replied:

'My dear N.,
　　'The less you say about it, the better. I think the man has had sufficient punishment for any offence, however great.'

Talking of natives sticking up to Europeans, the following I can vouch for:

H., of the 30th, had struck his matey boy in the presence of witnesses. The native took out a summons against his master, who was fined by the cantonment magistrate. Such a thing as a native hauling up his master for a blow was unheard of in those days, and H. bided his time; he said nothing, and kept the boy on as if nothing had happened. One day when his servant brought him his early cup of tea, H. jumped out of bed, and, fastening the door, said: 'You infernal blackguard! I'll teach you to haul me up before a magistrate; there are no witnesses, and I'll give you a d——d good thrashing.' The man pretended to cry, wiping his eyes on his sleeve, and blubbered out: 'Master sure no witnesses got?' 'Quite sure,' replied H. 'Then,' said the matey boy, dropping all pretence, 'I give master one big hiding,' and, to his astonishment, walked into him in fine style. H. had not a chance; his boy was far stronger and a far better bruiser, and knocked his master into a cocked hat. H. was on the point of crying *peccavi*, when he bethought him that he had on a pair of stout shoes, so, as a last resource, he kicked up, caught the man in a very tender part, and doubled him up. Just then two of us came up to see H.; the door was burst open, and a native rushed out writhing in agony, howling, 'Master not fight fair; done kick me there!' As for H., his mother would not have known him, and we could scarcely distinguish one feature from another. He had to go on the sick-list. His boy, who, we learned afterwards, had been a cook-boy in a battery of artillery, disappeared; and in after-life, if we wanted to get a rise out of H., we had only to stoop with our hands low down and whimper 'Master not fight fair,' to drive him nearly mad.

Our Colonel, who had lately joined, had been in the Commissariat and Mysore Commission over thirty years. The late Commandant thought more of horse-racing than of military matters, and the corps was in a very disorganized state; it was generally thought that one who had been in semi-military, semi-civil employment for so many years was not exactly the man to choose to put matters straight, and one or two of the officers presumed on that supposition to try and thwart him, and to do as they liked. But our new Colonel soon showed that he was fully competent to command, and that they must obey. He was certainly the best commanding officer I ever served under. Religious himself, he did not obtrude his opinions on others, but sought to rule more by example than by precept. He was most consistent, and showed neither favour nor affection to one more than to another. He soon effected a change for the better. The man who opposed him the most was a captain, who had been tried by a court-martial as before mentioned. He had lately rejoined, and did his best to set us all at loggerheads, and to ignore his commanding officer, who, however, continued on the even tenor of his way, and, whilst enforcing discipline, took no notice of the many acts, petty in their way, by which attempts were made to annoy him.

The native regiments wore sandals, and after a field-day the parade-ground would be strewn with these apologies for shoes. The Colonel had a few pairs of ammunition boots made, and distributed them amongst the non-commissioned officers and a few of the men, and talked to them of the advantages of being properly shod. But the natives are very averse to change; their forefathers had worn sandals, they said; the boots would cost more, they cramped the feet, it was against their custom, besides other objections to the contemplated change, and I fear that they were encouraged to rebel by M. But the Colonel allowed a thorough trial of the boots he had issued, and then ordered a parade. He talked to the men in their own dialects, for he was equally at home in Hindoostani, Tamil, and Teleego, pointing out the advantages of boots over the native slippers, and promised that if they were adopted the price of the first issue should not exceed that of the sandals, and that one pair of boots would last twice as long as the others. He commenced with the right-hand man of the Grenadiers, and asked if he would wear them. The man refused. 'Make a prisoner of him,' said the Colonel. Then he asked the next man, and so on, to the end of the line, and there was not another refusal. Our regiment thus became one of the first to be properly shod. The officer already referred to then took to putting scurrilous advertisements in the Madras papers, one being: 'Old boots, old boots! Apply to the Colonel commanding N.I., Secunderabad.' This having no effect on the Colonel, the company commander thought he could play other tricks with equal impunity, so he refused to pay his subscription to the billiard fund, to which he had belonged for over twenty years, and accompanied his refusal by writing that the Colonel had no more right to levy this tax upon him than he had to put his hand into his pocket and pick it. The Adjutant was sent to him with a written order to attend the commanding officer's quarters at once, and then, in presence of the Major, the Colonel gave him such a lecture that he left in a very humble state, applied for six months' leave on urgent private affairs, and never joined us again. Through family interest he was pitchforked into some staff employ, where he could do little harm. We were well rid of him, and the tone of the corps improved day by day.

I had been reported duly qualified, and had just fallen in with the regiment, when our Commander-in-Chief came up to inspect the troops. In opening out to quarter-distance column, I did not calculate the distance exactly, and in wheeling into line there would have been a gap had not two of the rear rank men promptly stepped to the front. It was so well done, I did not think anyone had noticed the error; but the old chief, who was a Peninsular and Waterloo veteran, galloped up at once, and said: 'It won't do, young fellow; I have done that trick too often myself to be deceived.' 'Mark those men for extra drill!' thundered out our Colonel. 'Do nothing of the kind,' said the kind old General; 'they were quite right to try and save their officer.'

A very sad occurrence took place soon after I joined. The Adjutant of the 3rd Madras Cavalry was shot dead whilst at dinner with his young wife. His back was towards the door, which was ajar to allow the servants to bring in the dishes; his wife was seated opposite to him; she heard a report, and saw her husband fall forward. He was dead—shot through the back. A trooper was tried for the offence, and found guilty; but there were great doubts as to whether he was the real culprit, although no doubt he was in the swim and knew all about it, so he was not executed, but transported, which was to him far worse than death. Beyond being somewhat strict, there was nothing against the officer, and it has ever been a puzzle why the dastardly crime was committed.

There was much sport to be had in those days in the Nizam's dominions, and I learnt to shoot fairly, and to hold my own across country. Once a year the great horseracing meet took place at Mole Ally. The saturnalia lasted a week, but the races were only on alternate days. A week before the meet, the plain round the course would be covered with tents of all sizes—the modest bichoba of the subaltern, the mess-tents of the different regiments, and the gorgeous and palatial structures erected for the Resident, the Prime Minister, and other native notabilities from the city. The scene, whilst it lasted, was most gay and enjoyable. The Princes and the officers of the Irregular Cavalry vied with one another in sumptuous array, and even they, grand as they were, were put somewhat into the shade by the nautch-girls, who appeared in public 'for that occasion only.' As a rule, they never left the city. Many of them were the favourites of the rich nobles, and were themselves very wealthy, covered with jewels worth many thousands of pounds. These girls alone were worth going many miles to see. Young in years, pretty, perfect in shape, they all belonged to one profession, which in the East is not held in abomination as it is in the West. Many of these girls were very fair; they never ventured into the sun except in enclosed palanquins; they take as much care of their complexions as many a Court beauty, and as for their figures, their equal is not to be found in Europe. They resemble living Galateas, as perfect as any of the finest representations of Venus in Greek statuary.

One of the most noted horses of those days was XL., originally bought by Child of my corps for a mere song; but Child was no rider, and the horse a very violent one; he ran away with his rider one day over the Maidan, and Bucksee B., of the 40th, a racing man, noticing what a stride the horse had, offered 500 rupees for him, which his owner gladly accepted. He was put into training, and for two or three years he won all the principal races and put many thousands of rupees into the pockets of the lucky purchaser.

The two best jockeys were Major Hughes, of the 47th Native Infantry, and Captain Phillips, of the 3rd Madras Cavalry. There was not much to choose between them, but on the whole I think Hughes won more races; he was a keen sportsman, and is said to have killed five hundred tigers; but how far that is true I do not know. Whenever he was off duty he donned a scarlet coat, and with his dogs hunted either a fox or a jackal.

At times caged leopards, and now and then a bear, would be let loose on Mole Ally, and be speared from horseback. It was on one of these occasions, many years after the time I am alluding to, that Nightingale met with his death. He had just speared a leopard, was seen to reel and fall off his horse, and was picked up dead of heart disease. A sad ending for a man who had braved death in every shape for years, who had served with distinction throughout the Mutiny in Central India, had killed scores of tigers, speared several thousands of hogs and hundreds of bears, and was certainly an accomplished sportsman and soldier.

There was not much gambling in those days. There was a retired Major, who could turn up the king at écarté whenever he liked, and belonged to a fraternity of professional sharpers and gamblers. He was well known, and generally avoided. But the son of a grandee, who had won some 4,000 rupees at a race-meeting, and had an idea he could play cards, foolishly challenged this gentleman, who declined at first, as he said he had learned the game in France, and was probably too strong a player; but his opponent thereon became doubly pressing, so the Major, chuckling inwardly, consented. They played for high stakes, and at first the youngster kept winning; the stakes were doubled and trebled, and, as might have been expected, the result was that he not only lost all his winnings by racing, but a very large sum besides, which his father had to pay.

I spent two or three years very pleasantly in Secunderabad, and then my regiment was ordered to a single station in the Northern Division. We marched by wings; I was in the left, but accompanied the right as far as Oopal. I was riding a great brute of a horse I had lately bought from an officer. Seeing some antelopes, I put him after them; he pitched on his head, threw me some distance, dislocated my right arm, and at the same time cut both knees badly, and I was glad to send him to an auction and sell him for a few rupees. I obtained three months' leave on sick certificate, and was left behind. As soon as I recovered the use of my arm, I left Secunderabad, and wandered about the country shooting and hunting. I had three horses and a Mahratta pony and a good battery of guns and rifles, and if ever there was a man madly fond of sport it was I. I travelled leisurely and got to Samulcottah a day or two before the expiration of my leave. During the next two years I spent a good deal of my time on detachment duty at Condapilly. I liked the life and its independence. It was rather solitary, it is true; but when the weather did not permit of my going out hunting and shooting, I found ample solace in reading and drawing. I had some capital pig-sticking, too, as will be related further on. I got on well with my brother officers, and flatter myself I was rather a favourite with our old Colonel.

Early in 1853 a new Commander-in-Chief arrived. He had known my great-uncle and was intimate with Lord Raglan, at whose request he promised to do what he could for my advancement in the service. Soon after his arrival I got a letter from his military secretary, asking in what way his Excellency could serve me. I had only passed in the vernacular to qualify for holding a company, but had neglected to pass the higher examination which qualified for staff employment. In fact, I was the greatest duffer possible in learning languages, and although as a child I believe I spoke three dialects as well as any native, I never could master them again after I returned to India. Although unqualified for the general staff, I was eligible for employment with the Sappers and Miners, whose headquarters were generally at Mercara, a noted place for big game, but the whole regiment was at that time employed in Burma. So I wrote back thanking his Excellency, and asked to be appointed to the Sappers and Miners, and was duly gazetted on March 31, 1853. But I had to remain at my post until relieved; then the only steamer plying along the coast, the *Hugh Lindsay*, broke down, and I was told to find my way across to Rangoon the best way I could. I sent off a letter to a friend at Cocanada to know if there was any vessel leaving for Calcutta, and got back a reply to go at once, as a ship would be leaving in a few days. I dâked there, only to find that the destination of the vessel was changed, and that a schooner, the *Zapna-Paneah*, would start in a day or two for Pondicherry, touching at Madras. Besides myself, there were three other passengers, viz., Colonel Clarke, of my corps, who had been appointed Brigadier at Aden; Dent, of the 11th, going home on furlough; and Tyrrell, of the 18th. The skipper agreed to land us at Madras for 150 rupees each, and said he thought we should get there in three days at the most. So we paid our money and embarked, but no sooner had we started than the south-west monsoon commenced, and we had to tack against it. At the expiration of fifteen days we were apparently no nearer to our destination than when we left. We were heartily sick of the vessel; all the live stock, beer and wine were expended; salt junk we did not admire, and all were anxious to get to the journey's end. I asked the captain when we should get to Madras. 'Oh,' he replied, 'I am halfway between it and Pondicherry, and as the port dues are very heavy, I shall be a considerable loser if I touch there, so I shall go on to Pondicherry, and you can dâk back to Madras.'

I was astounded at his impudence, but our agreement was only a verbal one, and we were entirely in his power. I spoke to the Colonel, and he was equally disgusted, and said, 'If it is a case of money, find out what he wants, and I'd rather pay it myself than be kept longer in this vessel.' The skipper asked 100 rupees, to which we agreed at once. The Colonel wished to pay the whole, but we three paid 50 rupees, whilst he paid the other moiety; the ship was put about, and by dark we were at anchor in the roads. We landed early next morning, and it was the only time I have seen that coast free of surf—for a wonder, the sea was as smooth as a mill-pond.

I duly reported myself in person at the Adjutant-General's office. 'Why, what brings you here?' was the query. 'We sent you orders at Masulipatam to cross over in the *Feroze* with the — Regiment.' 'I never got the order, sir,' I replied. 'Well, it can't be helped now; but a vessel will be leaving with detachments for Rangoon in a few days, and you can cross over in her.' So 'more haste, the less speed' was verified in my case. The regiment I ought to have crossed with arrived at Moulmein on June 30; it never moved out of the station or heard a shot fired, but got both the batta and medal. But I, who, owing to the dilatoriness of the post, lost that opportunity, and reached Rangoon on July 2, got neither, although for two years I was actively engaged on the Irrawadie side, because Lord Dalhousie had declared that the war was to cease on June 30, after which all Burmese found with arms in their hands were to be treated as Dacoits. This was a sop to the 'peace-at-any-price' party at home, but the war continued for fully two years more. It did not lessen our action against the enemy, or put a stop to their struggle against us, and only deprived a few of the medal and batta who had earned them better than many of those who got them.

I received an order to embark on the *Teazer*. When hostilities broke out with the Court of Ava, this vessel had been offered to our Government for sale for 80,000 rupees, but it was declined, and the vessel was chartered by the month, and I was assured by one of the owners afterwards that by the time her services were dispensed with the owners had cleared 150,000 rupees, and still had the vessel in hand.

The detachments for Burma consisted principally of artillerymen to replace those who had died or been killed in action. The officers at the Mount took that opportunity of getting rid of all the worst of the bad characters, and a more shady lot than those who paraded for embarkation were, I believe, never seen. Every man was drunk, and a disgrace to the very name of a soldier.

As I had not been appointed to do duty with the troops crossing over, I did not see the need of appearing in uniform, especially as the day was very rough, and the surf mountains high, and we were sure of a ducking. I waited on the beach until I could find room in some boat. The staff officer who had to see to the embarkation of the troops was not in the sweetest of tempers—small blame to him!—for the behaviour and appearance of the men would have driven an angel wild. It was no use his swearing at the drunken crew, and perceiving me, he asked gruffly what I was doing there. I told him I was going across in the *Teaser*. 'Why are you not in uniform?' he thundered. I replied that I was not appointed to do duty with the troops, but was crossing over as a passenger to join the Sappers. He was beginning to vent his wrath on me, when there was a fresh outbreak on the part of the gunners, and he rushed off to curse them and their officers, and I seized the opportunity to jump into a boat and to get on board ship without prolonging my interview with the irate official. Johnson (brother of Sir W. Johnson, a Canadian and an old schoolfellow of mine), two other officers and two medical officers, formed the party on board. We started about midnight, and early in the morning a half-naked black native came into the saloon and announced himself as the skipper! On shore he would have been taken for a common coolie, and we were astonished at his appearance; but when we came to know him better, we found he was not a bad fellow at all, a capable officer, and kept a good and liberal table.

A few days after we left the anchorage cholera appeared on board. We lost many of the crew, some of the artillerymen, and several of the Eurasian clerks. Our first mate, a very powerful Highlander in the prime of life, had been on deck nearly forty-eight hours, drenched to the skin the whole time, for we were caught in a cyclone as well, and, being fagged out, asked permission to go to his berth, which was at once granted. But the poor fellow never left it alive, as he died of cholera before daybreak and was buried at sea. No sooner had we shaken off the epidemic and got rid of the cyclone than a terrific storm overtook us off the Andamans, and some seven or eight of the Horse Artillery horses, worth 700 rupees each, were knocked about the decks, where they had been picketed, without even a box to hold them, and were so damaged that we had to shoot three and throw them overboard. The others were useless for army purposes, and were sold off as 'casters' shortly afterwards. Whoever shipped those valuable horses ought to have been severely punished. The monsoon was well on, and any fool ought to have known the weather we must encounter in crossing the bay, yet not a horse-box had been provided.

It was a most unfortunate voyage altogether. The day we entered the mouth of the Rangoon branch of the great Irrawadie River, the stream was running like a sluice, the periodical freshes being well on, and just at dark there was a great hubbub: the gunners had broken into the ship's stores, and were very drunk and riotous. We had to go down armed with handspikes, and to knock down and put in irons the greater part of the men. Whilst this tumult was going on below, a cry arose, 'Man overboard!' The night was as dark as pitch; the man was borne swiftly past by the current, uttering the most heartrending cries for help—these in a few minutes became fainter and fainter, and at last ceased. Boats had been lowered as quickly as possible, but the crew consisted of Lascars only, and in the absence of Europeans, who were all below quelling the mutiny, there was some delay in getting the boats away. A quarter of an hour after the first cry there was another: a second gunner, very drunk, jumped overboard to save his comrade, whose cries had ceased fully ten minutes before. There were no more boats to launch, and his cries also ceased. The boats got back with great difficulty, owing to the swiftness of the current, after searching about for two hours, but not a sign of either man had been seen. The river swarmed with sharks and alligators, and we all thought that if the men had not been drowned, they had been carried out to sea and devoured. No one got to sleep that night till the small hours, and at daylight, when I appeared on deck, I found the anchor being weighed. I asked the captain if he did not mean to have another search for the men by daylight; but he pointed to the stream, which was racing past us, and against which our two anchors could hardly hold, adding, 'What is the use? The men must have been drowned or devoured long ago; but if you like to take a party of gunners—I can't spare any of the Lascars —you can have a boat, and I'll wait a couple of hours for you.'

Just then Charlie Johnson, my old schoolfellow, appeared. I asked him if he would come; he replied, 'Certainly;' we got hold of four of the best and most sober of the artillerymen, and set out on our apparently hopeless task. We had gone about a mile, skirting the eastern shore, when we saw a sampan, manned by Chinamen, coming towards us, and bringing with them the first of the two men who had gone overboard. A junk was anchored about two miles below us, and the crew, hearing cries, nobly put out in a boat, and were just in time to save the gunner. He, ungrateful brute! was not quite sober even then, and cursed us and his rescuers most impartially. Telling the Celestials to take him to the *Teazer*, we pulled towards the right bank, with the expectation of finding the body of the second man.

We had gone probably three miles, when a human being rose out of the water close to the bank, as red as a lobster. It was the second man. The tide had taken him along and had cast him ashore, but he was so punished by mosquitoes that he had gone back and laid down in the water to avoid them. He was a wretched-looking object when we picked him up. I had taken a flask containing some brandy. I offered it to him, and a good nip considerably revived him. He was naked as on the day he was born; but he tied the turban off my hat round his loins like a nigger, and my coat afforded his shivering body some warmth, and I told him to take an oar and pull for his life. We got back to the vessel, and found the skipper in rather a temper at being detained so long, but when he saw the man and heard our explanation he was pacified. Although both these men escaped death for a time in a marvellous manner, I heard that they died shortly afterwards of fever, brought on by intemperance and exposure.

CHAPTER IV.

BURMA FORTY YEARS AGO.

Rangoon in 1853—Voyage up the Irrawadie—Prome—Famine—Sad sights—Death of Maddigan and Latter—Cruelty of Burmese—Construct a stockade—Officers, gallant and otherwise—Carpet-knights on service—Burmese tactics—Ramghur Irregular Cavalry — Dacoits — A girl outraged and murdered — Lord Dalhousie — Gallantry of Engineer officers — Loot — Bengal troops compared with those of Madras—Red-tape in Madras—The sappers—Am transferred to the Engineer department—A boxing-match—A British soldier hanged—Attempts to proselytize sepoys—Injudicious officers.

RANGOON in 1853 was about as filthy a place as can well be imagined. The English had held it for about a year, but very little had then been done to improve it. Soon after my arrival I had been dining on board a vessel in the river, and on returning to shore about 10 p.m., I found a Chinaman fishing in a drain which had lately been dug. It was a bright moonlight night, and I watched his proceedings, wondering what he was trying to catch. To my surprise, I saw him haul up bandicoots (huge foul-feeding gutter rats), one after another, knock them on the head, and string them, much as a fisherman might do fish. I asked him what he was going to do with them. He replied he would make them into pies, and sell them next day, adding,

'They very good eating'; but I'll be bound he neither partook of them himself nor would he inform his customers of what the pies were made. The Chinese and Burmese are omnivorous; but although they will eat even the carcase of a pony that has died of glanders, or putrid elephant's flesh, they draw the line at these gutter rats. But there is a rodent very similar in appearance, called the bamboo rat, which is a pure vegetarian, and I believe is very good eating.

Rangoon is now one of the finest cities in the East; the streets are broad, and laid out at right angles with one another, and planted with trees. This was commenced in 1858, whilst I was officiating as Executive Engineer. Knowing nothing of botany, I had still kept my eyes open, and seen natives plant various trees from cuttings, etc., so had an idea how it ought to be done. The Forest Department official was absent on one of his inspecting tours, but his wife, who really knew as much of the subject as I did, and no more, and had nothing to say to our department, used to inundate me with letters, suggesting that such a tree, or some other—all with long Latin names ending in *grandiflora*—should be planted in one street, and another *grandiflora* in the next, and so on, until the correspondence became a nuisance. I was then living with an Engineer officer, and showed him the lady's letters. 'Why,' said he, 'she knows nothing of what she is writing about. Wait a bit, and we will pay her off in her own coin.' So we concocted fearful words, all ending in *grandiflora*, saying that, although such and such a tree as she proposed would doubtless do when facing east or west, it would die if planted north or south, as the case might be; but—here we used fearful words, the like of which had never been heard of by botanists, but which sounded grand—would answer better. For every letter containing a dozen learned names, we, in my name, sent her twenty-four, until she shut up, and told people she had no idea I was so well up in botany.

My stay in Rangoon was very short, for the headquarters of the sappers and miners were at Prome, so I embarked on a steamer belonging to the Irrawadie flotilla, which also towed up a huge flat. We had to pay the skipper 8 rupees a day for table expenses, and it was an extraordinary fact that our progress would be in the inverse ratio to the number of passengers on board. The general excuse was the heavy fogs, but one day, when it was quite bright, and there were no signs of our moving, one of us asked the cause of the delay. 'Oh, I am waiting to see if the fog will get up,' replied the commander.

A trip up the Irrawadie is always pleasant, and ours would have been very enjoyable had it not been for the multitude of the mosquitoes and the virulence and persistency of their attacks. In the Panlong Creek they were in tens of thousands; the current was very swift, and our progress very slow. The artillery horses kicked, screamed, and bit at one another; the gunners swore worse than our army were said to have done in Flanders. Those who had good curtains, and retired inside them betimes, did not fare so badly.

Owing to the war against us, and the levy *en masse* of the male population, very little of the country had been cultivated, and the greater part of the alluvial

5

country had been left fallow. The Burmese, being an improvident people, had stored up no grain for times of scarcity, and a terrible famine struck the land. As we steamed slowly up, the river banks in the vicinity of towns and village would be lined by men, women, and children, beseeching alms. We carried rice for distribution, but what was the amount aboard amongst so many? Hundreds of cattle could be seen, fat and sleek, grazing on the deserted fields; but the rigid Buddhists would not deprive these animals of their lives even to save themselves from starvation. We had no such compunctions, and shot several, and no sooner was life extinct than the people would rush at the animal like wild beasts, tear it asunder, and devour great pieces of the flesh—raw!

The Government gave grants, and all, from the Commissioner down to the smallest drummer-boy, contributed to a general fund to alleviate the wants of the very poor. Work was provided for the able-bodied; yet it was not an uncommon occurrence to hear of the bodies of men, women and children being found dead of starvation round about Prome.

When the organized forces of the King retired, men of influence carried on an internecine war. They did not attempt to meet our men in the field, but harassed our outposts, burnt towns and villages, and made it as unpleasant as possible for all who had submitted to us, thus rendering a settled form of government and the collection of taxes impossible. No man's life was worth a straw.

The Burmese, by their religion, are forbidden to take life; they will not tread upon a worm if they can help it, yet will butcher men, women, and children with the most revolting cruelties. Whilst barracks were in course of erection, the officers and men were billeted in *kyoungs* and *zyats*, which were fortunately very numerous in all the suburbs of the larger towns. Many attempts were made to assassinate the European officers, and it is a wonder there were not more victims. Poor Maddigan, of the 84th, was cut to pieces in his tent. Latter, the Deputy-Commissioner of Prome, one of the bravest of men, was murdered by a party of men dressed up as women. The Quartermaster-Sergeant of the Horse Artillery, sleeping in a tent next to mine, was stabbed, and barely escaped with his life. If these so-called Dacoits could pounce down upon any native official appointed by us, they would tie him down, bore holes through him with red-hot irons, and inflict other cruelties too disgusting to mention. Once we were marching between Pounday and Tapoon, along a narrow path, and came upon a lot of poor wretches who had been crucified, impaled, ripped open, and partially burnt, all arranged in a row, their only crime being a suspicion that they had given us some information. As they had been dead some two days, the effluvium was dreadful and the sight sickening, for birds of prey had been at them, and many of our men fell out and vomited.

The Burmese, individually, are plucky enough, but collectively they are useless, as they are too impatient to bear control or to be disciplined, and fail to support one another in action. Every man fights for himself, and if he gets the worst of it, runs away, believing that it is better to live to fight another day.

I was in command of the Sappers on an expedition into the interior. We came to a large town with a strong stockade, protected on three sides by a considerable river. The ford was *pangied;* that is, it had spikes of bamboo driven into its bed. The bridge had been broken down in the centre. The stockade was well loopholed; a musket protruded out of each opening, muzzles of cannon could be seen on the salient angles, and we thought we were in for a stubborn fight. The troops were ordered to seek shelter, and to line the fringe of jungle along the river face; the guns unlimbered, but the orders were given not to open fire until the enemy fired the first shot. The word was given 'Sappers to the front to repair bridge.' So whilst all my comrades, most of whom had undergone the baptism of fire many a time in the Sutlej and Punjaub campaigns, and were well used to being fired at, were under shelter, I, poor devil! just twenty-one, having heard but a few shots fired in anger, had to go on to the bridge to see what was required to render it passable, and to remain there until I could pronounce it passable for the troops.

The muskets out of the loopholes swayed to and fro, looking as if they covered me every movement, yet not a shot was fired. The tension was almost more than I could bear. But for the disgrace of the thing, I verily believe I should have fairly cut and run. I should have preferred if the enemy had opened fire; I could have then retaliated, for I was well armed; but to stand there looking down those barrels, and expecting every moment to be potted, was not pleasant. The Sappers soon cut down some trees; we repaired the gap, and at last I was able to roar out that the bridge was passable, only too pleased to take a part in the rush that took place, in preference to remaining an idle spectator. We made a dash at the stockade, and were clambering over the walls, when someone called out that the place was undermined, and a momentary pause took place; but the hesitation only lasted for a second, and the next we were scrambling over and jumping into the stockade, wondering why the enemy did not fire or resist, to find that the place was deserted! There was not a living creature in. The muskets and cannon were dummies, slung by canes from the inside, and, as every breath of air swayed them to and fro, it gave them an appearance of being pointed at us. After it was all over, how I was chaffed!

It was the worst quarter of an hour I ever spent in my life. I have often been in far greater danger since, as on that occasion I was as safe as if I had been in bed; yet, as anticipation is far worse than reality, I found that it was not pleasant to stand inactive within fifty yards of a row of muskets, believing them to be loaded, and to be in the hands of the enemy. Whilst in action you have no time to think, and you are animated by a spirit of destruction. Passive inaction is very different; in the one case you do not think of danger, and in the other you do.

After the occupation of this place I was ordered to demolish the old stockade and to construct a new one on more scientific principles at a turn of the river, so as to command the reaches on either side and prevent Burmese war-boats from ascending or descending. Whilst constructing this defensive post there used to be a most abominable smell, which we put down to the natives using the ditch for latrines; no filth was visible, but the stench continued. I had left a splendid tree, which afforded a grateful shade, inside the stockade. In a storm a branch of this tree, covered with flowers, was blown down, and the odour from its blossoms was most overpowering, so it was condemned and hewn down; but a small tamarind-tree on the opposite side of the river was spared, as it was not in our way, and the sepoys were very fond of its astringent fruit. About a year and a half afterwards I again visited the locality (I was then surveying for a line of road between Prome and Rangoon, which has since been adopted for the railroad). I found no stockade on the original site, but half a mile inland, where it was of very little use, and badly constructed. On visiting the officer in command I asked why the stockade had been moved to its present useless site. 'You are a nice fellow to construct a fort!' he replied; 'you left a tree on the further bank of the river, up which the Burmese used to climb at night and fire down upon us, so we moved the stockade.' 'Would it not have been easier to cut down the tree?' I asked. 'By Jove!' replied my friend, slapping his thigh, 'we never thought of that.'

Burma was considered very sickly in 1852-53. The change from a hot, dry climate to a damp one affected very many of the senior officers; commands frequently fell vacant and had to be filled up. One of the finest fellows in Prome was Cotton, of the 67th Bengal Native Infantry, who so greatly distinguished himself afterwards in the Mutiny. When Armstrong, who commanded the 4th Sikhs, was so severely wounded in the final attack on Mea Toon's stronghold, and had to leave on sick certificate, Cotton ought to have got the temporary command. But one of another corps, who had the reputation of being a drill-sergeant sort of officer, was preferred, and was put in as officiating. He was ordered with the gallant Sikhs into the interior, and told to establish stations and to harass the Burmese whenever he heard of any of them collecting together. M., of the 2nd Bengal Fusiliers, a strong, plucky fellow, accompanied the regiment. Somehow he doubted the personal courage of his Commandant, and worked on his nerves by telling him frightful tales of Burmese cruelty and pluck, warning him to beware of every bush in a jungle, as Burmese sharpshooters lurked there and picked off the commanding officers. They reached Tapoon, and only a few shots had been fired at them; this M. accounted for by saying the whole Burmese force was concentrated in the teak forest between that place and Pounday. The wretched martinet, rather than encounter this force (which existed in M.'s imagination alone), pretended to commit suicide, and when the troops fell in next morning to move on, he was found in his bed covered with blood. He had stabbed himself harmlessly in many places with his penknife, so the second in command assumed his place, and sent him back sick to Prome. A court of inquiry was held, and he was directed to send in his papers.

During the first attack on Mea Toon, which was a failure, a certain Major was in command of the troops: he had been private secretary to a Lieutenant-Governor for many years, and had forgotten his drill. A party of blue-jackets was to accompany the force, under command of a distinguished naval officer. 'Do you or I take command?' asked the gallant sailor. 'You, by all means!' said the soldier. 'Then, follow me!' said the sailor, and off he dashed, followed by his men. He fell into an ambuscade, was shot down with many of his men, but was carried off the field by the survivors. The troops fell into confusion, and would, I believe, have been annihilated had not M., of the 67th, taken command and covered the retreat with the rifle company of his regiment. Young Boileau behaved gallantly, but was killed with two other officers in the second attack.

The second Burmese War opened the eyes of the authorities to the difference between ornamental and practical soldiers. Great things were expected of two or three of the Madras officers who had written learned books on the art of war, and were the pets of the ladies in the drawing and ball rooms. These men were gallant enough and theoretically good men, but they seldom braved the inclemency of the climate, and when called upon to fight for their country they succumbed at once to the heat, and were struck down by the sun. To qualify himself for service, a man from his entrance should accustom himself to the sun, and to brave the hardships attendant on a campaign, which comes easiest to those fond of wild sport. Doubtless many die, but the fittest survive; and our most successful Generals have always preferred sportsmen to carpet knights as leaders of men.

Moreover, in following wild beasts, men get accustomed to danger, learn to act promptly, and have their wits about them. They acquire a quick eye, and in moments of peril do not lose their heads. If they have hunted with their men they learn to know them, and the soldiers learn to know and have confidence in their officers.

The Burmese seldom attacked us by day; when moving through vast prairies, they once or twice set the long grass on fire, but we too burnt in our turn, and cleared spaces to which we could retire until the conflagration had exhausted itself, when we resumed our march. Twice these flames came rather unpleasantly close, and we got somewhat scorched.

But on one occasion some eight or nine Burmese who had lain in ambush could not resist firing into our column, which was marching along quite unconscious of danger. After blazing into us, they apparently lost their senses, for they attempted to escape by running across some dry paddy-fields towards the forest beyond. Some dozen sowars of the Ramghur battalion were after them at once. The paddy-fields in Burma in the dry season are as slippery as ice, and as full of cracks as the cotton soil of India, and anything but pleasant to ride over. But the Pathans are reckless on horseback, and went full pelt after the Burmese; a few fell, but the rest overtook the enemy and speared them one by one. One Burman, seeing escape impossible, pulled up; he had loaded his gun as he ran, and, facing round, waited for his adversary. The sowar did not deviate an inch, but rode as straight as a dart. It was a toss-up which would conquer, but the Burman had the advantage. When the horse was within five or six paces, the Mongolian levelled his gun and fired. We saw a bit of the sowar's turban fly off, and the next moment the Buddhist lay dead, with a spear-thrust through him. These fellows received a well-merited cheer on their return. Several of our men had been hit by the discharge, for the enemy fired at a distance of some twenty paces off; these were soon attended to, and we continued our advance, taking greater precautions in future. In all these expeditions the Sappers were hard worked. They marched in heavy marching order, carrying their entrenching tools in addition to their weapons, and it was a constant cry of 'Sappers to the front!' to clear the road of trees felled across it to retard our progress, or natural obstructions impassable for artillery. We had a couple of guns of the Madras Horse Artillery with us.

Going from Rangoon to Prome by steamer, we had some adventures on the way. About 4 p.m. we reached a considerable town, Meannoung, afterwards the headquarters of the Pegu Light Infantry, and saw some men attempting to crucify another in the veranda of a house alongside the river. The steamer was run into the bank and moored; a few of us jumped on shore and fired a shot or two, and released the man, and then we rushed after the would-be murderers. I don't think we had a spare cartridge between us. Presently we came upon a pagoda, with a parapet built round it and full of armed men, and we prudently retired; but why the Burmese did not sally forth and cut us to pieces I do not know. Probably they thought we had a force at our backs. Not satisfied with our demonstration, the skipper must needs remove several valuable bells, which was contrary to orders. This was reported to the Commissioner, and he was removed from the command of his vessel.

Further on, near Ka-in-gain, or some such name—a large town where we had a detachment—we found Moung Goung Gye in force; he was burning all the villages, and had such a large force with him that the few troops we had there were almost useless. As we had a detachment of Horse Artillery on board, we were asked to co-operate, and we blazed into the jungles right and left, the Dacoits firing at us from the elephant grass. Our commander and some three of us stood on the paddle-boxes, and fired shot after shot with arms of precision at the rebels, but I only saw one man hit. We found their fleet, consisting of several hundred boats, destroyed some, and sent the rest adrift; but we heard afterwards that the Burmese had swum off and rescued the greater part. Some of the *poonghie* houses were full of the insurgents, and the artillerymen made some very pretty practice, and sent a shell or two into them. The people inside rushed out like a swarm of bees, but the projectiles failed to burst, and but little damage was done. Finding the enemy too numerous to be satisfactorily dealt with, our skipper received orders to go off post-haste to Prome for more troops. But before the reinforcements arrived, Goung Gye had the audacity to make a night attack on our troops; he was beaten back with loss, but we lost a few men. Before the new force could act, the rebels had disappeared like so many will-o'-the-wisps, only to reappear miles and miles away.

Directly Latter heard our news he got into a *loung* (a fast Burmese boat), and went off to the scene of the disturbance. On arriving at Meannoung he sent for the *myo-oke*, or head-man. He swaggered up, accompanied by a numerous retinue of armed men, and stood erect, instead of squatting down in accordance with Burmese customs; for no inferior must stand before a superior, but grovel down as a sign of humility. Latter had only three or four peons with him; he did not hesitate a second, but seized his impertinent subordinate, tied him up to a post of the veranda, and gave him fifty lashes; the men who had accompanied their chief, and had doubtless intended to brave the Deputy-Commissioner's authority, if not to murder him, went down on their knees, begged for mercy, and at once came over to the side of order and authority. Had Latter been a less determined man, he would have been killed there and then, as the people of that town, thinking our power on the wane, had sided with Goung Gye.

Numerous attempts had been made to murder this fearless and most able officer. He was more dreaded at Ava than any other member of the Commission, and a large reward was offered for his head by the King of Burma. Unfortunately, his partiality for the fair sex was taken advantage of. Three men were sent down from Umrapoora to murder him. After dining at the mess of the 4th Sikhs, he and I went a part of the way together; we then separated. He went on to his own house (a *kyoung*), and I got on to my pony and rode out to Namyan, five miles off, which was my headquarters. It was very late; Latter had drunk as much wine as was good for him, but he was perfectly sober, though doubtless a little sleepy. The sentry over his quarters had orders not to interfere with any of the fair sex visiting them. The three men, dressed like women, had been waiting under the *poonghie* house for his return. A Jew named Cohen had heard that some men had come down to murder Latter, and went twice to his house to warn him, but found he was out, and was seeking him elsewhere, when Latter returned home and at once went to bed. About an hour after the three disguised men went into his bedroom; the sentry heard a crash, but thought nothing of it; then he heard groans, and called out; receiving no answer, he lifted the curtain and found the Deputy-Commissioner leaning on one elbow, with the blood pouring from his throat. He gave the alarm, but before a medical officer arrived poor Latter was dead and the murderers escaped.

Every Burman carries a sharp-pointed knife, about six inches long. This is used for cutting up food, or for stabbing in brawls. The favourite spot for a blow, and one perfectly deadly, is a downward thrust at the junction of the two collar-bones; bleeding takes place internally, and the person dies of suffocation in a few seconds.

I was out once shooting at Shoaydoung; I heard a girl crying, and should not have thought anything of it had it not continued, so I made my way towards the place, but it was some time before I could find the means of crossing over a deep, muddy nullah. When at last I came upon the remains of a bridge, I found but one plank, about nine inches broad, spanning a stream some hundred feet broad and about fifty feet deep, a ticklish place to cross over, and I took some little time in doing it. When I got across, I found a poor girl, in the first bloom of womanhood, weltering in her blood. The brute had probably seen me, and, fearing the girl would give information which would lead to his capture, had stuck his knife into the fatal spot, and she was barely dead when I found her. I searched for that monster everywhere, and had I come upon him I think I should have shot him like a mad dog. I gave information to the native judge, but the culprit was never found.

The Burmese are most expert thieves. They used to steal the muskets from the quarter-guards of the European regiments. I was once in a very large *poonghie* house: my bed was in one corner; in the centre, on a table, was a light, and a sentry was walking up and down. The sides of the house lifted up and down, and there was a veranda, surrounded by a railing, three feet high, the floor being fully eight feet off the ground. I awoke one night with a sense of danger, and thought someone was trying to steal my guns from under my cot; I called out to the sentry to bring me a light, but he said, 'It is nothing, sahib, only rats.' I listened for some time; as the noise was not repeated, I got out of bed, with a revolver in my hand, ascertained that my gun-cases were all right, and then went into the bath-room. Whilst there I heard a crash, and rushed back, only to find that a box, which had been on the floor at the foot of the bed, had been dragged by someone inserting his hand underneath the jambs; but, as the veranda was a foot lower than the main floor, the box had slipped over and caused the noise. I was out in a moment, but could see no one; but, on examination, I found that a good English blanket, which had been resting, folded up, on the lid of the box, had been walked off with.

These fellows used to insert their hands inside and drag out the uniforms of the sepoys, cut the buttons off, and walk off with the coats. My boy was a capital cook, and used to convert a number of young cocks to capons. These thieves had the impudence not only to steal, but to kill and pluck them, and once they even cooked some a little way off.

Men pretending to sell precious stones used to go about to spy out the nakedness of the land, and then rob right and left. They stole horses from the artillery, but would not touch our elephants, which, they said, did not understand their language. Every officer in Shoaydoung was robbed. I lived about a couple of miles off. My domicile was an open *zyat*, and, as I had a sentry and a strong guard, I did not think it was possible for anyone to loot me, for the sentry could see right through the house, yet I awoke one morning to find that I had been cleaned out. I lost my grandfather's presentation sword, my father's, and my own, and property worth some seven or eight hundred rupees more, and never recovered a farthing's worth, nor did I get any compensation. One officer thought he would catch the robbers. He ostentatiously strapped down a box with chains (first filling it with stones), as if it contained valuables, and, sure enough, one night two men entered his apartment and made for the box. He was out of his bed in a moment, and rushed at them, but, quick as he was, the robbers were quicker; as they ran out, followed closely by the proprietor, they flung back with all their force the massive teak door, which caught their pursuer fairly in the face and floored him. Robberies were so frequent, and the detection of the criminals so rare, that the Deputy-Commissioner told the *myo-oke* if he did not put a stop to them he would be dismissed. Still, not a night passed without some house having been entered. The native magistrate, driven to desperation, got up about midnight, and, with a couple of peons, took up his position under a bridge I had constructed on the new road, about two miles from Shoaydoung, and lay in wait there. About 4 a.m. the party heard voices, and saw several men coming towards them; when quite close they stepped out and shot a couple dead, who, by the merest chance, turned out to be noted robbers, with stolen goods on them. The gang, thinking they had been betrayed, dispersed, and for some time there were no more thefts in that neighbourhood. It was lucky for the official that he shot the right people; they might have been innocent travellers.

So clever and audacious were the thieves at Thayetmyo, that a cordon of sentries had to be formed round the station at dark. One night someone ran amuck; the sentry, one of the 8th Irregular Cavalry, challenged, but as the individual still rushed

on, he gave him two cuts that laid open each shoulder
so that the lungs could be seen, and to his horror found
he had cut down a man of the 2nd Bengal Fusiliers.
Great was his grief, for the Europeans and sowars
were the best of friends, at finding what he had done;
but the whole native regiment subscribed handsomely,
and, wonderful to relate, the fusilier partially recovered
and was pensioned.

The Ramghurs, who had done good service, were
very badly treated. When they returned to India,
their horses — their own property — were sold by
auction, and as there was no demand for them, they
realized only a few rupees each. I bought three. For
one I gave 5 rupees; she was a perfectly black mare,
with good points and quite young. For a gray I gave
1 rupee, and for a roan 2 rupees. The mare I sold
for 50 rupees within a few days. I gave away the
gray, but the roan I kept, and rode him out twenty-
six miles the next day. I used him for a year, and
was then offered 100 rupees for him; but I gave him
to an officer of our 19th, with whom I was living at
that time in Rangoon, and he became afterwards the
property of Dr. B.

This poor fellow met with a sad death. He was
going out to dine, and his young wife, being very near
her confinement, stayed at home. He asked her to
leave out a couple of pills for him to take on his
return. 'But where shall I find them?' asked the
poor girl, who had not been married a year. 'In my
looking-glass drawer,' he replied. So she put out the
first two pills she saw: B. swallowed them and died.
He had quite forgotten that in that drawer he had put

some strychnine pills which he had prepared for killing pariah dogs.

The Ramghurs were replaced by the 8th Bengal Irregular Cavalry, commanded by R., who so distinguished himself at the taking of Mooltan. They were a very fine set of men, and were as much pampered as the Ramghurs had been the reverse, nor had they the same chances of distinguishing themselves as the corps they relieved. They got quite out of the Governor-General's good books by refusing to serve longer in his pet province when their term of service had expired, and were ordered to march back to Bengal by the Tongoop road before it had been half completed.

Lord Dalhousie, perhaps the ablest man who ever ruled India, could not bear anyone to differ in opinion with him. When he visited Prome, he asked our chaplain what he could do for him. 'Take me out of this province, your lordship,' incautiously replied the divine. This angered his lordship, and he would not speak to the chaplain again. He was very fond of Major Fraser, R.E., our chief engineer, and with good reason, for a finer fellow never lived. Old as he was, he looked older, owing to a long white beard which he wore, yet he led the assault on the White House picket at the taking of Rangoon, when the assaulting party of the 51st temporarily hesitated, owing to the death of their leader. He and some six engineers rushed forward, and, calling on the Madras Sappers to follow them, erected the ladders, and took the place by escalade before the other troops had recovered from the confusion into which they had fallen. I remember his saying, at mess, he should have considered it an insult had anyone seized him by his long beard, but that when Lord Dalhousie had done so, in a late interview, he had felt anything but offended. He was a dear old man; he came to the front during the Mutiny, and died Acting Lieutenant-Governor of the North-West Provinces, a post never before or since held by a military man.

I don't know how it is, but most of the old Indian Engineers were fine fellows. Cunningham, who succeeded Fraser, was almost as much liked as his predecessor. W. Trevor ought to have had the Victoria Cross for Burma, only it had not then been established, but he afterwards got it for Bhootan. All the engineers were well to the front in every fight. Opposite to Prome, the hills are seven or eight hundred feet high. On one there were several superb bells, one of which Sir J. C., our leader, greatly admired; but the looting of them had been forbidden by the Commissioner, as he wished to conciliate the people. One engineer—I forget his name for the moment—who also had an eye on that bell, took a company of Sappers with him in broad daylight, brought the bell down, packed it up and sent it off before anything had been said on the subject, because everybody thought it had been taken by the General, and disposed of it, I heard, for £800. The General and Phayre were furious when they heard of it, but the culprit was away, and they could not bring it home to him. For cool audacity, that beat most things.

The Burmese, when they build their pagodas, bury a lot of images of Gaudama just underneath the bell part. In building barracks, we had to remove very many pagodas, and many Engineer and Sapper officers made good hauls; but I, who had the demolishing of perhaps more pagodas than any man of my time, had very bad luck, or the Sappers were too sharp for me, for although I got thousands of small images of thin veneered silver and lead, I only got one of gold, which my agents disposed of for, I think, 300 rupees.

With the exception of the Sappers and Horse Artillery, the force on the Irrawadie consisted of Bengal troops. There has always been a great deal of jealousy between the troops of the two Presidencies. In the earlier part of the century the greater part of the fighting fell to the coast army, but for very many years, except during occasional fighting in petty outbreaks within the limits of the Presidency, and now and then in China, the Madras Army saw little or no service. We played at soldiers. There was too much red-tape. A junior officer ran the risk of being put under arrest if he differed from his senior, even on a matter of weather. I was once reprimanded for appearing at mess with my neckerchief tied once instead of twice round the neck, although such became the universal custom very shortly afterwards. Just after the Crimean war, the rules regarding infantry officers wearing moustaches were relaxed; before that only the Cavalry and Horse Artillery were entitled to them. One day a divisional order was circulated that it had been brought to the notice of the General that some officers had permitted those under them to grow the objectionable hirsute ornament, which was contrary to General Order so-and-so, and directing a discontinuation of the practice at once. So we had all to shave. But a fortnight afterwards the same General issued an order that, having vindicated his authority in a divisional order, he was now graciously pleased to cancel the same, and that in future moustaches might be cultivated. At mess we were as strictly under discipline as on parade.

The Hindoostani we learned was Dekhani—very different from the pure Oordoo of the Bengalies—who spoke the language far better than we did, because they were forced to learn it thoroughly, whilst in Madras every other native spoke or understood English. In time, as the Bengal Presidency increased, the Bengalese troops vacated several Southern stations, and Madrassies were sent to replace them. The contrast between the Poorbiahs and the short Madras men was great. The former were a tall, handsome, broad-shouldered race, and possessed of a martial bearing. Our men looked pigmies beside them. The Bengal troops were well dressed and accoutred; our men were the very reverse, and with their ridiculous headdress were the laughing-stock of the officers of the greater Presidency. The Madras officers, jealous of the better appearance of the Oude men, sought to recruit them too, but only succeeded to a very limited extent: and the few men we had in the Madras regiments from the other Presidency were invariably the best men, and made the best native officers. But the Oude men did not care to go so far South, so, as they could not be got in sufficient numbers, the commanding officers looked about them; those who had been stationed in the Northern Division noticed that the Talenga men were taller, and if dressed in uniform would look better on parade than the Southern Division men, who were short, but came of the fighting castes of Southern India.

It was acknowledged by all Generals that the Madras Sappers and Miners were second to no troops in India; they had done splendid service from Afghan downwards, and from Abyssinia and Persia to China; they were of the pure Southern fighting castes. But the men of the Northern Division were a long-legged race, without fighting traditions, and more fitted to carry palanquins and to be fishermen than soldiers; but because they looked better on parade, they were enlisted freely, and the fighting castes left out. To such an extent had this mania spread that the only reliable troops we possessed, viz., the Sappers and Miners, were very nearly being ruined; their headquarters were moved from Merkara to Dowlaishwarum, and the long-legged Talenga enlisted. But the new element was not found equal to the old. Time proved the uselessness of the new recruits, and before very much harm had been done the Sappers were removed back to Mysore, and the old class of men re-enlisted. To show what these sturdy little fellows could do, when the first Chinese war broke out two companies of Sappers marched from Merkara to Madras, some three hundred miles, in a week, going almost day and night. In Burma some of the companies suffered terribly. My own company landed 103 strong, and I think only three of the originals went back alive.

In the final advances on Mea Toon, a nullah had

to be crossed, and rafts were being constructed by the Sappers; but the fire from the opposite side was so heavy that the European Sapper sergeant discontinued the work. Jemadar Appiah stepped to the front, lantern in hand, tested each knot, and, though exposed to the heaviest fire, did not desist till the raft was ready, and then stepped on shore and reported all complete.

In 1853 we, the few Madrassies, amidst a great number of Bengalies, had to stand a good deal of chaff from our more fortunate brethren; but I liked the Bengal officers and men very much. It is true that the discipline in the ranks was laxer than ours, but on service they had always fought well, though there was a little too much caste about the men. Their messes, too, far inferior to ours in organization, kit, plate, etc., were pleasanter than ours, and more like well-regulated clubs, free from undue restraint. All met on equality, and I never saw but once, and that only when the necessity arose, an officer rebuke another at the mess table. This was a very agreeable change from the stiff routine of similar establishments in Madras.

Our mess in Prome consisted of the Engineers, Sappers, and staff officers, and a very jolly time we had of it. The Bengal and Madras Artillery had a mess to themselves, but on service the Artillery and Sappers messed together, unless invited to become honorary members of the mess of some regiment, which was generally the case.

On various expeditions into the interior, I had helped to map out the country. I passed in surveying, civil and military engineering, and was offered an appointment by Sir Arthur Phayre in the Department of Public Works. For some years I carried on the duties of a sapper and also of a civil engineer, and as my duties led me into remote districts, and I had also to survey from Prome to Rangoon, I began to discover the whereabouts of game, whence my career as a sportsman may be said to have commenced. I was always fond of sport. My experience as a child may have strengthened a natural inclination that way, and living as I did often for months and months together in the jungles, blessed with youth, a good constitution, and almost total independence, I lost no opportunities of hunting the wild beasts of the East.

I got a bad attack of fever marching down to Rangoon, and had to go to Moulmein for a change. The scenery round that town is lovely, and I enjoyed my month's stay there greatly. At the mess one night, P., of the 30th—a fine, well-grown young fellow—began to lay down the law on boxing, maintaining that no small man had a chance against a bigger one in boxing. 'Why, P.,' said I, 'come and breakfast with O. and myself to-morrow, and I'll bring a man of the 2nd Bengal Fusiliers, much shorter than yourself, who will lick you into a cocked hat in half an hour.' I asked Paddy C. to come over; the room was cleared, the gloves put on, but poor P. was 'nowhere.' All the officers of the 1st and 2nd Fusiliers were expert boxers, and by constant practice had become adepts at the noble art of self-defence. In a few minutes C. had P.'s head in chancery, and O. and I cried with laughter at the unequal combat, which was conducted on both sides with the greatest good temper.

After that I never heard P. brag again. One day two tigers strayed into the hills inside the town, and after an exciting chase we accounted for them both.

One of the saddest of my reminiscences of Burma is one connected with the execution of a soldier of H.M.'s 29th Regiment by hanging. The man undoubtedly deserved death; he had deliberately stabbed a comrade. They had been drinking, and then played cards. The man lost, left the table, procured a knife, and returned and killed his late opponent.

This occurred in 1857, about the time the great Mutiny commenced. He was tried and sentenced to death by a general court-martial. For some reason or another the proceedings went backwards and forwards between Calcutta and the headquarters of his regiment, then at Thayetmyo. Before the sentence was confirmed fully a year had elapsed, during which the man had lingered in gaol. During the interval India was convulsed, and our power all but paralyzed by the Mutiny. We required the services of every available white man, and the culprit, then a reformed character, who had heartily repented him of his crime, begged to be sent to the front to meet a soldier's death, fighting for his country, and not to be hanged like a dog. The man he had stabbed was dead, and could not be brought to life again. The chaplain and all his officers interceded in his behalf, but one day the order came for his execution. The first difficulty was to erect a scaffold. Directly the Burmese carpenters found out what it was for they struck work; the Chinese also refused. Sir T. W., the executive engineer, had the greatest difficulty in getting the job finished in time for the carrying out of the sentence of the law. He had to engage Indians and Europeans of the Artillery at exorbitant rates, and then the scaffold was not completed till 6 a.m. A hollow square was formed; the 29th faced the gibbet, the two sides being formed by the Artillery, Sappers, and Native Infantry. The condemned man, a strong, sturdy fellow in the prime of life, appeared with his hands tied in front of him; his coffin was borne just ahead, and the chaplain accompanied him, reading the prayers for the dead. The man showed neither fear nor bravado, but bore himself as a soldier, ready to meet his death. I, as a Sapper, was the closest to the place of execution. He was marched round the three sides of the square; as he came in front of his own regiment, several of the men and an officer fainted. When he came to the scaffold, he ascended without help; he begged the sergeant of the guard to adjust the rope round his neck, as he objected to being touched by the native sweeper. The cap was drawn over his face, the bolt withdrawn, and he fell some six feet. The troops were then marched past the dead body, still suspended, and all was over. I cannot help thinking that, however necessary an example as a deterrent to others may at times be, under the peculiar circumstances of the case his life might have been spared, and his wish to die for his country, fighting against the mutineers, been gratified.

In the days when the East India Company had unlimited sway over India, no missionaries were allowed into the country; but we are a meddlesome people, and can never let well alone. Gradually the powers of the ruling body were relaxed, and missionaries admitted, but, though the greater part of them had the sense not to attempt to interfere with the religion of our mercenaries, still, the small end of the wedge was introduced. The old officers were fighting men, devoted to their profession; the greater the daredevil, the more he was worshipped by his men. But for a few years before 1857 several officers, who had evidently mistaken their vocation, took to preaching, not only to the outside natives, but to their men, and a few were injudicious enough to show favour and affection to a pervert, or convert, whichever you please to style the renegade from the religion of his fathers. This unsettled the minds of the high-caste Brahmin and Mussulman sepoys, and led them to believe anything said to our detriment. Had the proselytizing officers been publicly dismissed, as they ought to have been, confidence might have been restored; but when the Enfield rifle was introduced, with its greased cartridges, the men were only too ready to believe anything the disaffected told them about our intentions to destroy their caste. The Hindoos were told the cartridges were greased with the fat of cows, the Mussulmans that pig's fat was being used; the men became the dupes, and broke out in rebellion. When will the subsequent horrors ever be forgotten? or how can the violation and murder of so many of our countrywomen and children ever be expiated?

CHAPTER V.

BURMESE LIFE.

Failure of missionaries among the Burmese—Their success among the Karens—Matrimony in Burma—Relation of the sexes—Origin of the Burmese—Their freedom from caste—Their manners, customs and characteristics—A romp in the river—Burmese fondness for children—Their courtship—Their priests—Roman Catholic nuns—The Buddhist religion—Karens—Burmese theatricals and dancing girls—The Assamese—Half-breeds—The Kachens—Fires in Burma—An affray—A soldier punished for doing his duty—Sir A. Phayre—'Dismal Jemmy'—His treatment of me—A gallant Brigadier—One of another kind—Anecdotes—How the two Brigadiers left Tongo—Our chief engineer—Roguery of subordinates—Public works—Abandonment of Namyan—Sir Trevor Wheler astonishes a Burman—Gallantry of 'the Sweep'—A mad doctor.

It is very well to attempt to convert the heathen, but there is plenty of work to do among the ungodly in our own country. Why invade a country like India, which had religions of its own long before the dawn of Christianity? The Hindoos do worship idols, but the Mussulmans don't. As for the Buddhists, their religion is very similar to ours, only much older. Him whom we call Christ they designate as Buddha. Many of the sayings attributed to our Saviour in the New Testament are but copies from the sayings of Buddha, written down in Pali seven hundred years before the Christian era. No one can convert high-caste Brahmins, or Mussulmans, or Buddhists, who understand the tenets of their own faith. Preaching the Gospel in India only unsettles the minds of the natives, and makes them doubt our good faith. I remember a lamentable case in a Sikh corps. The Commandant converted a man, and showed him every indulgence. He was allowed a small tent to himself, but not a soul in the ranks would speak to him, or eat or drink with him—his life was a burden. His comrades used to defile his tent, and the poor fellow had to act as his own sweeper, and clear out the garbage every morning. His life was a long misery. Very many of these proselytizing officers were no doubt sincere and consistent, but all were not so. In India you cannot sneeze without its being known all over the bazaar, and what must the natives have thought of some of those Christians who privately led impure lives?

There was an officer of our Artillery who had a long-standing feud with the principal medical officer of the station; they detested one another. One day I met him at dinner at the house of a common friend, with whom I was then living. After dinner, B., the officer in question, said, 'D.,' addressing his host, who was as thorough and as good a Christian as ever lived, 'shall we read a chapter?' Then, turning round to me, he added, 'That is, if Pollok does not object.' 'Don't mind me,' I replied; 'go a-head.' B. produced a huge Bible; each page had but one or two verses of the Holy Scriptures; the rest was a commentary in very small type, by somebody who evidently thought God's word needed explanation, and that he was better qualified to interpret the sayings of our Lord than either He or His disciples. B. commenced, 'The man who hateth his brother hath committed murder in his heart.' I forget the exact words. He then put down the Bible, and said, in a sanctimonious and self-satisfied tone, 'Well, thank God I was never guilty of that.' 'Come, come, B.,' said I, 'what about the late Superintendent Surgeon? I am sure you hated him enough.' 'No, no,' said B., 'I did not hate him, but I must own I disliked him very much.' 'Well,' said I, 'we will call that manslaughter. Go on.' But somehow B.'s power of elocution failed him, and after praying for the souls of regenerate sinners, amongst whom I have no doubt he included me, he took his departure.

Very many of the missionaries, in Burma especially, were from America; they were scarcely the class to prevail with such a fastidious race as the Bhuddists of that land. Many of them were of exceedingly humble origin, who had tried their hands at many trades in their own country, and, failing in all, fell back on teaching the acutest people on earth the doctrines of a faith which they themselves scarcely understood.

Whilst the missionaries amongst the Burmese all but starved on their small stipends, unless they did a bit of private trading, which many did, those sent to convert the Karens lived in clover. These people had no fixed religion, but they cherished a legend that the true faith would be revealed to them through a people ruled by a woman. The missionaries, knowing this, claimed to have come from our Queen, and these ignorant people accepted the Gospel blindly in batches of fifty and more.

The missionaries no doubt have done good among the Karens, but they have not had a like success amongst the Burmese. At one large town, where there was a large school for the education of Burmese and other girls, the only abandoned females were found there. The Burmese are not immaculate, but they look upon it as shameful to visit any man for money; they will do so readily enough if there has been any affection between them, and do not think that degrading; but as for professional profligacy, it was unknown in those days.

Matrimony is a light bond in Burma. A couple who live together publicly are recognised as man and wife, but the tie can always be dissolved at pleasure. Marriage, as it exists among them, is a matter generally of free choice, and is attended by a good deal of courtship on the part of the man, and coquetry on that of the girl. As long as a woman is well treated, she is generally faithful; but if she has had a lover before marriage, she considers that he has a prior claim on her, and will not hesitate to renew relations with him, if he wishes it. In ordinary life she is her husband's equal, and vastly his superior in the house, for she buys and sells at pleasure, mixes in all society, goes about unshackled, and leads a happy, contented life. So bounteous is Mother Earth in Burma, that poverty is all but unknown there; by labouring for three months a family can subsist in idleness for the remaining nine. Fish is to be had in plenty, and some of it—for instance, the *hilsa*—is even superior to salmon. Many of the coarser kinds of the finny tribe are converted into *gnapee*, a favourite dish of theirs. It is composed of fish pounded up with salt, and then preserved; the odour is most offensive, and the very thought of it nearly makes me feel sick.

The Burmese have no caste. They are of Tartar origin, have high cheek-bones, and the broad faces, flat noses, and slanting eyes peculiar to the Mongolian race.

A Burman is not wanting in pluck; he is generally under the middle height, slightly but compactly built, possessing considerable strength. He is fond of wrestling and boxing, in which kicking is permitted, and plays at football, which is also in vogue in the neighbouring countries, and in Malaya and Siam. But by nature he is indolent, and will not work unless forced by necessity, and then he will labour like a slave, propelling a heavy boat up-stream all day. He learns to smoke and to swim before he is weaned from his mother's breast, and is tattooed from the waist to a little below the knee as a sign of manhood. He is a born gambler, and will bet his bottom rupee on a boat-race, a main of cocks, or a spurt on ponies. He is a daring and expert robber, fond of raids by day or night; when his evil passions are not aroused, he is kind-hearted and as merry as a cricket. He is very cleanly in his person, and delights in gorgeous apparel. He is also affectionate to his offspring, seldom possessing more than one, or at the most two wives, for the women are jealous and do not care to share a man between them. His complexion is fair for an Eastern; he shows marks of respect by sitting down unbidden, instead of standing up like most Orientals. He is a capital pedestrian, but will seldom walk if he can ride or get a lift. Indolent and averse to all exertion as he is generally, he can exert himself if he chooses. He will sit up night after night, listening to one of their interminable *pooays*, or theatrical performances. He smokes incessantly, and does not object to a tot of grog. Should he take service, he will freely help himself to his master's tobacco, tea or sugar, and not consider this pilfering.

He is proud of his hair, which is very long, luxuriant, and worn tied up in a knot at the top of his head, with perhaps a gaudy handkerchief coiled round it in lieu of the customary turban. His ears are pierced, and the holes in the lobes extended until he can insert a good-sized cheroot therein. Unless very poor, he condescends to wear nothing but silk *putsoos*, a cloth which is tied round the waist, hangs down to the knees, and is then drawn up tight between the thighs, the end being inserted in the waistband behind. In lieu of a coat he wears a long flowing jacket. He excels as a carver of wood and in carpentering generally, and shows considerable architectural skill and taste in the construction of his monasteries or *poonghie* houses. He is charity itself—never accumulates wealth, unless it be in the ornaments he lavishes on his wife and children. If by a stroke of luck he realizes a fortune, he forthwith spends it in works of charity, and in building *kyoungs* for his priests, and *zyats*, or resting-houses, for the weary. Along all the roads, at intervals, there are small elevated sheds in which are daily deposited pots of water to refresh the traveller.

7

Every lad is taught to read and write his own language. Every village and town has its monastery, wherein each boy is taught free of charge. School commences about an hour before daybreak. Suddenly every boy commences to shout out his lessons at the top of his voice, and a babel commences which, to say the least of it, is startling to one unaccustomed to it. I know, the first time I heard it, I thought it was an attack by Dacoits, and jumped out of bed and quickly dressed to repel the marauders. With the exception of the very poor, who bury their dead because they cannot afford to cremate them, the Burman burns his, and has a grand ceremony over the event. When a member of a family dies, professional women howl the death-chant over him or her, the coffin is constructed in the street outside the house, and a pyre is prepared as near as possible; the defunct is carried there, and reduced to ashes amidst the cries and lamentations of the relations.

But in the case of a priest, especially if he is of any note, the remains are embalmed. The body is deposited in a house built expressly for that purpose, with bamboo tubes to convey the gases from the body to the earth. The corpse is kept there for a year, carefully guarded by neophytes. The whole population then turns out. Many dummy coffins are made, besides the one containing the defunct, and neatly arranged in a cluster in an adjoining plain. The principal pyre is conspicuous from its greater size and the gorgeousness of its surroundings. Some time before the day fixed for the final scene booths are erected, hundreds of carts with their living freights assemble, the people camp out, and a regular fair is held. On the appointed day, the car containing the dead is drawn in state to its final resting-place. When near its destination, ropes are attached to the car, front and rear, and a mock struggle takes place, one party propelling and the other retarding the coffin. Generally it is only a farce, but at times the two sides get excited, the car is upset, and its ghastly contents are thrown out. At last those holding back give in, and amid deafening shouts the deceased is placed over the pyre which has been prepared for him. This is constructed of the most inflammable materials, and has, moreover, some gunpowder hidden in it. Long horizontal ropes are stretched, and to them rockets are attached, and all endeavour to set it on fire, for whoever first succeeds is deemed most fortunate. All this time a brisk trade is carried on. Every man, woman, girl, and child is dressed in holiday costume. There is nothing but mirth around. No stranger would dream that it was a funeral of a high-priest. The hubbub and noise are deafening, the dust fearful. The ground is covered with flagstaffs, flags, banners, and general jollification is the order of the day.

At last the pyre, with a slight report, as a rocket goes home to the magazine, is alight, the fire quickly spreads, and all the adjacent structures, as well as the one containing the coffin, so tastefully got up at a considerable cost, are burnt to the ground; in half an hour nothing is left but ashes and smoke from the smouldering ruins. The crowd disperses; the priests collect the charred remains of their defunct brother, and put them into a small shell of silver or gold, which they either bury in the bosom of Gaudama or deposit in the tumulus in a pagoda. The scene, however repugnant to our feelings, is a very gay one whilst it lasts. The apparel of the men and women, the numerous emblems displayed, and the beauty of the flimsy structures so gaily painted and resplendent with tinsel, silk, and gold and silver leaf, help to light up what ought to be a sombre scene.

As I have before said, the Burmese are inveterate gamblers, the women being as bad as the men. During their sports they all mix together freely, and bet right and left. Their excitement at a close race, especially in a boat contest, cannot be imagined by anyone who has not witnessed one: the people go wild, backing one side or the other. They will bet everything they possess, and more. Many a girl, after losing all her jewellery and what money she possessed, will, if attractive, stake herself against what she considers her value, and, if she loses, will follow the winner (she generally, on such an occasion, takes good care to bet with a bachelor not unpleasing to herself), and becomes his wife or concubine, for the two are synonymous in Burma.

The Burmese, unlike the natives of India (who delight in marrying children), prefer their wives to be full-grown and matured, and capable of bearing healthy children. A Burman is a man of contradictions; his good qualities about balance his bad, but, with all his faults, I prefer him to a native of Southern India. As for the women, they are not pretty; at first their peculiar features detract from their charms, but when one gets used to their physiognomy, they are very taking.

They are small, but perfectly formed. They have not the voluptuous forms of the best of the Hindoo girls, but are well knit together, and until they become mothers, none could be better moulded in proportion to their height; their busts, arms, and feet might serve as models to the most exigent of sculptors. It is considered exceedingly improper for a girl to expose her bosom, but directly she has a child she thinks nothing of nursing in public. They are the quintessence of cleanliness, and always bathe once, generally twice, and in the hot weather even three times a day. The hair of the head is their glory; they take the greatest care of it, and dress it *à la Chinoise*, with a garland of sweet-smelling flowers entwined.

The unmarried girls wear an under-jacket, which fits tight to the figure and supports the bust, and a flowing jacket over; for show, a gaudy scarf hangs down on either side over the shoulders, partially concealing the perfect contour of the bosom. From the waist downwards they wear a silk *tamien* of most elaborate pattern, which exposes the inside of the right leg halfway up the thigh, or a *loongee*, which is more of a petticoat, exposing no part of the person. The lobes of their small and shapely ears are distended like the men's, and in them they insert elongated amber earrings or costly gold ones. Their fingers are covered with rings; their pretty arms and necks are covered with as many bracelets and necklets as they can get together. Their love for finery is, like that of the rest of the sex elsewhere, inordinate. They all smoke, and chew betel-nut and *saparie*, but have nice, white, even teeth. They can all swim, and delight in dabbling about in water.

On their New Year's Day, which corresponds with our April 1, the girls go about with pots of water and drench all they meet. On one occasion, knowing the custom, Worsley, of the 47th Bengal Native Infantry, and I, donning the shabbiest garments we possessed, mounted our ponies and rode into the town of Prome. We told our syces to keep close. We had not gone far when a bevy of girls, who were drawn up on either side of the road we had to pass, doused us. We were off our ponies in a moment, and after them like lightning. The girls, finding us overtaking them, took to the river; there were vast rafts of teak timber moored alongside the bank, and as we plunged in after them, they tried to dodge us amongst the logs. But Worsley and I were then only about twenty-one; we could both swim and dive as well as the best amongst the girls, and we soon caught and ducked them well. At first they were very wroth, as it is not usual to take reprisals on these occasions, but finding that we did it only in fun, they retaliated, and some dozen of them setting on us at once, ducked us in return, and for a good quarter of an hour I never had greater fun in my life. We were fighting, as it were, for bare life against many. In the scrimmage the slender raiment of the girls, which was but wrapped round them and looped loosely across the bosom and at the waist, soon got adrift, and there were we surrounded by a merry crew of as beautifully made sprites as one could wish to see. A great crowd had assembled on the beach enjoying the fun, and when we thought we had taken our revenge, we helped the girls to collect their garments and to clothe them. We all landed like so many half-drowned rats; but a wetting in the East, especially in April, does little harm. We soon found a booth kept by a Madrassie, who sold hot coffee and tea, and a few cups of the fragrant infusion soon diffused warmth into the bosoms of our fair opponents and ourselves. The Burmese are the only people, except the Chinese, in the East, who understand or appreciate a joke. They are merry by nature, and the least absurdity will tickle their risible faculties.

When we first occupied the country, the greatest favour you could confer on a girl was to give her a cake of soap. They had an idea that the white lather helped to make Europeans fair. They greatly admire a white, healthy skin, especially if accompanied by dark eyes and hair and a hairless face. They do not admire hairy men, as they say they remind them of apes. The Burmese as a race never cultivate hair about their faces or their bodies—in fact, they are nearly devoid of all hair except such as grows on their heads.

Burmese women and girls are free to visit European families; a bevy of girls will not hesitate to visit even a bachelor, just to show themselves off and their ornaments, and perhaps to attract an admirer, for these little women have no objection to accept a *kala* (a foreigner) as a husband according to their laws and customs—and very good wives they make, too. The Burmese men are not unduly jealous of their women. They say if a woman wishes to be unfaithful, nothing will prevent her all the watching and prying in the world will be thrown away—and it is therefore better to trust them than to be always doubting them.

A girl's great ambition is to keep a stall in a bazaar. It is her introduction into society, and is equivalent to our own girls being brought out, and a sign that she is of a marriageable age. During a courtship, if a girl lights her admirer's cheroot, giving it a few puffs herself, it is a sign that she is willing to accept him, but if she refuses, he had better go elsewhere.

There is not a prettier sight in the world than to see a crowd of Burmese on a gala-day, as they go in procession to one of their shrines; their gay dresses, pretty figures, smiling faces, banners flying, flags streaming, make a display difficult to beat anywhere; add to it the beauty of the surrounding scenery, the elegant proportions of their shrines, the architecture of their *kyoungs*, and the merry voices of the young, and you have a scene difficult to match. The sides of the roads along which they march are covered with booths containing offerings for the gods, or as propitiations to the *nats* (evil spirits); there is not a dull moment until the apex of the hillock on which the pagoda stands is reached. Then there is a solemn silence: they kneel down in groups, and with upraised, clasped hands they supplicate the deity. The women cannot read or write, as their priests are not only forbidden to teach them, but must not speak to them, or even look at them.

A priest cannot possess any property. He is a genuine mendicant, dependent for daily food and raiment on the charity of his flock. Lads dressed in yellow, with bowls suspended round their necks or on their breasts, go round daily. They do not supplicate alms, but the people put into the bowls such offerings as they can spare, and the mendicants then silently pursue their course till every house has been visited.

The priests can eat but once a day, and drink nothing but water, and lead strictly moral lives. There are no nunneries near their abodes, but what struck me as the height of cruelty was seeing young, comely girls exported as Roman Catholic nuns to the Gaboon, a climate deadly enough for males, but certain death to these poor creatures, who linger a year or so, die out, and are replaced by others. As they do nothing towards the curing of souls of the African heathens, there can be but one reason for locating them in such a pestilential climate.

The Burmese priest is perforce condemned to celibacy, for no woman could be induced to permit his addresses. If such a thing occurred and was found out, not only would she be killed, but every one of her relations would expect to be tortured in their several places of punishment after death for generations. After a man has become a priest, if he tires of the sacred calling, he can throw off his sacerdotal garb, resume the ordinary dress of a Burman, and become a layman. Very few, however, ever do so, and no one who had once thrown off the garb would ever be allowed to resume it again.

The Buddhist religion, if acted up to, is as pure as most doctrines, and more comforting than many in some respects. It teaches belief in a Supreme Spirit, which created and creates all things, Buddha being his impersonification on earth. There is no eternal punishment; no one is pure; there is innate sin, which must be expiated, and this is done by the transmigration of souls. People are punished in accordance with the sins they committed when on earth, and are gradually purged thereof. Eventually, when they have expiated their sins, they are again absorbed in the godhead whence they sprung, which is called Nibban. This does not mean annihilation, but simply an absorption into the Power which originally created. The doctrines of Buddha were preached fully a thousand years before the commencement of the Christian era. The pagodas at Rangoon and Pegu were in course of construction when Remus jumped over the walls of Rome, and very many of the sayings attributed to our Saviour are to be found in Buddhist books, written some hundreds of years before His advent. The Buddhist priests laugh when a Protestant missionary tries to convert him, and say, 'You call Him Christ, we call Him Buddha—same person. Your religion,' they remark, 'is only copied from ours. You stick to your version, and we will stick to ours.' I look upon it as impossible to make a sincere convert of either a Mussulman, a Brahmin, or a Buddhist, because their religions suit them; they thoroughly believe in them, and under them they have thriven very many thousand years.

The Karens who lived on the highlands on the borders of Burma are quite a distinct race, more closely resembling the Cossyahs and the Jynteahs on the confines of Assam, whilst the Cacharies of the plains of Assam are no doubt the descendants of the Burmese, who overran the valley of the Brahmapootra for many years. The hill tribes are a fine, manly race, possessed of great bodily strength, and capable of carrying as heavy weights as the *hamals* of Constantinople or of Syria.

Their loads are supported by means of straps hooked on to the shoulders and a band across the forehead. Their dress somewhat resembles the tunic worn by the ancient Romans. The women, especially those of the Darjeeling Terai, are credited with being able to carry heavier weights even than the men. There is a legend that a gentleman, wishing to have a piano carried up to the station, showed it to a porter, who tried the weight, shook his head, and said, 'Although I cannot take it myself, I think my sister can,' which it is said she did. The women are massively built, but with Christianity they have not imbibed the habits of cleanliness. Unless caught young, and trained in the house of a European, they are too filthy to look at; but with the ayahs of Shillong and the Karen attendants on missionaries in Burma cleanliness has become a habit, and many of the young girls are passably pretty and well made.

Feuds are common amongst the savage Karens, who are divided into white, red and black. Their war-gongs are peculiar, and are greatly prized, and the secret of their manufacture has almost died out. They are cylindrical in shape, made of metal, and have only one head, on which metal frogs are soldered. Those with a ring of single frogs can strike a note that can be heard over one range of hills; those that have a row of two frogs, one on the top of the other, can be heard over two ranges; whilst those with three, which are very rare and proportionately prized, are good to give warning over three ranges, and have been the cause of many feuds, the tribes fighting amongst themselves for the possession of one.

They are given to raiding; the buying and selling of boys and girls, and slavery in a mitigated form, are prevalent. The Karen country is principally valuable for its teak forests. At times all these hill people have given us a good deal of trouble; they erect strong stockades and *pangy* the approaches. A *pangy* is a small bamboo stake driven into the ground, with the point an inch above ground. This point is hardened by fire and barbed, and will go through the sole of an ordinary ammunition boot. These obstructions they cover over with leaves, etc., and they make most formidable defences.

None of the Burmese think it immoral for one of their women to live with a European, as she is considered his wife by the custom of the country. If her protector dies or leaves the country, the girl soon finds a native husband. She has generally accumulated some property, has jewellery, and perhaps a house has been given her. She is considered, like many a widow at home, a decided catch. If there be a child or children by the European, it is no bar to her in marrying again. These children are taken care of fully as well, if not better, than any children she may have by her second venture. The women especially, but also the men, are very fond of children whiter than themselves. But somehow the progeny of the pure European with any of these races does not come up in comeliness to those born of Moguls, or traders from the Persian Gulf, or even to the offspring of a Chinaman and his Burmese wife.

The stigma which attaches to dancing-girls in India does not extend to Burmese girls taking a part in a *pooay*. The Burmese are far more musical than the Indians, have sweet voices both in singing and in speaking, and their musical instruments are all tuned and graded like our own, though outlandish to look at. A celebrated actress (and all the girls are born actresses), who had a great name in Burma, was performing a *shoaydung* before a large audience. There were many of us looking on. Amongst other things, to show the pliability of her body, she had to stand on a mark. A small coin was put a foot or so behind her heels, and she had to go over and pick it up with her teeth. Whilst in this position, in which it looked as if she would break in two, a big officer of the 2nd Fusiliers stepped forward, put his hand under her, and, with a movement of his hand and arm, tossed her on to her feet. She performed, of course, a complete somersault, and was taken quite unawares. Instead of being angry or disconcerted, the moment she lit on her feet she went on dancing in her most approved style, and fairly brought down what should have been the house, only that we were in the open air.

The Assamese are probably the most debased and effeminate race under our control in India. The young girls of the better class in Assam are often pretty and well made, but frightfully immoral.

About eighteen miles from Gowhatty, there is a celebrated shrine called Hazoo. People of all creeds

—even Mussulmans, who abhor idols—crowd thither. The Bhootians, with their praying wheels and their baggage animals (sheep), assemble there; but I believe it is more to worship at the shrine of Venus than to perform religious rites, for, with the exception of the priests, no men are allowed to live there permanently. The three villages consist of women, girls, and children only. These women are remarkably well made and good-featured, and dress more like Madrassies than Assamese, and are all courtezans.

Every Hindoo temple has its votaries in the shape of very many dancing-girls, considered, like Mohammed's houries in Paradise, perpetual virgins. The Cacheries are a jolly, drunken race, but much oppressed by the Mouzadars, who are all Hindoos, and who force them to do all the porterage of the province. They are pressed and taken miles and miles from their homes, often without food, to carry the baggage of some sahib, whilst the lazy opium-eating and spirit-drinking Assamese are spared. The Cachins of Burma are supposed to be the descendants of the original inhabitants of the country. They were much oppressed in former years by their conquerors, and fled into the hills and other remote places. They tattoo the faces of their women, and give as a reason that they were so admired by the Burmese that periodical raids were made by the stronger race, and their women carried off on account of their beauty. What they may have been in former days I do not know; but an uglier set it would be difficult to meet nowadays anywhere, and the tribe may rest assured that no future raids for wives will ever be made on them. The Garrowes are savages pure and simple, going about without a stitch of clothing.

The women wear iron and brass rings in their ears, and the lobes often reach to the shoulder. To show how vindictive and determined the Burmese are in avenging an injury, I may state the following: I was living with an officer of the 4th Sikhs at Eeingmah, twenty-seven miles from Prome. About half-past four in the morning we heard the most dismal howling from a village about half a mile off. Thinking it was a case of dacoity, we hastily dressed, and, armed with revolvers, made for the hamlet, sending orders to the guard for a party of armed sepoys to follow us. We found a man had been murdered, his throat having been cut from ear to ear. He was sleeping between his two wives, one of whom recognised the murderer as he made off, and we learnt the following particulars afterwards: About a year before there was a case of dacoity, and the murdered man had given evidence which led to the conviction of the murderer, who was sentenced to be imprisoned in the Prome gaol for a number of years. The night of the murder, this Dacoit had clambered over the gaol wall, some fifteen feet high, had walked out to his village, revenged himself on the informer, and got off scot-free.

No one can realize a fire in a town in Burma, or even the periodical burnings of the vast savannas, without having seen one. In three years Prome, a town extending along the river bank for fully three-quarters of a mile, and over a quarter of a mile broad, was twice burnt down, scarcely a single house escaping.

On one occasion Worsley, of the 47th, and I got to

the Cutcherry with great difficulty; the flames were sweeping across the streets, igniting the opposite houses. We had to run and dodge, and got to the court-house to find the Deputy-Commissioner wringing his hands and saying that all his records would be destroyed.

We climbed on to the roof, and with hands and feet tore off the thatch, throwing it down. Flakes of lighted combustibles constantly fell on our building, and we had to rush to the place and cast down the inflammable materials. We worked like slaves, and could get no one to assist us; they were not salamanders, they said. The thatch was at last off the original wooden roof, for the building was an old *poonghie* house; but the mat sides, which had been added by us, began to smoke, and we thought it was all up with this palace of justice. The Deputy-Commissioner was still crying out what should he do. In fun I said, 'Do! Why, let it burn, and, as certain commissariat officers were supposed to have done in China after periodical fires, make your fortune.' 'What do you mean?' screamed the irate official. 'Why,' said I, 'when the records are destroyed, pocket the money, and retire as a millionaire.' He was speechless with rage at my supposing, as he thought, that he was capable of such an act of infamy, and would not speak to me for some time afterwards; but our actions contradicted our words, for if anything saved those records it was the joint exertions of Worsley and myself, and we were afterwards thanked for what we had done by the Commissioner. In these fires, cats, dogs, numerous *tuck-*

toos (large lizards), and now and then men, women, and children would be burnt to death. I saw an old woman who had been roasted alive, and her skin crackled like that of a roast pig. But the people are not much cast down by these conflagrations; they pick up the pieces, and set to work to rebuild without a murmur. The only result is that the price of all bamboos and thatching materials goes up a bit.

The Deputy-Commissioner was very consequential, and thought no end of himself and his position. A party of Sappers, under a naigue belonging to my company, were marching along; the cash-chest (empty) was on a cart being dragged by a pair of bullocks. The Burmese, recognising the box, and thinking it was full of rupees, attacked. The naigue, after due warning, gave the word to fire; one man fell, and the rest ran away. A complaint was lodged before the Deputy, who, on the *ex parte* statement, sent me an official order to send the 'murderers' in. I replied that I objected to any soldier being styled a murderer until it had been proved that he was one; that I was astonished that he, who would have to try the case, should thus prejudge it, and declined to comply with his request under the circumstances, adding that his letter and mine would be sent on to the General to be laid before the Commissioner. I knew this would drive him mad, for he considered himself infallible, and stood a great deal on his dignity.

So I got on to my pony the next day and rode straight up to his quarters. In came the Deputy with his nose in the air, and greeted me with, 'My God, man! what do you mean by writing me such a letter?'

'My God, man!' I replied, 'what did *you* mean by calling a man under my orders a murderer?' So at it we went, hammer and tongs; but as I would not budge an inch, he offered to withdraw his letter if I would withdraw mine, and as I had written it with a view of taking a rise out of him, I consented, and we breakfasted together amicably.

The naigue was tried and sentenced by the Deputy to imprisonment, but we appealed, and the Commissioner said he should have acquitted the man had the chest contained any money; as it was empty, he thought the act of firing unjustifiable, but commuted his sentence to six months' simple imprisonment, and at the same time made him officiating jemadar of the gaol, which carried certain emoluments with it, so the naigue was rather the gainer. But I consider he only did his duty when he repelled the attack, and I do not see what the chest being empty had to do with it one way or the other. When attacked a soldier should use his arms, and to punish him for so doing is to degrade him.

Our Commissioner was a fire-eater. He called out two officers under him because they differed from him, and he also challenged the General commanding the division to a duel, who, instead of accepting this polite invitation of pistols for two and coffee for one, reported him to the Government. But the Commissioner was too valuable an officer to be dispensed with, and he was only reminded that the days of duelling were over. This General was a Plymouth Brother, and, unless report did him great injustice, he had been in his youth as wild as he was now sanctimonious. He went by the name of Dismal Jemmy. I suspected him of doing what he could to prevent my advancement, as he had once been put under arrest by my grandfather for some breach of discipline in his youth. He kept me back when I received orders to take the command of my old company, then under orders for Persia, and whenever I was applied for he had some excuse to give for not placing my services at the disposal of the Civil Government.

The Brigadier I served under at Tongho was as fine a soldier as ever lived. He had seen considerable service, and had greatly distinguished himself in the Kaffir war under Somerset and Sir Harry Smith. He had been a noted athlete, a splendid shot, and a good all-round sportsman, and everybody believed in him. He was not long with us, and when he left on promotion every soldier, European and native, went to see him off. His successor bore a character the very reverse. He had not distinguished himself in the wars at the Cape. During one hot action, his Colonel, not seeing him, asked where he was. 'I don't know where he is,' said a soldier close by, 'but I think them's his boots,' pointing to a pair just visible out of a dense bush. 'By God, sir!' said the Colonel, 'this is not the first time I have seen you show the white feather, and if I live, I'll try you by a court-martial.' But almost a moment after the Colonel was shot through the head, and the person he had threatened, as the next senior officer, took the regiment out of action and got a brevet! On another occasion the Brigadier complained to a gallant Scotchman, then in command of the regiment, that one of the officers had called him engineer. I made my draughtsman copy these out exactly, and sent it in. It was returned scored all over in pencil, with such remarks as 'most defective' here, and 'out of proportion' there, all of which amused me greatly. So I replied that, while I regretted exceedingly that the plan was so defective, it was a facsimile of one drawn by so-and-so, and erected by so-and-so — both celebrated in their respective professions.

But the chief engineer bore no malice. He and his wife were staying with me soon afterwards, during one of his tours of inspection. He was busy writing in a room I had placed at his disposal; his wife and several other ladies and gentlemen were lunching with us, and the conversation turned on official correspondence.

'Well,' said the engineer's lady, 'all the executives say that when my husband has occasion to find fault he does it in such a nice way no offence is ever taken.'

'The deuce he does!' said I. 'I never read such blackguard letters as his in my life.'

Up she jumped, and ran into the next room, crying out:

'Chay dear, do you hear what Captain Pollok says —that you write the most blackguard letters?'

'I dare say I do,' replied her husband, not the least put out; 'and he writes back the most impertinent replies.'

Poor fellow! He died a few years afterwards of liver. He never would allow one of his officers to be sat upon by anyone but himself.

Laughable incidents come to me as I write. There

was a man very anxious to get into the Quartermaster-General's department, who flooded army headquarters with plans supposed to have been prepared from surveys conducted under great difficulty by himself. He was a very good draughtsman. We all knew that these maps had been copied from the works of others. He one day sent in to the draughtsman of the chief engineer a map —— and its environs, surveyed and drawn by ——. This was more than Harris, of the Bengal Engineers, could stand, so he printed after the preamble, 'Oh yes, tell another!' The copyist knew no English; he merely printed the inscription as he found it, and the aspirant's indignation may be imagined when he got the fair copy, with an addition he had not bargained for! He made a great fuss over the incident, but the Engineers stuck together, and asked him to prove what part, if any, he had actually surveyed. If he pointed to a part, 'No, you did not,' one would say, 'for I did that myself under heavy fire, and it is not over-correct;' and so on with every bit of it, with the exception of a few yards along one of the main roads, which they admitted he might or might not have surveyed, as it consisted of a mere straight line of an inch or two in length. In the end he had to own that he had compiled his plan from the work of others.

Softening of the brain was a common complaint for a time in Burma. Many officers went off their heads, and had to retire. One, a most upright, honourable man, would insist that he had robbed the Treasury, when there was not a farthing missing from it; but nothing would persuade him to the contrary. As is usual in such cases, a man who once gets this disease seldom lives long, and he, poor fellow! died persisting in his self-accusation.

I was the first officer sent to lay out Namyan, which was then to be the big station on the Irrawadie. The place was covered with giant tamarind-trees; their leaves, most astringent, had fallen for a hundred years, if not more; nor had the sun reached the ground beneath them for nearly as long. To build barracks and to construct roads, these trees had to be cut down. I had as many as a hundred saws at work cutting up teak logs for timber required by the Engineer department. These men were supervised by a sapper, who put in the number of men employed daily in Tamil, and the Burman headman put the numbers in in Burmese, whilst the European overseer did so in English. There was thus a nominal check, but it required a great deal of inspection and knowledge of the languages to compare all the figures. I had a man, a private of one of her Majesty's regiments, sent to me from across the river, from the Tongoop road works, as overseer. He had not enough money on his arrival to pay for his boat-hire across, and asked me for it. I was very busy that month, and an officer of Engineers had arrived, and was living with me. He was superintendent, and I his assistant, in the construction of the Prome and Rangoon road. At the end of the month I told the clerk to make up the accounts, and threw him the vouchers sent in by the subordinates. He took a long time deciphering them, and at last said he could make nothing of them, so I examined them myself, and found the figures had all been altered, but so clumsily that the originals could still be seen. I thus found an overcharge in the overseer's accounts of 1,000 rupees. Not bad for one month's peculation! I sent for the overseer, who, suspecting nothing, came over. I astounded him by demanding the key of his cash chest. He refused to give it up, so I told the havildar of the guard to make a prisoner of him. He then gave the key up, and asked permission to go home and bring his account-book. I sent a guard with him, and had the treasure-chest brought over, and when the overseer returned with his books there was an interpolation in ink, scarcely dry, 'Deposited by Private S., one thousand rupees.' The contents of the cash-box were counted over, and we found in the box the exact sum which had been overcharged, which would have been appropriated in a few days, had I not by the merest chance discovered his defalcation and taken prompt action. I kept him under arrest, and sent all the papers to Rangoon, but it was decided not to try him, but order him back to his regiment. When he got to Madras he had the impertinence to send me a lawyer's letter :

'Whereas it has been presented to us by our client, Private S., of her Majesty's — Regiment, that you did by force seize and appropriate a sum of 1,000 rupees, belonging to the said private, and have retained it, you are herewith directed to remit the same to us at once, or we shall at once take proceedings for its recovery in the High Courts of Madras.'

I took no notice of their letter, nor did I ever hear again on the subject.

Another overseer was sent to me. He was a young gunner, born in the country of European parents. He had been educated in India, and not only spoke, but wrote, all the native languages—in fact, he was a clever fellow, and very prepossessing, and I rather liked his looks, and found him very useful, speaking so many languages. But it does not do to entrust these men with large sums of Government money. The rains were approaching, when all work had to be stopped, and as heavy embankments were in progress, which, if not completed, would be washed away by the floods, work had to be carried on on Sundays as well as on week-days. The new overseer had commenced well, but he soon picked up Burmese, and took a girl of the country as wife, and I found that he was lavishing jewels upon her. The money for their purchase could not have been honestly gained, but to pick a hole in the accounts of such an accomplished man was not easy. Every month I examined his chest and accounts, and could detect nothing wrong, yet I knew he was robbing right and left. I had to write to him to push on works even on Sundays. He wrote back he was not a heathen, and would not work on the Sabbath. I told my havildar, Cawthan, to mount one of my ponies, I got on to another, and in a couple of hours we most unexpectedly arrived. 'Did you write that letter?' I asked. 'Yes,' faltered the man. 'Then, you are relieved, and the havildar will take your place at once. Hand over the keys and books.' The consternation of the man was great; he begged to be forgiven, but I was obdurate, and on examining his books and chest I found 150 rupees deficient, which he had taken only that morning to buy his girl a necklet, and had not had time to manipulate his accounts, so I sent him about his business, and as there was due to him about 200 rupees, I deducted the deficiency, and sent him off with the balance. His commanding officer was very angry, because I wrote to him 'that Private K. had been dismissed from the Department of Public Works for dishonesty and impertinence,' and at first refused to admit him back to his battery. What became of him eventually I do not know.

Well, for two years we were hard at work at Namyan, lacs of rupees had been spent, and no sooner were the barracks ready than troops were moved into them. Colonel Fraser, C.B., warned the authorities. He said the place should not be occupied for another year or two. It had been cleared too recently, and malaria would prostrate the soldiers. But he was not listened to. The mortality that set in was appalling. Europeans died by the dozen, natives five and six a day. In three months there would not have been a single man of those who first occupied it alive, had not the General at once removed all the men, and Namyan was abandoned as a station. It was then decided to remove all the public buildings, and to erect them afresh at Thayet-myo. Officers had been put to great expense in building, yet not a penny was given to any of them in compensation. But one knowing man, who commanded the 47th, sent in a bill for compensation for removal of his house (not for constructing it), and got it, whilst those who asked for some reimbursement for the expenses they had been put to for building quarters never got a penny. I was the first and last man in Namyan. I escaped the fever till the very last, but then I, too, got a bad dose of it; but from twenty to twenty-five grains of quinine a day, and a shift of quarters, soon drove it out of me.

Sir Trevor Wheler, of the 1st Bengal Fusiliers, was executive engineer at Thayet-myo. He was a wonderfully powerful man, though he did not look it, and a first-rate bruiser. One day, in mustering the work-people, a Burman was rather obstreperous, so Sir Trevor gave him a push. The man turned round as quick as lightning with *dhaw* upraised, but a blow straight from Sir Trevor's shoulder sent him rolling head over heels. It resembled more the effects of a shot in the head of a rabbit than anything else. The man got up quite dazed, looked at Wheler in amazement, and then ran for his life.

We had a man called Smith, who was known by the name of 'the Sweep.' He was a gunner, had charge of the boats, and was a character. He wrote to McMaster, the Brigade Major, 'when he should have the *bote* ready.' Mac wrote back, 'Have the *boat* ready at such an hour.' When he went down with a party of ladies, he asked Smith how he spelt 'boat.' 'Some people spells it b-o-a-t, but I spells it b-o-t-e,' he replied.

The roof of the building which held the ammunition of one of the Native Infantry regiments caught fire. There was a general panic, but 'the Sweep' mounted the roof, pulled off the thatch, poured buckets of water as fast as they were handed to him over the flames, and saved the magazine, as plucky a thing as it was possible for a man to do, considering there was enough powder in the place to have wrecked half the station had it exploded.

Smith, like most Europeans, despised the natives. Though tall, and as plucky as it was possible for a man to be, he was not physically strong. Once in Banlong, in attendance on our Brigadier during a shooting expedition, 'the Sweep' struck or pushed Shoagjah, our best shekary. The Burman at once closed, threw his opponent a fearful cropper, for, like most of his race, he was a good wrestler, and considerably astonished the gunner at the promptitude of his retaliation.

A party of Europeans was placed over a doctor who had gone off his head. But madmen are very cunning; the lunatic got out of bed, said he wished to go into the bathroom, and directly he came to a window took a header through it, threw himself down a well, and was drowned before he could be rescued. No blame was attachable to the guard over him. A court of inquiry was held. The officer commanding the wing was president, and he bullied and badgered the sergeant to such an extent that he lost all patience, and said, 'Major ——, if you will tell me what you wish me to say, I'll say it and be done with it.' Then his commanding officer, after driving him to the verge of mutiny, complimented him on his straightforward evidence. So much for personal reminiscences. Now for records of sport.

first and last man in Nanyan. I escaped the fever till the very last, but then I, too, got a bad dose of it; but from twenty to twenty-five grains of quinine a day, and a shift of quarters, soon drove it out of me.

Sir Trevor Wheler, of the 1st Bengal Fusiliers, was executive engineer at Thayet-myo. He was a wonderfully powerful man, though he did not look it, and a first-rate bruiser. One day, in mustering the workpeople, a Burman was rather obstreperous, so Sir Trevor gave him a push. The man turned round as quick as lightning with *dhaw* upraised, but a blow straight from Sir Trevor's shoulder sent him rolling head over heels. It resembled more the effects of a shot in the head of a rabbit than anything else. The man got up quite dazed, looked at Wheler in amazement, and then ran for his life.

We had a man called Smith, who was known by the name of 'the Sweep.' He was a gunner, had charge of the boats, and was a character. He wrote to McMaster, the Brigade Major, 'when he should have the *bote* ready.' Mac wrote back, 'Have the *boat* ready at such an hour.' When he went down with a party of ladies, he asked Smith how he spelt 'boat.' 'Some people spells it *b-o-a-t*, but I spells it *b-o-t-e*,' he replied.

The roof of the building which held the ammunition of one of the Native Infantry regiments caught fire. There was a general panic, but 'the Sweep' mounted the roof, pulled off the thatch, poured buckets of water as fast as they were handed to him over the flames, and saved the magazine, as plucky a thing as it was possible for a man to do, considering there was enough powder in the place to have wrecked half the station had it exploded.

Smith, like most Europeans, despised the natives. Though tall, and as plucky as it was possible for a man to be, he was not physically strong. Once in Banlong, in attendance on our Brigadier during a shooting expedition, 'the Sweep' struck or pushed Shoagjah, our best shekary. The Burman at once closed, threw his opponent a fearful cropper, for, like most of his race, he was a good wrestler, and considerably astonished the gunner at the promptitude of his retaliation.

A party of Europeans was placed over a doctor who had gone off his head. But madmen are very cunning: the lunatic got out of bed, said he wished to go into the bathroom, and directly he came to a window took a header through it, threw himself down a well, and was drowned before he could be rescued. No blame was attachable to the guard over him. A court of inquiry was held. The officer commanding the wing was president, and he bullied and badgered the sergeant to such an extent that he lost all patience, and said, ' Major ——, if you will tell me what you wish me to say, I'll say it and be done with it.' Then his commanding officer, after driving him to the verge of mutiny, complimented him on his straightforward evidence. So much for personal reminiscences. Now for records of sport.

CHAPTER VI.

PIG-STICKING.

> 'The boar, the mighty boar's my theme,
>   Whate'er the wise may say :
> My morning thought, my midnight dream,
>   My hope throughout the day.'
>
> Old Song by MORRIS.

The first sport in the world—My first hunt—Hunting over an enclosed country—Extraordinary speed and endurance of wild-boar—How to ride a pig—Chased—A fall—Thirty-five minutes from start to finish—Another chase—Struggle for first spear—Not always to the fastest—A fighting boar—Narrow escape of a horse—Particulars of my first hunt—My comrade falls into a *dul-dul*—Kill the boar—A hunt near Guntoor—A good thrust—How to meet a charging boar—Spearing under difficulties—A horse killed.

So long as the people of these islands hold their supremacy in the East, never will the immortal verses, one of which heads this chapter, be forgotten. A man may have slain his hundreds of tigers, he may have killed a hecatomb of big game in Africa and elsewhere, but if he has not followed the mighty boar, he has not tasted the delights of the most fascinating and invigorating sport in the world.

Anyone may kill a tiger by potting him from a tree

or a *machan*, but it requires a *man* to ride down, and spear, a boar.

The vicissitudes and dangers of the sport are many. Man and horse are pitted against one of the most plucky and savage of wild beasts. The ground is generally execrable; there can be no craning; a hunter of the boar must ride not only straight, but his hardest, if he intends to try conclusions with his foe.

> 'Firm hand and eagle eye
> Must he acquire, who would aspire
> To see the wild-boar die.'

There is everything in its favour, and nothing to be said against it. There is jolly companionship, friendly rivalry, a health-giving sport, just sufficient danger to make it exciting, and a man must be past praying for who, having once tasted its delights, will forget it as long as he has life; and

> 'When age hath dimmed manhood's powers,
>   And every nerve unbraced,
> The joys of the past will still be ours,
>   In memory's tablets traced.
> For with the friends whom death hath spared,
>   When life's career is done,
> We'll talk of the dangers we have shared,
>   And the tushes we have won.'

Alas! when I think of the jolly days I passed in my youth, and compare them with the humdrum existence I am forced to undergo in this land of cold, mist, and rain, in penury and old age, I am almost inclined to quarrel with life, and to exclaim: 'Oh, why did I not die like so many better men of my time in that sunny clime, and in the days when I was happy and young?'

But repining is useless, and I will here endeavour to recall some hunting scenes of the distant and irrevocable past.

I have already said that before I was six years old I was familiar with hog-hunting as a spectator. I was under eighteen when I took my first spear, which was at Bedar, in the Nizam's dominions.

Some years afterwards a party of us went out about fifteen miles from Bezwada, to beat a couple of isolated hills; in front there was an extensive but enclosed plain, and in the rear and for some way on both sides heavy jungle, reported to be full of pig and spotted deer. All my comrades elected to use the rifle in preference to the spear. I was the only one mounted. Whilst they took up their positions on various rocks near the foot of the hills, I ensconced myself, horse, and syce with extra spear, behind a high hedge.

I have never seen a country similar to this in any other part of India. Owing to the numerous hogs, the cultivators had fenced in their fields with stiff hedges made of wattles and bamboos interlaced, which you either had to clear or come a cropper, for there was no hope of their giving way before the weight of man or beast. That they only partially answered the purpose for which they were erected was evident, for the fields of *dhall* and pulse showed signs of ravages by the porcine tribe. To get at the grain, the hogs must have sprung over the fences both in going in and coming out, so I knew that if any pigs broke, the work was cut out for me and my nag. Fortunately, I had trained my three horses to clear hurdles, for during my spare time in Condapilly I hardly knew how to dispose of my leisure; so they could all jump well, and had a fair turn of speed. I had two horses out that day. I was on a golden bay with black points which a friend had got for me from Bombay; the other, a chestnut, was in reserve. About three-quarters of an hour after the beat commenced, there was a great rattling of stones down the hillsides, and a *sounder* of fully twenty pigs broke, headed by a huge boar. There was a second boar, not very much inferior to the leader; the party broke into two, each led by a boar, and took across the open. As they did so, a perfect *feu d'enfer* broke out, and the bullets whistled unpleasantly close to my person. I was up and away, as much to escape the missiles of my comrades as to follow the pig. I was on the right side, and the boar, followed by three lanky sows, took the fence, a good four feet in height, like a bird. As he landed only about fifty yards from me, I went for him, and thought I should be into him before he could reach the next hedge, but no sooner did he perceive me, with a squint out of one eye, than he hesitated for a second whether to come at me or to continue his course. He was probably decided by seeing his wives rattling across the fields, and with a grunt, as much as to say, 'Look out, I have not done with you yet,' he followed them.

I was within two spears' length of him, but could not get an inch nearer. He bounded over the next fence, a particularly nasty one; I had to steady my horse a bit to enable him to negotiate the obstruction, which he did right well, flying over it, with a good foot to spare. The boar had gained a couple of spears' lengths, and yet seemed to be going well within himself at a long swinging canter. If you don't press your pig from the very start you'll never catch him. My horse required no spur to urge him on. He was in his prime, about six, full of pluck, and hard as nails, and we went fully a mile, jumping over obstacles every hundred or a hundred and fifty yards. The sows still led the way, the foam was dripping from the boar's chaps, and his old eyes every now and then looked at me out of the corner of the lids. He was getting riled. I saw him stumble for the first time over the next hedge, and knew he would not go much farther; as my horse flew over the same fence, the sows were visible, but where was the boar? I was not left long in doubt, for he had lain close to the hedge; no sooner had my nag's hoofs touched the ground than with a whoof, whoof! he thundered at our heels. For the next three or four minutes I had to use the persuaders to keep my horse from being cut. Instead of jumping over the next fence, I skirted it, followed by the boar not three feet behind me. Finding I had the legs of him, I drew in the reins and allowed my foe to get within a foot or so of my steed's quarters, then, turning round in the saddle, with a backward prod I stabbed the boar as hard as I could in the head; but the aim was not good, the blade went in a little below the eyes, through the base of the nostrils, glanced to the left, and it was as much as I could do to withdraw my weapon.

The boar stood shaking his head; the more he shook it, the more blood he got in his eyes, and during his indecision I wheeled round, and went at him as

"Turning round in the saddle with a backward prod I stabbed the bear."

fast as my horse could lay legs to the ground. Before I could close, he rushed, in his turn, at me. The spear caught him in the neck, just below the withers; the blade bent like a reed, and, tough as it was, it snapped in two, just saving me from being projected out of the saddle, for the force of the collision had all but unhorsed me. The broken shaft stuck upright, and with this in close proximity to my quarter I had to gallop off in search of another spear, the boar following me the while. I did not attempt to clear the obstruction I had already overcome, as my horse was getting done, but circled round and round the field until my syce, with the extra spear, should appear. At last I saw his turban on the safe side of the hedge, put on speed, seized the weapon, and making a circuit, I charged the boar again, but he avoided the blow, and with a stumble rolled over the next fence. My horse rose at it too, but taking a deep breath as he did so, his fore-feet caught in the topmost bar, and he rolled heels over head. I fell clear and scrambled out of the way, but was on my feet and had got hold of the reins ere the horse recovered himself.

The boar had seen our mishap, and with another 'whoof' came at us. There was no time to lose. I had frequently practised jumping on to the saddle whilst the horse was in motion, so taking a good hold of the mane, I sprang into my seat just in time to avoid the rush of the boar, who, however, was so close that the broken shaft struck the quarter of my steed. The pig was blown, so was my horse—his tumble had taken it out of him considerably; but he went with his ears still cocked, and, as I circled round, did not shirk the encounter. The boar almost sprang at me, but the blade caught him under the jaws and came out through the top of the neck, severing the spine, and he rolled over. I had to let go the spear, and my horse sprang clear of the foe.

I was glad the struggle was over. It had lasted just thirty-five minutes. I was perspiring like a 'frog on a log'; my horse could not have gone another mile at the same pace. I was off him, loosened the girths, turned his head to the wind, and carefully examined him. Fortunately, when he went such a cropper, he had fallen on his side, and his knees were untouched; but some of the splinters from the broken shaft had penetrated his quarter and gave me some trouble to extract.* My syce soon appeared, and went back for coolies. I had to rest my horse, for these fields had no gates as outlets. The natives clamber over the fences at certain places, where holes for their toes are left, and though it had been rather exciting during the hunt, with a fresh horse, taking these obstacles at a fly, it was very different in cold blood and on a fagged steed. However, picking out the lowest places, I negotiated them successfully, and got back to camp to find that my comrades had killed a couple of sows, and had breakfast ready. I did not take long to pour a few chatties of cold water over me, and then joined them at their meal.

In the afternoon I persuaded one of the Engineers

---

* Never leave a splinter from a bamboo in a wound. Some years afterwards one of the nicest fellows in the 68th Queen's died of lockjaw through a small splinter in his chin, which no one thought anything of.

to ride in preference to shooting. This time we separated, the shooters going one way and we two another.

I think a sounder that broke was headed by the second of the two boars we had disturbed in the morning. He took across a plain covered with thick prickly bushes, in which we lost sight of him several times, but recovered him after a while each time. He was making for the Kistna River, where there were a lot of islands, densely covered with long grass, where, if he once got in, he would be perfectly safe. I had the legs of my companion, but in such ground we had to ride at a moderate pace, for fear of overshooting our quarry. So we were never far apart, and when we got clear of the jungle, an uninterrupted plain, as flat as a board and as smooth as a lawn, lay before us. The boar was only a few hundred yards ahead. Here we raced for the spear; I got within prodding distance, my friend a few yards behind to my right. It is a mistake to poke at the pig; hold your spear steady, in a line directly behind the shoulder-blade, and let it go in with the impetus imparted to it by the speed of your horse. My blade was within half a foot; in another second the coveted spear would have been mine, but the boar turned at right angles. I overshot the mark, but the Engineer met the boar; his spear went right through him and into the ground, and such a cropper as horse, rider, and pig went over I never saw.

I thought the man would be killed at least, and his horse's back broken. The boar had broken the shaft and was clear of the spear, the blade portion of which was still sticking upright in the ground, and with a vicious glance around he made for my friend's prostrate body. I was round by that time and interposed, giving the foe a good dig and withdrawing the spear, on which he turned all his wrath on me. The beast seemed to bear a charmed life; the blood was pouring in a stream from the hole made by the first spear through his body. I had given him three thrusts well in, but he was still full of fight; in one headlong charge my spear went in at the back, just missing the spine, and came out between his hind-legs, yet he ran up the shaft and cut the sole of my boot with his left tusk as clean as if it had been done by a razor. I withdrew my weapon, and, using it as the Bengalese do theirs, I jobbed down, caught him just behind the head, in the centre of the neck, and down he fell to rise no more.

Whilst I was finishing the boar, my friend's horse had recovered his feet, and seemed to be none the worse for his spill. I found the rider stunned, and his left arm dislocated at the elbow, but he soon came to, and I got him into the saddle. Riding along the river bank, I hailed a boat, and gave the men a couple of rupees to row the invalid back to Bezwada, where the doctor soon put him to rights. Horse and rider had rolled over the pig and had not a scratch. I led the nag back, but my own stallion was rather inclined to fight, so I was not sorry to see a syce coming my way, to whom I consigned the waif.

My next hog-hunting adventure was at Bedar. I was shooting with Henegan, of the Artillery; the game was principally antelope. As the ground was pretty open, we took our horses and spears with us to run down any wounded buck. We found that an antelope even when wounded was not easy to overhaul, and all but impossible to touch in an unwounded state. But one day, just at daybreak, we came across a sounder of pig. Changing our rifles for the spears, off we went. We were fairly matched as to speed. I was the lighter weight, and kept my horse's head close to Henegan's girths, ready to rush in.

A native on horseback joined us, so we raced along. The ground looked good: it was undulating; the grass was only a few inches long, there were no cracks in the soil, the few rocks scattered about were easily avoided, and the bushes offered no impediment, as they were few and far between. We were pressing our nags to their utmost, fighting for the spear. The excitement was maddening; Henegan leant forward, hoping to draw first blood by a prick behind when the boar turned suddenly. I made a mad prod, and missed egregiously; but whilst Henegan's horse went on, mine turned like a dog. I heard a yell, but had no time to look round. I expected Henegan would be round every moment, and perhaps deprive me of the advantage I had gained, but I heard no thundering of hoofs behind me. The native was also not in sight, so giving my good steed the reins, I dashed alongside, drove my spear well in, wheeled to the left, withdrew it, and was just in time to meet the boar face to face. He ran on to my outstretched spear, spitting himself. I had to let go or be carried over the cantle of my saddle.

There was no other spear out, and I was afraid the quarry would escape us, when I was glad to see the boar roll over on his side, the shaft broken in two, and the beast at his last gasp. I did not think of Henegan, or what had become of him, until my prize had breathed his last, and, after admiring its grand proportions, I looked about for my friend. I could see him nowhere. The native was gesticulating, and off his horse; so I cantered back to see what had happened. Henegan was up to his neck in a puddle, his horse on his side a little on the right; but, on my inquiring what was the matter, the strange horseman said it was only a *dul-dul*, or quicksand. The syces ran up fast; we tied their turbans together, threw the end to Henegan, who held on whilst we hauled away with might and main, and soon had the pleasure of seeing him on firm ground. I told him to mount on my horse, and to ride back to camp to cleanse himself of the filth that clung to him.

The syces soon collected a lot of brushwood, and we were about to lay them on the surface to form a sort of bridge, when I saw a vulture sweeping down on to the boar. The horse seemed in no danger. I was not going to allow my boar to become the prey of these obscene birds; so, before extricating the nag, I made the syces drag the hog close to us. We then found that only the hind-legs of the horse were in the quicksand—his neck, fore-quarter, and head were on the hard—and that the *dul-dul* was of small extent. But he was a very large waler, not easy to move; and it took all our strength—and the strange native helped us right well—before we got him on to the solid earth. By this time the vultures had assembled in large flocks, and seemed inclined to dispute with us the possession of our quarry; so I had to remain on guard with a spear to keep them away, whilst the two syces slung the boar on a stout bamboo, and carried him to the bungalow.

A civilian whom we knew had a beat for hog near Guntoor. There were seldom pigs there; but occasionally a sounder would take possession of a half-dried tank, and commit depredations on the grain-fields. News was brought in of a sounder, and that fifty beaters would be ready next day to drive the pigs out. Once clear of the marsh, they would have to go at least three miles before finding any other cover, unless they broke back through the beaters; then there were a few small hills covered with low shrub, and here and there marshy places with long reeds and grass in which a solitary pig might take refuge, which they would not afford shelter to a sounder. It is the unforeseen that often happens. There were only three of us out—T., O., and I. T. was a civilian, a capital sportsman, and well mounted. O. and I were subalterns not overburdened with money. Our horses could go; but our three, when purchased, had not cost what any one of T.'s had done. T.'s were pure Arabs, but the race is not always to the swift. O. was one of the best riders I ever came across, a light weight, and as good a fellow as ever lived. We were kept on the move; the sows, many of them barren, kept breaking away, and we chased several before we discovered their sex. There is a boar attached to every sounder. If the sows are many, there may be two; but one is the master, and the other, though keeping company, gives the larger a wide berth. At last a great outcry and a scattering of the coolies denoted something unusual, and waving of arms and turban-cloths pointed the way we should go. Skirting the *bheel*, we rode as hard as we could; but, quick as we were, the boar had been quicker, for he was well ahead of us before we got clear of the marshy ground.

He had half a mile start of us; the hills were only a mile and a half off, and we rode as if our very lives depended on the result. But it was a hopeless task; the boar got into the scrub. However, we were not far behind him; and, instead of lying by or 'doing 'possum,' he crossed the low range, and made for some marshy bits beyond. T. had led; indeed, neither O. nor I had attempted to wrest the lead from him. It would be quite time enough to struggle for the spear when we got closer. Across the open T. got on terms with the boar, O. lying a length behind, whilst I had been thrown out, having been misled by a sow which broke away; but finding out my mistake, I had cleared a boulder on the hillside, and was making up leeway, when, just as T. was within prodding distance of the boar's side, his horse became rather restive. Hearing O. thundering along behind him, T. made a desperate lunge, cutting away a few bristles, but failing to show blood. The boar jinked; O. seized the opportunity, and drove his blade well in, and the first spear was won.

The boar now turned to bay, and as I had taken a short-cut, and was then the nearest, he made for me. O. and T. were then neck and neck, T. being not overpleased at the turn affairs had taken. He generally used to hunt alone, and had thus killed a fair number of pigs. He did not like the Lieutenant taking the spear

"My spear went through his brain, and he died."

from him. I met the boar fairly. I hoped to get my blade into the chest; but as the brute charged with his head protecting his body, my spear went through his brain, and he died incontinently.

The sounder with the other boar had been marked down, and after tiffin we looked him up. Scarcely had the beaters gone in, when there was a commotion, and a fair-sized boar charged me without any provocation. I had just time to urge my steed into a gallop (never receive a hog at a halt; charge at him), and speared him. O. and T. were neck and neck. The boar made for them; O. speared over the reins, T. on the off side, and they rolled the foe over, but both lost their weapons. I came up hand over hand; the boar, with two long spears in him, made for me, and to spear was impossible, for it was as much as I could do to avoid the two shafts, which swayed about like pendulums, and were heavily weighted at the butts. Then O. did a plucky thing: nearing the boar, he rushed past him, and, as the brute charged, cleverly seized one shaft, and though he got a nasty blow on the knee-cap with the other, he withdrew the one he had seized, came up from the rear, and, with a forward thrust, spitted the pig from end to end. We had no further luck that day; T. was disgusted, and did not exert himself either to show us more sport or to obtain it himself. So the next day we wished him adieu, with many thanks for the hospitality shown us; but he never asked any of us to join him in another hunt. He was very different from Tom Prendergast, who preferred that his guests should get the sport rather than that he should have the luck himself.

I will only give one more reminiscence: MacMaster, of the 36th, a noted sportsman and naturalist, a good shot and a clipping rider; Gostling, of the Civil Service; Clerk, of my corps; Weldon, of the Police, were out with me in some difficult ground, where occasionally a few pigs were to be found. We had fair luck; two boars had been killed, one spear falling to MacMaster, and the other to Gostling, who won it through the speed and bottom of his gray Arab (I bought the horse there and then, and he was the best for hog I ever rode). There was then an interval. In the afternoon's beat Weldon got the spear, but could not extract it again; the boar charged him before being touched, and over rolled man and horse. MacMaster was coming from one way; I was charging down from the very opposite. The horse struggled in vain to rise; the boar gave him another gash, and then went for his master, who was lying face downwards, apparently insensible. MacMaster and I both drove our spears well in, the former on the outer, and I on the inner side; the boar fell right on to Weldon, and MacMaster's horse cleared both. Just then Clerk saw a large boar, and gave chase. Gostling hesitated a moment whether he should come to our assistance, or dispute the spear with Clerk; he finally decided on the latter, but Clerk was too near, and won.

Gostling having killed the boar in his charge, MacMaster wheeled round, and we heard fearful utterances. Weldon was struggling to get clear of the incubus on the top of him, but could make no impression on the huge mass. We dismounted as quickly as we could, but it required all our strength to drag off the unclean beast (and unclean he was, too, in more respects than one, for he had been wallowing in the filthiest of mires). When our Irish friend got up, he was very irate to see us both laughing, as he could not see the joke of it. We prayed him to betake himself to the tents and get clean, but Pat would not till he had ascertained the fate of his beautiful mare; he had only owned her three or four months, and had paid 600 rupees for her, which is a fair price for an Australian, but she was past praying for. She had been twice ripped, once in the hock, and once along the abdomen, through which the entrails protruded. Pat had tears in his eyes, and saying, 'Will one of you put an end to her? I can't,' went off. I had already sent off for a gun, for I knew the poor creature had received her death-wound. On its arrival, putting the muzzle inside the ear, I pulled the trigger, and the gallant mare gave up the ghost without a sigh or a quiver.

CHAPTER VII.

ELEPHANTS.

Two varieties of Indian elephants—How to kill them—Game in the Prome district—Purchase of two rifles—Burmese shikaries—Their dislike of Europeans—Mosquitoes—How to circumvent them—My first elephant hunt—Tree-leeches—Native cookery dying out—Bag my first elephant—A sad disappointment—D'Oyly and Moung Goung Gye's state elephant—Gallantry of a young sowar—Habits of elephants—Anecdotes—Elephants do not breed in captivity—Difficulty of finding a good shekar elephant—Mahouts—Their duties—Death of Wedderburn—Necessity of elephants for shooting tigers—Their furniture—Battery for sport—How to manage elephants—A pitched battle.

THERE are two distinct species of elephant—the African and the Asiatic; but the latter are represented by two varieties—the *gondahs*, or those having tusks, and the *mucknahs*, or tuskless ones. The latter are found scattered abroad here, there and everywhere, but are principally to be found in Ceylon and Sumatra. There are men, like Sir Samuel Baker, Rogers, Garrow, Michael, and a few others, who can boast of having slain their hundreds of these pachyderms, but the sport is nearly a thing of the past in India. They are now protected throughout our provinces, but not a year passes that some rogue elephant does not take to killing people and destroying their granaries, and the collector of the district is only too glad to avail himself of the services of any man who will go out to slay the creature. It is as well, therefore, to know how to deal with them. The natives of Burma and Assam fire behind the shoulder, and I have seen many monsters who have been so killed, but as a rule the European confines himself to the head shots. There are six vulnerable places:

First, the bump between the eyes, which should be fired at from the front, low down and upwards.

Second, the temple, between the corner of the eye and top of ear. This shot should be fired either from the right or left half-face, from the front, slightly upwards and backwards, or in the centre of the hollow or temple, equidistant from the corner of the eye to the top of the ear. Of all shots, this is the easiest to kill with, and the safest to the hunter, because, being on one side, if the shot does not prove fatal, and the elephant either charges or involuntarily rushes forward, as most animals are apt to do on suddenly receiving a wound, the sportsman will not be in the line of charge or flight, and will be less liable to be trampled upon than in firing the front shot.

Third, a spot just behind the ear at the junction of the head; but this is a shot one seldom gets.

Fourth, a shot fired from a moderate height downwards in a forward direction, striking the back of the head close to the spine, when death will be instantaneous.

Fifth, straight across into the orifice of the ear. For this shot the gun should be on a level with the ear, and the ball should pass straight through.

Sixth, behind the shoulder at the point of the elbow. Also, a shot fired into an upraised foot will cripple the creature and make him an easy victim to succeeding shots.

To hunt these animals successfully on foot is very hard work, and requires a man not only to be in good training, sound of wind and limb, but also to be possessed of determination, undaunted pluck, a quick eye, and very sharp hearing. It is no child's play to slay these animals in their forest homes. Huge as they are, no beast is easier to kill, if a hunter comes across one on foot, and if he follow the directions already given. Not only must the spot to aim at be known, but the angle at which the shot is to be fired; one without the other is useless. Moreover, the distance should not exceed twenty yards; better if it be a good deal less. Many men prefer smooth bores—generally double eights, with hardened spherical bullets driven by eight or ten drachms of black powder. I myself have never used anything bigger than a ten two-groove rifle or a '577 express; either will kill if held straight, charged with six drachms of powder and a solid steel-tipped conical bullet, hardened with a small alloy of quicksilver.

The first elephant I ever killed was at Eeingmah, which was my headquarters for some years. I had seen a good deal of Burma by that time. I searched for sport from the very day of my arrival in Prome. I had soon discovered that the finest snipe-shooting in the world was to be found in the country between the middle of August and the end of October. Other small game, such as hares, francolins, jungle-fowl, and barking-deer, were plentiful about Namyan, and also at Eeingmah. But India and Burma differed so much that, however expert a shikarie a man might have been in India, he was no use in Burma. Now Grant Allan, the Deputy Quartermaster-General, was, or had been, a noted sportsman, and had brought his battery of rifles and guns to Burma. He had travelled more over the country than any other European, but had seen no game worth mentioning. So in disgust he offered me his whole battery for 500 rupees, though it was worth treble the money. But I only took a Lang double No. 10 two-groove rifle (which, having been made by the celebrated Joseph Lang in 1839 for Captain Gill, of Ellora fame, was in 1854 as good as new) and a four-bore single rifle by Blanche, for 400 rupees—half their value.

My work consisted principally in surveying and road-making. I had to explore the country to find out the best routes for the proposed lines. For this purpose I was provided with elephants, and in pushing my way across country through the vast plains, I found that deer were pretty abundant, especially on the borders of marshy places or in *quins* (clearances surrounded by tree-jungle, but no longer cultivated). But I could get no Burmese shikaries to go with me; there are such men in plenty in the country, but it is their trade to kill deer and sell it to the village people. They are looked upon as outcasts for taking life, though that does not prevent the people from buying from them the spoils of the chase; but they are not shikaries as we understand that term in India. They do not like their preserves invaded, fear Europeans, and think if one was killed in a hunt they would probably be hanged.

Our sportsmen, with a very few exceptions, did not understand the language. The Burmese were accustomed to their own mode of sport, by torchlight and with bells at night, and did not comprehend the niceties of stalking or of shooting off elephants. I liked the people, and lived in their midst without fear. I encouraged them to bring me in *kubber* (news of game), and by giving trifling presents to the women and a little tobacco to the men I tried to conciliate them. I knew all the influential people of both sexes. There was not a village for miles around I had not visited, and wherever I went I kept my eyes open, behaved liberally, and begged them all to send me news of any game to be found in their neighbourhood.

I generally sat on a pad behind the mahout, with a Burman guide behind me, having no howdah then. I occasionally came across deer. At first I missed egregiously, for the knack of shooting off elephants is not acquired in a day; but now and then I made a lucky shot, and keeping but a little for myself and servants, I gave the greater part of the meat to the people at work under me.

Every day of my life, when not searching for new routes, I was up at daybreak, drank a cup of coffee, mounted my pony, and remained on the works until near sunset. I used then to pay the people, bathe, dine, and go to bed. There was plenty of small game; by going out for an hour or two I could always shoot a few francolins and hares, and in the season I could have lived on snipe. But my great ambition was to slay an elephant. I had seen killed, or helped to kill, everything else, but had never come across wild elephants, rhinoceroses, or buffaloes.

My house was within a hundred yards of a nullah, which, coming out of the Nāwen Creek, near Prome, went through the country parallel to the Irrawadie, and formed the Tlein creek lower down. Once in the rains, when the country was flooded and travelling impossible by what ought to have been land, I determined to reach Eeingmah by water. I was assured it could not be done, as creeks did not join the two streams together, but this was against common-sense. From the contour of the land I knew passages must exist, and after a great deal of trouble I got an old Dacoit to show me the way on a payment of 20 rupees. I had a quantity of pickaxes, shovels, spades, blasting tools, etc., to carry, and, as only small boats could go, I engaged nearly fifty of them, and with this flotilla reached my destination in three days. I had to cut my way here and there, as creepers had blocked some of the smaller creeks, but it was not a hard trip, after all, and saved a great deal of trouble and expense. The mosquitoes in Eeingmah were so bad we could not have existed, had we not found that they could not bite through newspapers ; so we got suits of loose wrappers from the soles of our boots to our necks, made of paper, and with a vigorous punkah overhead we bid them defiance, though the dinner-table would be at times black with them.

One day a Burman came to me and said he had seen an immense tusker elephant near the nullah, about five miles below. Telling my havildar to look after the works that day, and to pay the coolies if I was late, I got into the Burman's boat, and took nothing with me save my two weapons and ammunition.

Instead of taking me five, the man took me fully ten miles. We then landed, and walked through a nasty swampy tangled jungle for a couple of miles more, where leeches were very plentiful. We then entered a forest of *eein*, or bastard teak. These trees have huge leaves which are shed twice a year, decompose, and form rich vegetable mould, which in places is so deep that I have seen an elephant unable to go through it. There is seldom much undergrowth in these forests. We had trudged for an hour, and I was getting heartily sick at seeing nothing of our quarry, when presently the guide pointed out some fresh elephant droppings, and we also noticed their footmarks, which showed that the herd consisted of some four or five full-grown beasts and two small ones. As one track was much larger than any of the others, I presumed one was a bull, and the others his wives and children.

We followed the trail, which was plain enough, but it seemed as if we should never overtake the herd. We had started at 8 a.m. ; it was now 2 p.m. The heat was suffocating ; there was not a breath of wind, and the mosquitoes and horse-flies buzzed and hovered round us ; worst of all, we got among the tree-leeches, which, almost as fine as bits of thread, inserted themselves down our backs, up our legs, and hung about us in festoons, and with repletion soon swelled to respectable proportions. I was in good condition, but more accustomed to ride than walk, and began to feel pretty well dead beat.

I was cogitating whether I should give in, when the trumpet of an elephant, apparently not far off, instilled fresh life into me; so on we pushed again. It is extraordinary how far sound travels in a forest, and how deceptive it is. We walked a good hour and a half without sighting the herd. They were probably feeding away from us. I was tired, so I suppose I did not pick my footsteps with due care, for suddenly, right in front of us, we heard a shrill cry of alarm, a terrific rush, and the herd was off. We did not even catch sight of them, but, from the noise they made, it was evident they were thoroughly alarmed, and that we should not see them again that day. When elephants are not frightened, they go through jungle so quietly that they make not the least noise.

What to do I knew not. It was getting towards dusk, and we must have been at least twenty miles from Eeingmah, and ten in a direct line from our boat. The mosquitoes and sand-flies became very troublesome, and our position was anything but pleasant. My knowledge of the language was very limited then, but I knew a few phrases; and telling the guide to get back quickly, I followed him silently, and in time came to a village, where it was apparent I must spend the night. I was glad enough to rest my weary limbs; I had had no food all day, and the severe exercise had made me very hungry; besides, after the many miles I had walked, tormented by leeches and other vermin, I required a thorough rest.

The Burmese, as I have said before, are a hospitable

race. They gave me a clean house to go into, and commenced to rig up a bed for me; but a glance at the greasy pillow was enough—I preferred the clean bamboo floor, and a log for a support for the head. The village, a small one, was called Subaguay, and was situated on a small rivulet running into the Waygheechoung. I was soon dabbling in clear fresh water, which was too shallow for swimming, but nothing refreshes one so much as a plunge into cold water after a hard day's fag.

An old woman soon cooked me some rice, and, seeing some fresh fish hanging up, I got her to broil me a couple. The people offered me messes of their own; but, as *gnapee** predominated in them all, I declined them with thanks. I had no table appliances. My shikar knife was too large; but the woman gave me one of her own, and, using my fingers, I made a fair enough meal. But what would I have not given for a bottle of Bass! Sleep was out of the question, for, tired as I was, directly I dozed the mosquitoes settled on me in myriads. I dislike their buzzing even more than their bites, and had to do battle with them all night, thankful to see daylight when it came. I rushed into the rivulet, finding a deeper pool; but it was slightly muddy at the bottom, and I got a couple of leeches on me. The *gnabodeen* fish also took a nip or two out of me, but I felt greatly refreshed by the immersion. These gnabodeens swarm in most rivers in Burma. They are terrible pests. When taken out of the water, they blow themselves out like a balloon.

* *Gnapee* is a decoction of fish pounded in a mortar with salt, and is most offensive to Europeans.

The old woman who had taken me under her culinary charge brought me a cup of tea, of which the Burmese are very fond, drinking it plain, without sugar or milk. I robbed a hen-roost of an egg, and broke the yolk into the tea, stirred it well up, and put in a lump of molasses, and I had as good a cup of tea as I could wish for.

I told the guide to go back to Eeingmah, and, giving him the small cannon, I followed him with the double; but I soon saw that he had no intention of doing as I had bid him. He took me straight back to where we had lost the elephants the day before. I did not like giving up, for fear of never getting them to bring me news of big game again, for this was the very first occasion anyone in the country had volunteered to show sport. I did not want them to think me a laggard, and I myself was most anxious to slay Behemoth. I did not know at that time that the Burmese prefer the flesh of the elephant to all other, and thought the man's anxiety for me to be successful in our chase was due to his love of sport, whereas he was but hungering and thirsting after the flesh-pots.

As there was nothing else for it, I girded up my loins, and took up the trail afresh. We had started at 7 a.m., and toiled through interminable jungles till past twelve, when I called a halt. I had not been troubled with leeches to the same extent as on the day before, for, seeing the Burman smear his legs over with their crude petroleum, I did likewise, and it answered well as long as it remained on; but when the dew and wet leaves had saturated my gaiters, the smell wore off, and these pests soon found their way to my feet and ankles, so that I had to stop now and then to extract them. Another awful trick these leeches have is to drop off the bushes as you brush past them, crawl down your neck, and fasten themselves on to the small of your back.

The Burman had brought food with him in the shape of boiled rice, to which was added a little molasses, the whole being compressed into a bamboo, to be pushed out from the bottom like a sausage, and eaten. Natives will subsist on this for days. My guide offered me some, but I declined it : so while he ate his breakfast I wandered off a little way, had a good drink and a bathe.

We then resumed our tracking, and I was glad to find the pachyderms had taken a backward course, and were going in the direction of the village where I had put up the previous night. We walked along as fast as we could, consistent with making as little noise as possible, for the least unusual sound in a forest will send all wild animals off; not only are their olfactory nerves acute, but their hearing is of the best, and a man's footfall is soon recognised as something uncanny.

We were tormented as usual, and we seemed to be getting no nearer our quarry. So at 4 p.m. I again called a halt, and this time I made the man understand that he must take me back to the village, which he did most reluctantly. We arrived there at sunset, I dreading to have to pass another sleepless night, tortured by mosquitoes, and with no bed and no beer.

My delight may be imagined when I saw my boy waiting for me, my bed and curtains nicely rigged up, a small camp-table and chair arranged outside, a cold hump, a lot of beer, wine, etc., covered with thick quilted covers well sprinkled with water, hanging up to cool, and perceived the delicious smell of a prawn-curry, all but ready for the table.

To get a really good curry nowadays, even in India, is difficult. The native cooks, than whom there are no better in the world in learning to prepare what are called 'Europe' dishes, have to a great extent lost the art of preparing their own national ones. But in those days most Madras cooks would give you a different curry at each meal, and continue to vary them daily for a month. People at home must not imagine that the apology offered them nowadays is a good curry. It consists principally of turmeric and cayenne pepper that scarifies the roof of your mouth and tongue, and gives no pleasure in the eating. The Madrassies are the only people in India who really understand what a good curry should be. The ingredients should be fresh, differently apportioned for each kind, and newly ground every day. Fresh cocoa-nuts are also necessary. One of the commonest, yet perhaps the very best curry in India forty years ago, was an ordinary one in the Madras Club. It was made of tender cubes of mutton that would almost melt in the mouth, the ingredients were most appetizing and delicious, and not at all hot. When I visited the old haunts three or four years ago, the club butler did not even know it, and I had forgotten its native name. In a few dishes the Bengalies excel the Madrassies. Their *dalbat* is very good ; beefsteaks, made out of an old cock or a duck, are, I think, better than the juiciest steak obtainable in England; but they have no idea of a curry. When you consider that in camp a boy will prepare a dinner fit for a king, his cuisine consisting of a few earthenware pots, a tripod or two, a little charcoal, and a few sticks, and that he will give you a roast, side-dishes, soup, and fish if it is obtainable, winding up with the inevitable curry and rice, and poppadums, or Bombay ducks, it is a marvel how he manages it.

A long residence in the East, especially the India of old days, spoils a man for a life in Europe, where there is nothing real; everything is artificial. You can never depend on two days being alike, to say nothing of the blinding storms of snow, the bitter cold winds, and the miserable wet weather, so often experienced. In India we know exactly what to expect, and are prepared to meet it. There we live a life of ease, are not troubled with formalities or Mrs. Grundy, have jolly companions at hand, can enjoy good sport without troubling ourselves about game-licences or ascertaining whether we are trespassing or not. I am speaking of the India of old, before there were reserved lands, and before native rajahs took to preserving game and became expert sportsmen. Every old Indian finds out when too late what a mistake he has made in retiring to this detestable climate. Marriage has a good deal to do with it, and were it not for the children, few men would come home, instead of settling in India. The old directors were wise when they discouraged matrimony amongst their officers. But we live and learn, and often thoroughly repent.

That night I was in very good case. After a good

bathe and a hearty scrub, I put on clean clothes, enjoyed my meal, washing it down with a bottle of cool Bass, a liquor which in those days was far superior to what it is now. Before the overland route, thousands and thousands of casks of, first Hodson, and then of Bass and Allsopp Pale Ales, used to be sent round the Cape. Whether the long voyage improved the ale, I know not. Each mess had men specially skilled in bottling beer, which, when cooled in saltpetre, became nectar. One thing I do pride myself upon, and that is my knowledge of what constitutes, or does not, good ale. During a life, now, alas! getting on towards the seventies, I have never drunk spirits, not because I thought there was any harm in doing so in moderation, but because I had no taste for them; nor did I ever take to smoking, but I should like to have all that beer has cost me!

My people at Eeingmah, alarmed at my not returning by the evening of the day I had left, made inquiries the next day, and ascertained that I was at Subaguay, for boats were constantly passing both ways, so my man put my traps into my boat, and brought everything I required. I had not given him credit for so much sense, but he was an exceptional native, and about the best servant I ever had; at the end of four years, however, he got home-sick, and would go back to his own country. Both he and his son, who was my *chora*, or dressing-boy, picked up Burmese, and spoke it almost as well as the natives of the country. Through him I learned that some Burmese, watching their paddy-fields, had seen the elephants during the night and early that morning; that they were in a tree-forest bordering on the cultivation. So carefully cleaning out both rifles, I reloaded them. The great drawback to muzzle-loaders was the difficulty of extracting the charges prior to cleaning. To fire off heavily-charged weapons was to alarm the whole jungle, and it was not always easy to draw a bullet from a grooved tube. Mine were belted bullets that fitted so perfectly that I could easily pull them out with a stout loading-rod, but what a comfort breech-loaders are now! The less noise you make in camp, especially after dark, so much the greater chance of sport.

I took the double rifle; the guide carried the single. Not knowing how long we might be out, I took an extra hand, and made him carry some breakfast for me. On reaching the paddy-fields, it became evident that the watchers had spoken the truth, for a great deal of the corn had been eaten, and more trampled underfoot; and as the forest, consisting of trees and bamboo, was close by, and they had not been molested, I felt sure the elephants would not be far off, so took double precautions, and advanced with the greatest care. About 10 a.m. we first heard them, and advanced up-wind on them, as if our very lives depended on our caution. The breakfast coolie was left behind, and the guide and I crept on from tree to tree and bush to bush in the direction the animals were feeding, for we could hear them tearing down the young bamboo shoots. Even now the elephants were not nearly as close to us as we thought. Crawling along, with every sense stretched to the utmost, momentarily expecting to come upon them, we had to control our impatience for fully half an hour, when at last the herd appeared in sight. We could distinguish several females browsing on the young bamboos, but the male was nowhere visible. The beasts were somewhat scattered, and the Burman kept urging me to fire at the nearest. I wanted the bull, not a female that carries no trophies, but, never having then killed an elephant, I was very eager, and did not require much persuasion to make up my mind to kill one if possible. As for the guide, all he wanted was the meat, and the carcass of a female would be as good to him as that of a male. It is far easier to approach elephants when they are browsing in a bamboo jungle than anywhere else, for, if the wind be favourable, they themselves make such a noise in tearing down the young shoots, which snap with reports resembling pistol-shots, that they are not nearly so likely to hear a footfall as in other jungles where they themselves make less noise.

Having made up my mind to murder the nearest, a plump young female, I crawled up to within twenty yards of her, and squatted down under a bamboo clump, till she should afford me a shot at the proper angle and in the right place; for though I had never fired at an elephant in my life, I had read, I think, every book written on sport, had examined numerous skulls, consulted many sportsmen, and was pretty confident where and how the ball should strike to kill.

Whilst thus waiting patiently, I heard a slight noise, so slight that at first I paid no attention to it, but hearing it repeated, I looked round, and there, gradually approaching me, with his ears cocked and trunk raised, was a fine tusker. It is one thing to stalk an animal, and quite another being stalked. I suppose the animal had got a taint, though a very slight one, of me, and could not make out what it was, so was carefully approaching to ascertain who had dared to come between the wind and his nobility. He would stop every second or two, throwing his trunk about in every direction, scenting the air, but refraining from giving the warning cry. Perhaps the very fact of my being behind the clump of bamboos, lying flat on the ground, while his trunk was raised so high, prevented his scenting me thoroughly. From his previous eagerness, I presumed the attendant with the four-bore was close by me, and wishing to give the tusker a taste of my quality, I held out my hand for the single rifle, but both man and weapon had disappeared. He had left me in the lurch. Not that it mattered in the least, for I was perfectly safe, the clump was dense enough to resist a cannon ball, and much too low for an elephant to charge underneath it, so I waited for the brute to come close enough with the utmost coolness. The elephant kept gradually advancing, halting, intently listening, using its extraordinary olfactory powers to the utmost, yet it was puzzled: perhaps the variable currents of air balked him, I cannot tell, but at last he halted not more than six or eight paces from me; he seemed disgusted and dissatisfied, and put down his trunk to strike the warning note on the ground. This was my opportunity; the temple was exposed, though not quite at the exact angle. If he had been a couple of feet more forward it would have been better, but at such close quarters I knew the bullet. hardened by a mixture of quicksilver, and driven by six drachms of Pegou and Wilkes' best rifle powder, would go through and through, and penetrate the brain; so, taking a quick but steady aim, I let drive. The monster rushed forward a pace, and fell head foremost in a clump of bamboos. I was so delighted at my luck that I quite forgot to fire the left barrel at the cow, and although the Burman appeared as if by magic, and thrust the cannon into my hand, I never dreamt of using it, or firing at any of the others, though they were so dumfounded by the report of the rifle, and the fall of their lord and master, that they clustered together, and I might have killed one or more had I used the weapons at my command.

The Burman was disgusted at my not exterminating the herd. I did not understand the ins and outs then; but the more I had slain, the more he would have got from the villagers for the flesh. The guide went off to get people to cut out the tusks, which were very thick, but not long, and I sat down not far off and breakfasted. In a very short time the inhabitants of the neighbouring villages turned up armed with dhaws and knives. They had a long palaver, and apparently high words, with my shikarie, finally rushing upon the carcass, weapons in hand, hacking and cutting away, each trying for certain tit-bits which are found in the inside only, and endeavouring to collect together as much meat as possible. This was a sight I could not endure, so I walked back to the village, packed up my traps, and returned to my headquarters in my own boat.

It was not till some time afterwards I discovered

that the shikarie had sold the carcass of the elephant I had shot to the villagers by auction, getting not only his share of the meat, but some 50 rupees, by the transaction. That was the palaver that preceded the rush for the meat, and I have seen the same scene reacted on several occasions afterwards.

Having told of a successful hunt, I will relate the story of one very much the reverse, when I was at Lepangyoung, on the Pabay Choung, north-west of Tongho, where several elephants had been killed. This was a capital locality for sport, as not only elephants, but gaur, sambur, tigers, and leopards were fairly abundant. Starting early one morning, we got on the fresh trail of a solitary elephant. As he fed as he went along, and showed no signs of being in a hurry, I was in hopes we should soon overtake him, but we walked a good fifteen miles before we sighted him. He was standing in the bed of a small rivulet, pulling down and eating the stalks of wild-plantains. The wind blew directly from him to us, so I crawled up within twenty yards and sat down. His huge quarter was staring me in the face, and I could not see any vulnerable spot, but occasionally, as he swung his immense head about to flick off the flies, he exposed a splendid pair of ivories. I must have watched him more than twenty minutes; he had eaten all the esculent morsels in the front, and to get at others he would have to present his broadside. So with both barrels on full cock, and finger on trigger, I bided my time. Suddenly, without the least warning, he spun round facing me. I threw up the rifle in a hurry; a drooping bamboo struck the barrel; the rifle exploded

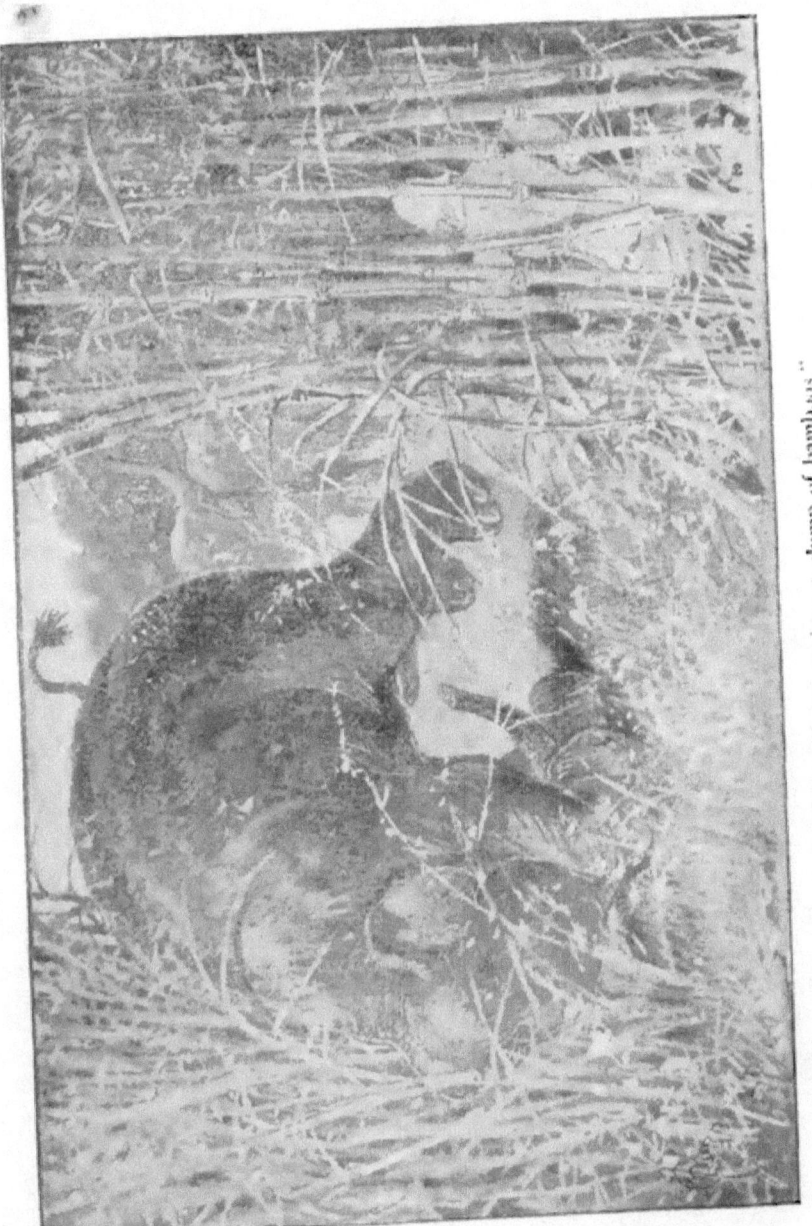

"Fell head foremost into a clump of bamboos."

in mid-air; I had made a clean miss. Before I could use the left barrel all the vulnerable points were safe under cover, and I was not cruel enough to fire at his carcass. Thus this monster with most splendid tusks got away untouched. The memory of that wretched miss rankled for many a day in my bosom, and even now my mouth waters when I think of the trophies that ought to have been mine.

In 1854 Colonel Cotton, C.B., sent a force out from Tapoon, which, travelling all day and night on elephants, surprised Moung Goung Gee, the rebel leader, and his camp. It was just upon dusk; the Burmese bolted one way, our force the other. The enemy left everything behind. Some men of the gallant 2nd Bengal Fusiliers found, as they thought, ingots of lead, and scattered them about the jungle; but one or two of the old stagers who kept some found out that they were pure silver. The officer in command, though personally brave enough, was not a man of decision, and allowed himself to be swayed by an officer who afterwards in India got no end of a name for gallantry, but who on this and other occasions in Burma was not conspicuous for that quality. He urged the Commandant not to remain in possession of Goung Gee's camp, as it was surrounded by jungle, from which the Burmese would pepper us all night, but to retreat to more open ground some miles to the rear. D'Oyly, who was political officer, combated these views, but without avail. A disgraceful retreat was decided upon. D'Oyly then begged to be left with only a company to follow up the day's success, but even that was denied him. He, however, recaptured two of our

Artillery horses, which the Burmese had stolen; but a huge tusker, Goung Gee's state elephant, escaped. The Burmese, on our retreat, repossessed themselves of their camp and goods, and were nowhere to be found the next day.

In 1855 Colonel David Brown was Deputy-Commissioner of Tharawaddie, with powers of life and death. D'Oyly was his assistant, and Twinam in command of the forces. These officers stood no nonsense, and made no retrograde movements; they followed the enemy day and night, soon broke up the whole gang, caught the chief's eldest son, hanged him, and restored the province to peace and quietness. But the state elephant, a magnificent brute with splendid tusks but of very uncertain temper, as he had killed several mahouts, again escaped. D'Oyly determined to capture him if possible; if not, to destroy him. He took one of our best mahouts and a plucky Burman with him, and thinking to find him in the neighbourhood, he started with only a biscuit or two in his pocket, and armed with his fowling-piece, an old Joe Manton No. 17 bore, loaded with a spherical bullet and two and a quarter drachms of powder.

The elephant, an old wanderer, had walked off a long way. For two days and nights his pursuers stuck to his trail, subsisting on what they could get in the jungles, before they came upon him. Their endeavours to catch him were futile; neither the keddah-jemadar* nor the Burman could do anything with him; he charged them all round, and they had

---

* Keddah-jemadar—man in charge of the elephant establishment.

very many narrow escapes. At last, thoroughly worn out, and despairing of capturing the beast, D'Oyly determined to shoot him. He had never fired at an elephant in his life, but he was perhaps the only man I ever met who was totally fearless. He did not know what fear was, and at the same time he was one of the most modest and unassuming of men. The animal charged down on him across a shallow nullah. Kneeling down, D'Oyly waited until the elephant was within a few yards of him, and fired for the bump between the eyes. The first bullet struck a little too high, and did not check the animal's career for a moment, but the second, fired a little lower down, penetrated the brain, and the monster fell dead at his feet.

Talking of D'Oyly, I must here relate a narrow escape he had of his life. He and I were encamped at Pounday—he employed on his civil duties, and I on surveying. Information was brought to him that some of Goung Gee's lieutenants were in a deserted *poonghie* house, a few miles off. He asked me if I would like to go too, but I declined, for I had had enough of such expeditions; and it was a common dodge for the Burmese to bring in false intelligence with a view of sending us on wild-goose chases, while they attacked and looted villages near our camp. D'Oyly himself, having undergone such experiences many a time, was not sanguine of success, but, having nothing particular to do just then, thought he would ride out and have a try once more. He was going totally unarmed. With some difficulty I persuaded him to take my shikar knife, the only available weapon we possessed between us, for our revolvers were in Prome, and he would not be bothered with a gun. He started at 5 a.m., followed by about eight sowars of the 8th Irregular Cavalry, which had only just arrived in Burma to replace the Ramghurs, who had returned to India. The *poonghie* house turned out to be, not a few miles, but a good eighteen from Pounday, and the track lay over paddy-fields for the greater part, which in Burma are particularly nasty to ride over, as when they dry up after the rains the surface is as slippery as ice, and full of cracks.

D'Oyly led the way, guided by a man also mounted on a Burmese pony, and they soon left the escort behind. On arrival at their destination, D'Oyly jumped off his pony, and rushed into the house, to find himself confronted by four Burmese fully armed with their formidable *dahels*, or two-handed swords. Nothing daunted, D'Oyly stood in the narrow doorway, with the shikar knife as his only weapon. His resolute bearing had its effect on the rebels; they hesitated a moment before rushing in upon him, and that second proved his salvation, and the destruction of two of the Burmese. A shot was fired—a man fell dead; a hop, skip, and jump, the flashing of a *tulwar*, and another man fell headless, whilst the other two took headers out of the outer veranda into the long grass below and escaped. So prompt was the rescue that the danger was past before D'Oyly had time to realize it. A gallant young sowar, little more than a lad, outstripping the others, had ridden up just in time to see his leader's jeopardy. To unsling his carbine, shoot one man down, to bound into the house, sword in hand, and to account for another, was with him the work of a few seconds, and lucky it was for D'Oyly that he had such a gallant and prompt follower, or his career might then and there have ended. This sowar, a Pathan, one of the most warlike races of India, did not think he had done anything out of the common, though it was probably the first time he had drawn his sword in earnest. The report D'Oyly made of his conduct ensured his immediate promotion, but whether he remained faithful to his salt, or whether he was led astray during the fearful crisis in 1857, I know not. I have forgotten even his name, but a finer fellow never graced the ranks of the Bengal Irregular Cavalry, rich as that branch is in gallant soldiers. I trust he still follows our standard; but whatever his subsequent conduct or career may have been, surely that one gallant deed will be recorded in his favour at the Last Day.

Elephants are at all times a wandering race. They consume so much, and waste so much more, that no single forest would long suffice for their wants. During the rains in Burma, when they cannot well be molested, owing to the swampy nature of the country, they are especially destructive to the paddy crops. After the harvest they retire to their hill fastnesses, subsisting on wild cardamoms and plaintains, long grass, bamboos, and the leaves of various trees, which are all very plentiful in many parts of Burma.

Colonel McMaster, a well-known sportsman and naturalist, writes as follows: 'Those who only think of elephants as they have seen these domestic giants working at any of the innumerable tasks on which these almost reasoning slaves may be employed, can hardly imagine how puzzling a matter it is to distinguish them amongst the dark shadows and irregular outlines that fill up any portion of a landscape in their forest haunts. I was for some moments, it seemed to me hours, waiting in long grass and reeds within a few *feet*, not yards, of the head of a fine elephant, without being able to get a satisfactory shot at him, or even to see more than an indistinct dusky outline of form, or a dark shadow, as his trunk was raised aloft, when the mighty beast, a magnificent tusker, suspected that he scented mischief. Having at length made sure that there was something uncanny near him, he uttered a shrill cry, and wheeled right round on the very spot on which he stood, without exposing any more vulnerable target than his enormous hind-quarters, at which it would have been wicked and wanton cruelty to fire, rushed down the hill, followed by his family (eight or ten unwieldy wives and sturdy children), whose progress, as they crashed through the dense underwood and undergrowth of long grass caused a noise sufficient to startle anyone whose nerves were not tightly braced, and which my pen is certainly too weak to describe.'

The height of an elephant is equal to double the circumference of the fore-foot as it rests on the ground. These gigantic mammals differ much in size—one ten feet high is very rare; but there is a skeleton of an elephant in the Calcutta Museum eleven feet three inches in height. The African variety is taller, and probably stronger, than the Asiatic, but not so handsome or graceful. In habits, too, they are dissimilar— the Indian species dislikes too much of the sun, and retires to forests during the heat of the day; not so the African, of which both males and females have tusks.

The two varieties of Indian elephants seldom herd together, and are readily distinguishable. The *goonda* has a broader expanse across the forehead; the hump between the eyes and at the root of the trunk is more prominent; but the hollow between the eye and ear, commonly called the temple, is less marked. Its countenance is more pleasing, its eye brighter and kinder-looking; it seldom reaches the height or bulk of the other.

The *mucknah* has the head much longer and narrower, the temple very much depressed. The trunk is longer and very ponderous, possessing immense strength, as if to compensate the animal for the want of the formidable tusks possessed by its rival. Although the mucknah is styled tuskless, that is true but of few; for the majority have rudimentary tusks, like those of the females, growing downwards, with which, by jobbing down, they can inflict fearful wounds. Its eyes are small and sleepy-looking, and its general appearance morose; even when quite young it has an old look. Mucknahs are taller and more bulky, as a rule, than goondas. These peculiarities are not confined to the males, but extend to the females. The two varieties interbreed, no doubt, and perhaps this accounts for the difference perceptible even amongst goondas. Some animals of huge size have tusks, but not as good as they ought to have; these are a cross, I should say, between the goonda and the mucknah. The true goondas have far better tusks, the true mucknahs only rudimentary ones. If Nature has not given intellect to these animals, it has given them a remarkably keen instinct. One has only to hunt them in their wilds to learn how wonderfully Providence has taught them to choose the most favourable ground, whether for feeding or encamping, and to resort to jungles, where their ponderous bodies so resemble rocks or the dark foliage that it is difficult for the sportsman to distinguish them from surrounding objects, whilst their feet are so made that they can tramp over any kind of ground, whether hard or soft, thorny or smooth, without causing a sound. Some of their encamping grounds are models of ingenuity, surrounded on three sides by a tortuous river, impassable for ordinary mortals by reason either of depth of water, precipitate banks, quicksands, or entangling weeds; whilst the fourth side may be protected by a tangled brake or a quagmire. In such a locality the elephants are perfectly safe, for they cannot be attacked without due warning being given them. To get within this enclosure, they will scramble down the bank where the water is deepest, and then, either wading or swimming up or down stream, ascend the opposite bank a half-mile or more above where they descended. Their instinct is wonderful, and their memory must be most retentive. There may not be an elephant within fifty miles or more of a place; but when certain trees there produce a fruit to which they are partial, they will return thither at the exact time year after year.

Elephants have not bred with us in captivity; but wild-elephants are soon tamed after capture, and there are still thousands available in Burma, Assam, and other countries, to supply all our wants for the next thousand years, and probably much longer. A thoroughly trustworthy elephant for all kinds of sport, and at all times, does not exist. The best of them show the white feather at times without cause. I remember when Jung Bahadoor bought an elephant at Burpetta, and gave 18,000 rupees for him, for the Duke of Edinburgh's shikar in the Nepaal Terai, it was looked upon as a monstrous price; but since the rich Princes and zemindars of India have taken to sport, and strictly preserve all game in their territories, far larger prices have been paid, and I have no doubt that there are many elephants now in the possession of native chiefs which they would not part with for double the sum paid by Jung. There is splendid sport to be had in Burma and Assam; but without elephants it is much wiser not to go to those remote provinces for shooting, for without these necessary slaves you can neither see nor approach the localities where game abounds.

Always stick to the same mahout if possible. Every horseman knows how differently a horse behaves at different times, and that his behaviour is but a reflex of that of the man on his back. So with the elephant, only he is more timid and more impressionable than a horse, and therefore less to be depended upon. Do not keep a cowardly mahout; he will ruin your beast. But mahouts, as a rule, are plucky. It must be remembered that the sportsman in the howdah runs or incurs little risk, whilst the mahout, sitting on the elephant's neck, with his legs dangling down, is in considerable danger from a charging tiger. He is unarmed, save with his driving-hook, and the frequency of accidents proves that his berth is not a sinecure; moreover, the friction caused by sitting on the animal's neck, perhaps for a whole day, is excessive. He also gets bitten by numerous gadflies and mosquitoes, is exposed to the sun all day, and he has, perhaps, to take off and readjust the howdah several times during the journey, if it gets out of the perpendicular, as is too often the case. Take a howdah ladder with you, such as may be got in Bombay, and with one as a pattern, any carpenter will manufacture more for you. When folded, the rungs fit into a hollow, and the whole is about eight feet long and under a foot in circumference, and lies alongside the howdah on the guddie until required for use. Making the elephant kneel down constantly is very apt to disarrange the howdah, and to make it lopsided.

In the management of his beast a mahout should not be interfered with too much. More can be done by firmness and judicious treatment than by bullying or nagging, but, when necessary, do not hesitate to make a severe example of a man who wilfully disobeys your orders or takes advantage of your kindness. Many of the mahouts enter into the spirit of the chase, and like a successful sportsman for a master. At the end of a trip I always divided all the Government rewards amongst them, the one on my riding-elephant getting rather more than the rest. Usually this more than doubled their pay for the time they were out, and instilled greater zeal, for the more dangerous beasts I killed, the more they got, and without the hearty co-operation of your mahouts, more particularly of the one with you, you will get little or no sport.

As a rule, domesticated elephants are timid, quiet and inoffensive; but in the wild state, when wounded, or in a state of *must*, their fury knows no bounds.

It behoves men when in chase of the wild denizens of the forest to have common prudence. If a sportsman possess coolness, good nerve, quick eye and hearing, and has been in the habit of handling his gun and rifle, he need fear nothing that roams the jungles of any country. Every hunter must be plucky, but he need not be foolhardy. Wedderburn, of our 37th Native Infantry, was one of the best shots in Southern India; in his first essays at elephant-shooting he was phenomenally lucky, flooring many an animal right and left. Yet on one occasion, having failed to kill as easily as had been his wont, he lost his head and his temper, and met with his death. At Teppacadoo news was brought to him by some Corumbers (jungle people of the Wynaad) that there was a rogue elephant in the neighbourhood. Wedderburn took the field, accompanied by Oocha, a celebrated shikarie and plucky tracker, himself the slayer of many elephants, and a stanch gun-carrier, and by a dog-boy also noted for his steadiness in elephant-shooting. He soon came across the rogue, a huge mucknah, and floored it; it got up again, and was again knocked down. Still it would not die, and a running fight ensued, which was kept up till all Wedderburn's ammunition was expended with the exception of one barrel of his rifle, a double Purdey. The dog-boy had been sent back for more ammunition, but had not returned. The mucknah, though weak, was irate to a degree, and made up its mind to die fighting, or to beat off the foe. Retiring to an open space, the animal stood at bay. Wedderburn proposed to Oocha to accompany him into this glade, but that experienced shikarie said, 'Sahib, I have never known any elephant take so many bullets. He is a shaitan [a devil]. We are in bad luck to-day—leave him alone. He has no tusks, and, besides, he is sure to die. You have but one barrel loaded—my rifle is empty; there is not a tree near, and the *janwar* means fighting.'

Wedderburn, who ought to have known better, for the old man's courage was proverbial, and he had been the best shikarie of Michael (the great elephant shot of India in those days), called him a coward, and said, 'Well, stay here, and see how I will kill him,' and rushed on to his fate. The rogue allowed Wedderburn to get close up to him, and then wheeled round to the charge. Wedderburn fired, failed to stop him, turned to run, and, though the sward was as smooth as a lawn, he tripped and fell. Before the smoke cleared away, his body was a shapeless mass of clay. The beast was found dead the next day with twenty-two bullets in him, any one of which Oocha declared would have killed an ordinary animal.

For tiger-shooting in the plains of the East elephants are a necessity, and to make the best use of them it is of importance that the furniture should be of the best and lightest compatible with strength. Now that breech-loading rifles and guns are in universal use, double howdahs are no longer required. Even in former days, when there was some excuse for them, they were a nuisance, for a man behind you often interfered with a shot at a beast in full chase after your steed, and I have often saved my animal from being cut by turning round in the howdah and dropping a beast when close to the elephant's quarter, which I could not have done had there been a man behind. Besides, the less weight you have on your riding beast's back the better; therefore get a howdah made as light as possible. The portion of the howdah which rests over the elephant's spine should be hollowed out. The weight should be equally distributed on either side of the spine longitudinally, with the bars resting on the pad, which should be specially made and fitted for each elephant, and stuffed with pith, which can be got in almost every marsh. Under the pad there should be a well-stuffed *guddelah*—wool is better than cotton for stuffing—and another similar one above the pad, on which the howdah rests to prevent it from slipping. The longitudinal bars have iron rings through which ropes with pieces of leather softened by elbow grease are attached, and passed under the throat and tail—securely tied—to prevent the howdah from shifting backwards or forwards. The floor of the howdah should be raised at least four inches above these longitudinal bars, to keep it clear of the pad. I prefer planking the bottom of a howdah, for then the motion is not so much felt, though some people dispense with it; but if you stand on the pad, you will feel the motion of the elephant far more than if you stand on a boarded floor. Round the sides of the howdah nail strong *char-sootie* cloth, which can be bought in any bazaar, and give it two coats of green paint, which renders it waterproof, and prevents rain drifting on to your guns and tackle. To protect your guns farther, sew two strips of waterproof cloth on to the top iron bars, to serve as flaps to be thrown over the guns in case rain comes on. The lower portion should be weighted by lead, to prevent its being blown off. By taking this simple precaution I have kept my weapons perfectly dry in the wettest weather. The front of the howdah should not be too high, and should suit the height of the sportsman, allowing his elbows to be clear of the highest portion. A howdah made for a man six feet two inches would not suit a man of five feet eight inches, and *vice versâ*. The back should be about a foot less in height than the front. But the most essential part is the height of the seat from the floor: it should fit exactly inside the bend of the knee of the rider. If lower, should the elephant jerk suddenly forward, the rider is apt to go backwards out of the howdah; if higher, the constant friction against the back of the thigh is very annoying, and is apt to throw one forward—whereas if fitted as recommended, your body sways to and fro, and you acquire the swing so necessary for correct shooting. Four guns in a howdah are ample—two on each side. Racks are fitted on which the rifle stocks rest, and the closer and tighter they fit, the better; the bar in front on which the barrels rest should be of wood, and the notches for the barrels should be cut just large enough and no more, and lined with felt, so as to avoid the least rattling. In front there should be a long box with compartments for cartridges, also lined with felt. To avoid confusion, have your weapons of the same bore, with perhaps one exception, and that a ·577; but the cartridges for an express are easily distinguishable from all others. I think No. 12 bores are probably the best, as cartridges of that calibre can always be got almost everywhere; the rifles should weigh twelve pounds, and the gun eight pounds. The gun should be cylindrical, or, better still, a 'paradox,' which is equally suitable for ball or shot. If you are short of elephants, you can have a compartment under your seat, for carrying your breakfast or lunch, but the less you have on your own elephant, the better. Very few beasts, in a country where elephants are used, care for the noise one of these animals makes in forcing his way through the long grass, because they are accustomed to such noises, but if in addition they hear the rattling of plates or guns, they soon make themselves scarce, for they know such noises are unusual, and caused by their enemy—man.

If your elephant takes to eating earth, stop his grain food, and in a few days he will pass a quantity of bots or worms. Never picket your elephants in the same place long, for the foul ground will soon soften or rot the soles of their feet, which, though apparently spongy, ought at the same time to be as hard as ivory. Mahouts can generally treat the ailments to which their charges are liable, and it is better if you have a stud to keep a headman, or jemadar, and make him answerable for their medical treatment; but it is as well for you to see them fed personally, otherwise the temptation to steal some portion of the rice will prove too strong for the men. Generally, a *seer*[*] per foot of height for each elephant per diem is enough, but if working them for many hours daily, you will not be

---

[*] *Seer*—two pounds.

wrong if you give each double. Thus, an elephant ten feet in height will get daily ten seers in camp, but when hunting daily twenty seers, in addition to his *charah*,* which should be varied as often as possible. Feeding elephants always on the same fodder does not answer.

Never give an elephant a sore back; it not only incapacitates him for the time being, but renders him less stanch afterwards. Lancing the back of an elephant to let out the pus certainly helps to deteriorate him and to lessen his courage. Never allow your elephant to make a football of a fallen beast; it is apt to make him vicious. Naturally, one of these giants would not hurt a worm, but he can be taught anything, and for hunting purposes I would sooner own a coward than a vicious beast.

One of the narrowest escapes I ever had was at the foot of the Yomahs. We had been following up *Tsine*,† and were entering a tunnelled space, with a lot of bamboos on one side and a huge buttress-tree on the other. We were not expecting elephants; indeed, we had seen no footmarks of them the whole day. I had the double Lyell in my hand, and Shoay Jah had the Lang, when with a fiendish shriek a large tusker charged us suddenly. I always carry my weapons on full cock; the rifle was a very handy one with short barrels, No. 10 bore. I had just time to fire a right and left, and to throw myself over a buttress, and the shikarie followed suit. The impetus of the brute took him on fully fifty yards. The bullets

---

* *Charah*—green food for elephants.
† *Tsine*—wild cattle.

were well placed; the first, in the bump between the eyes, would have killed him had I been kneeling down, but not having time for that, I fired from the shoulder standing up, at a distance of only five or six yards. The left shot was higher, and over the left eye. The blood pouring down did not improve his vision; the smoke, too, hung, and enabled us to crawl round and to get behind a regular bulwark of buttresses.* This fiend of an elephant regularly hunted us; but the oil-trees were close; in his half-dazed and half-blind state he was rather abroad, and I gave him several shots. None of them, however, were at the proper angle, and finding that he could not get at us, he retreated. Upon this we took up his footsteps, and seeing a space where huge bamboos grew without undergrowth, we ran ahead, and took up a position behind a clump of male bamboos, of which the stems are far stronger than those of the female or hollow kind. I waited patiently until he afforded a temple shot, and then the Lang brought him down dead.

Whilst in the Bassein district, I was asked to shoot a must mucknah, and I followed his trail for five days, tormented to death by mosquitoes, leeches, and ticks. This elephant was credited with having killed some dozen men. He had been a tame elephant belonging to a mozadar,† but had escaped, and had become the terror of the district. He had lost all fear of man,

---

* These are trees yielding an oil which the natives greatly prize; their roots are often five feet high, and run considerable distances at right angles.

† *Mozadar*—a native official.

and three shikaries, who on different occasions had gone after him for the sake of the reward offered—200 rupees—had never returned. At last the officials could not induce any of the natives to go after him. He used to go great distances at night, and to destroy immense quantities of grain, not only in the ear but in granaries. It was the monsoon, and although D'Oyly and I had tried elephant-shooting in the rains with signal failure, the poor people were so urgent that I broke through my resolve not to hunt at that season, and taking a few Karens with me to carry my baggage, I crossed over to Dalhousie, whence by devious paths I was taken to Cape Negrais. Foot-marks of elephants were plentiful, but none of them belonged to the one we were in search of. On the morning of the third day we entered a ravine, full of rocks and water-courses, where the leeches were enough to drive one frantic. Here we first came upon the homicide's trail. There was a little cultivation belonging to some Karens about four miles away, and the poor people had blocked every pass but one, and that was too wide. They were going to cut a deep ditch across it, when I arrived, but I told them not to do so, as I would take up my post on a bare granite rock, fully fifteen feet high, with scarped sides, except to the rear, where, as it sloped a bit, we could climb up by means of bamboo ladders. I chose this spot because, being a sheet of rock, there were no leeches on it, and I had already suffered so grievously that with a few more such in-flictions I should be unable to put foot to the ground; for these pests get into every part of one's body, but seem more particularly to prefer taking up their abode between the toes, and to fasten in festoons on to the ankles. From this rock there was a narrow track, which went down fully two hundred feet into a gully, and it was up this pathway the monster used to wend his way to the cultivation. He had been fired at innumerable times, but the native guns were not powerful enough, and the bullets had done little more than just sting him; however, with my heavy battery, it would be a different tale. His habits were nocturnal, and he was back into his lair before daylight, so for two days, although he took his usual constitutional, I had failed to get a sight of him, and the exposure had landed me in a sharp attack of fever. During the day I had attempted to find his whereabouts, and had totally failed. I could not stand this much longer, and told the men with me I should remain only two days more.

One day three men went down into the gully before daylight whilst I watched from my perch; but the elephant must have passed before they went down. One of them came back and reported that the other two were following him up. I was thinking of descending and having a try too, when there was an appalling yell, and the monster appeared scrambling up the ravine face. The man with me was so excited he all but fell backwards as I opened fire. Shooting down from the front was useless, but I trusted to his turning and exposing the back of his head. Bullet after bullet struck the immense head; the *hathi* seemed only to get more frantic, and attempted to get at us; he even pulled down a couple of trees; but all his efforts were vain—we were impregnable. I fired at least a dozen No. 10 belted bullets into his head without much effect; but when the second tree gave way, and he fell backwards, in scrambling up he exposed the junction of the head and spine, where a ball from the Joseph Lang caught him a crack which resounded through the jungle. Next moment he sank down on his knees —dead—but not before he had killed one of the two men who had followed him.

Marching from Prome to Rangoon, surveying, as I went along in the Hensada district the people complained bitterly of the damage done to their crops. Having been pretty well disarmed by Colonel D. Brown, the Deputy-Commissioner, they complained that they were now helpless, and that, if the herds of elephants were not driven off, they would lose all their paddy, and would have to starve. They had heard from my interpreter that I was very fond of shooting: would I come to the rescue? I told them I had no time to spare, as I had to meet Scott, of the Engineers, in Rangoon on a certain day; and besides, if I did kill an elephant or two, it would not avail them much, as they seemed to be in herds, judging by the marks they had left.

'Not so, Tuckin,'* they said; 'the leaders are two tuskers, the image of one another; they are the prime movers, and do not fear man; they are close by; if you will shoot them the rest will run away.'

'What do you call close?' I asked.

'We will take you up to them in a couple of hours,' they said. 'These two always remain together and apart from the rest; if you will kill them we can drive the rest

* *Tuckin*—the equivalent of ' my lord.'

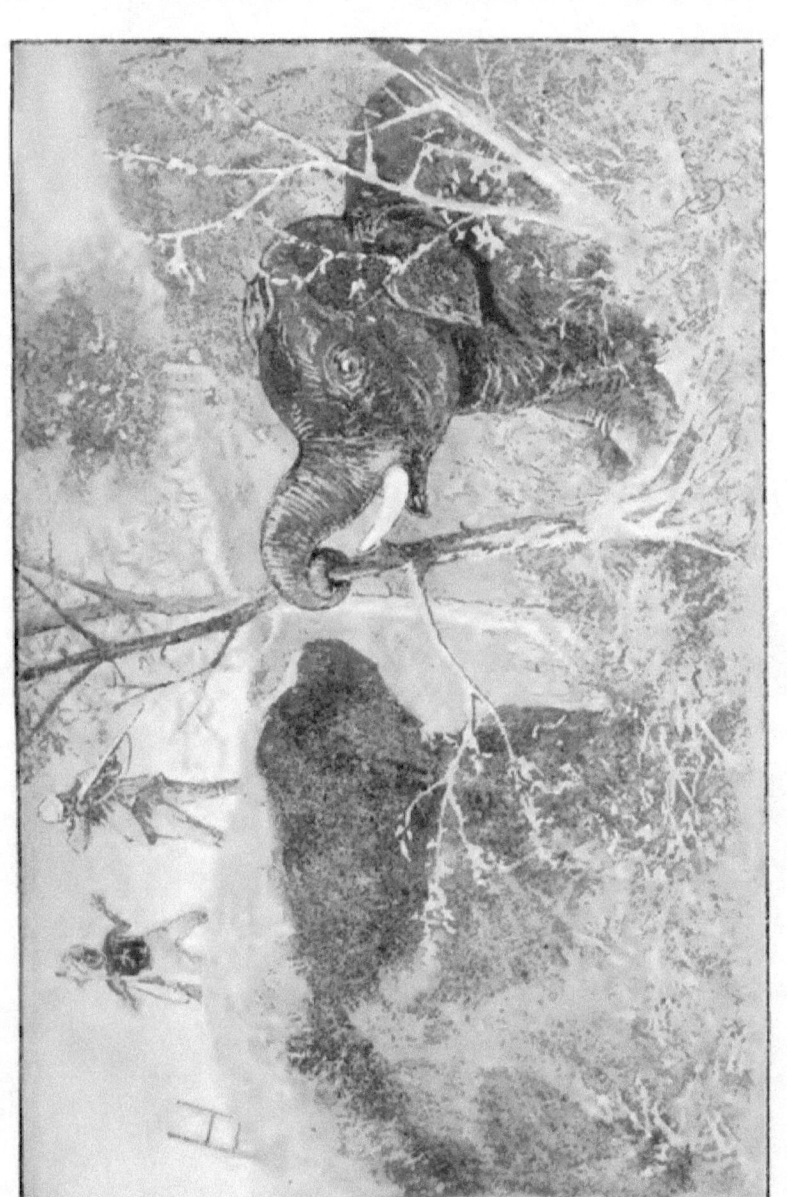

"The monster appeared scrambling up the ravine face."

away: they are all either females or young males and little ones. We don't fear them, but the tuskers we cannot manage.'

I had not much to do that day, so I agreed to go with them, never thinking that I should see those elephants, or any others, for these old rogues know how to take care of themselves; but at the same time a walk would do me no harm, and I heard some Burmese partridges calling. I took the two Lang rifles, the men leading the way across a plain towards some knolls and a forest of trees; and, true enough, within a couple of hours I saw two magnificent tuskers standing on a *teelah* (a small hillock) under the shade of a couple of trees. The wind was favourable; there was a huge tree, and, keeping it between me and my prey, I advanced rapidly, followed by one of the men carrying the extra rifle. There was a kind of pool between me and the hillock on which the elephants were reposing, and the trunk of the saul-tree afforded a capital rest. I got to within fifteen yards, when the nearest lifted up his trunk to scent us; the other went on feeding, but exposing the temple. A careful shot, and down he went; the left barrel caught his comrade a crack, but as I fired he threw up his head, and the ball missed the brain. As he spun round I got hold of the other rifle, and gave him two shots behind the shoulder, but he went on. The man with me touched me and beckoned me to follow him; he went almost at right angles, dived into a small nullah, ran along it until he came to another which fell into the one we were in at an acute angle, up which I followed him hurriedly. Leaving the dry rivulet, my guide clambered up a hillock, and scrambled along a narrow path till I was quite blown. I was right glad when he halted in a very narrow ravine and ensconced himself behind a huge rock, giving me opportunity of a much-needed rest.

'He will pass this,' the man said, so I waited patiently with both rifles on the full cock. Presently the elephant appeared, looking very dismal, and letting him get opposite, and distant only about six paces, I put both balls into his ear, and he too dropped dead

CHAPTER VIII.

BUFFALOES.

Wild buffaloes more dangerous than tigers—Very difficult to kill—
Plentiful in Burma and Assam—How wild bulls appropriate
herds—D'Oyly and his pony tossed—Archie Campbell's elephant
overthrown—His critical position—I am called to his rescue—A
savage encounter—A runaway elephant—Meet a tiger—Encounter with a bull which fights desperately—A pugnacious herd
—Charged by a couple of bulls.

I WOULD sooner meet a tiger on foot in the open than a buffalo. I look upon buffaloes, either in the East or in Africa, as the most savage of all objects of chase. Sometimes they are easy enough to kill, but far more frequently they seem to bear a charmed life, and the more they are riddled, the more lively and savage they get. They are fairly plentiful in Burma, but swarm in Assam. In Southern India they are only found in a wild state in the northern Sircars, near Daraconda and in Bustar.

The ordinary buffaloes in bondage, except on the Neilgherries, are poor-looking, half-starved brutes, bred in and in. But across the Bay of Bengal the people keep no tame bulls, and turn out their numerous herds into the vast prairies, and trust to the wild bulls to keep up the supply. A wild bull takes up with ten or fifteen cows. At first he is shy, and only associates with them during the day, but gradually he loses all timidity, and accompanies them to the place where they are tethered at night, and hovers about them until they are released at daybreak after milking, when he retires to graze with them during the day. In time he cares so little for the people that he won't allow the keepers to go to their cows, and has then to be killed, for to drive him off is an impossibility. The people resort to many devices to effect his death, and mostly succeed; but if there be any European sportsman about, they seek his aid. Although I dislike the Assamese very much, yet I have often rid them of this nuisance, more willingly because these bulls are generally the pick of a wild herd, and carry good heads.

There is very little difference in size and ferocity between the domesticated and the jungle buffaloes in these countries. Both in Burma and Assam a tame cow will go for a European, whilst she will allow the smallest native lad to drive her about and to whack her to his heart's content. Whilst snipe-shooting, I have been chased many times and escaped with difficulty. D'Oyly, of the Commission in Burma, thinking to intimidate one, charged her on horseback, but she tossed him and his pony, and did for the latter. Archibald Campbell, in Assam, had a very narrow escape. He was out shooting on a smallish elephant on a pad; he wounded a bull which charged and overthrew the elephant, and kept prodding it viciously whilst it lay on the ground; this enabled Campbell to crawl away. It was in the old muzzle-loading days;

he and his powder-horn became separated. He had fired both barrels, and had only his empty gun in his hand, but he made off at his best pace towards a solitary tree in the distance.

His horror may be imagined when, on looking back, he saw the bull with his nose close to the ground following his footsteps much as a bloodhound might have done. He availed himself of every little cover he could find; he plunged through morasses, forced his way through patches of high grass, yet the avenger was surely and rapidly gaining on him. Between him and the tree he was making for was an open plain, perhaps two hundred yards in breadth; the bull was only about half that distance behind. Campbell took off his coat and hung it over a bush, and then ran as he never had run before for his life. The bull charged the decoy, trampled it under foot, but finding that he had been deceived, took up the scent and followed at a gallop, for now he could see his enemy, and he bellowed with rage, snorting a kind of view-holloa. Campbell got to the tree, and scrambled up only just in time, for less than a second after the trunk received a blow that shook it to its roots. He held on like grim death; again and again the monster butted. The tree was not very large, and at times almost bent over; but it was Campbell's only hope. In the meantime the mahout recovered his elephant. Odd to say, though he had been overthrown, too, and had sought refuge in a clump of grass close by, the bull took no notice of him, but pursued his master, so the man on his dilapidated elephant hurried back to camp and related what had happened. Campbell's followers did not know what to do, or whether their master was dead or alive. There was not a gun; of the two with Campbell, one had been left where the encounter had taken place, and the other he had dropped at the bottom of the tree in which he had taken refuge.

I was about eight miles off, superintending the construction of a bridge. Campbell's elephant was badly hurt, and the others had gone for their fodder; but a couple of men set out on foot with the mahout, and reached me about 3 p.m. with the news that Campbell had been killed. I got on to my elephant as quickly as I could, mounted two of the messengers to serve as guides, and made for the scene of action direct across country. Fortunately Campbell's mahout was a Cacharie, who knew the country and guided me straight; but I had many nasty nullahs to cross, and it was close on six before I got to my destination. I had no difficulty in following the trail; the bull had left marks of blood behind him, and soon I had the pleasure of seeing my friend perched on the tree, and the bull on guard over him. I was on a large elephant, generally stanch, and notwithstanding the shaking of the head and the pawing of the ground, all denoting hostile intentions, I made straight for the bull. When I was about fifty paces off, he came for me. At first he carried his nose well up in the air, moving at a canter, with his massive horns thrown back over his broad back; but as he got closer his pace increased, and when less than ten yards off he lowered his head. This was the opportunity I had been waiting for. As I fired, my elephant wheeled round; he had been so steady hitherto, I had not anticipated such a move on his part. My bullet took effect, but not in a mortal part, and the next moment the elephant's quarter was acting the part of a buffer, into which the bull drove his mighty horns with all the force at his command. After the first blow my elephant was in full flight, but the bull easily kept up with him, prodding him behind as a gentle hint not to slacken his pace.

In the meanwhile, finding the coast clear, Campbell had called out to the people on my spare elephant to come to him, and he mounted it off the tree. As we passed the place where he had been overthrown, his mahout had picked up his spare rifle and powder-flask, and he lost no time in recovering the one he had dropped, and followed in chase. I had not been idle; the beast I was on was very rough, and whilst going at full speed it was not easy to shoot correctly—to reload far harder, for mine were all muzzle-loading guns—but I gave him a stinger or two, which made him shake his head in great disapproval. Directly he heard the approaching footsteps of the other elephant, he left off following me, and hid behind a clump. I yelled out to Campbell to look out, for the beast was close at hand; and it was as well that I did so, or he might have been taken unawares, for where we now were there was grass sufficiently high to hide even the colossal body of an *arni* (buffalo).

Campbell was seated on the pad just behind the mahout, and in front of the guides. It is not easy to shoot off a pad excepting to the left front. When the bull charged from the right, Campbell used his rifle like a pistol, firing both barrels without effect.

The bull closed, and struck the elephant on the shoulder, the horns going on either side of the foreleg, grazing the skin of the belly and chest only. The blow fairly staggered the elephant, but for a wonder she turned and butted her assailant, knocking him clean down. I was coming back as fast as I could, but the infuriated bull, not a bit abashed, picked himself up, receiving a shot from Campbell as he did so, and bore down on me as fast as he could in his enfeebled state, for he had at least seven or eight bullets in him. Calling out to my mahout that I would flay him alive if he allowed his beast to turn, I opened fire; I had four double rifles, but had managed to reload but two. Campbell turned his elephant, so that he could fire also. My third shot caught the buffalo fairly in the spine of the neck, and over he went, a complete somersault, his huge quarters alighting on the ground within a foot of my elephant's trunk. This was more than the beast could stand, and, notwithstanding all the exertions of the mahout, he turned tail, and would not pull up until he reached my camp, having crossed many very nasty nullahs at full speed and in the dark, for at the conclusion of the fight the light of day had passed away. Campbell turned up about an hour afterwards, and spent the night with me. Next day we went back and recovered our quarry. Campbell took the head, the finest but one I have ever seen; the horns were very massive, and measured from tip to tip and across the forehead twelve feet three inches, which for a bull is enormous. The cows have the longest horns, and the best head I ever saw was thirteen feet eight inches along the horns and forehead and six feet six inches between the tips.

The shooting in Burma was very uncertain; no one could tell what we should come across during the day. We left at daylight, and having settled beforehand the direction we were to go, we beat steadily across country. I had a house built at Myetquin, about eight miles inland; the nearest inhabited spot was a small Karen village consisting of about six or eight houses. They do a little shooting, wandering a good deal, thus soon learning their way about the jungles. They informed me that if I would go due west for six miles I should come across plenty of buffaloes and other game, and that I could not fail to find my way, as I had only to go towards a peak of the Yomahs which could be seen from our camp. So one day, directing the leading elephants and the shikaries to follow with a couple of the Karens, to whom I promised plenty of meat, I started in the dark, wishing to secure a good specimen of the *thamin*, which graze in the open in the early morning, but retire into the forests during the heat of the day. I had passed the marsh, gone through the belt of forest which surrounded the *quin*, or open space, and was advancing slowly and straining my eyes in search of a good stag. Passing a heavy clump of grass, I heard a rustling, and the next moment a tiger came at me openmouthed, uttering his guttural roars. Why he came at me I cannot imagine, but it was evident he was 'spoiling for a fight.' I was on an elephant that did not care two pins for a tiger, but who would fly for her life at the sight of a pony cantering towards her.

She stood as steady as a rock, so I was able to put in a right and left, and the beast rolled over, almost touching the hind-legs of my elephant, who let out at him with one foot, and sent him flying. He was not dead, and tried to charge again, but a couple more pills settled him. When my people came up, they brought important letters which had just arrived, and I had to go back to Tongho at once; but I returned with two others in a week, and then visited Gna-Ecin.

I had killed much and varied game before I came across buffaloes in Burma. The truth is, during the months which we devoted to sport, the *bubali* were in the marshy lands in the Yomahs and other hilly districts; they only came into the plains when the rains commenced, just as we were leaving off shooting. Thus, although anything but scarce, we seldom saw them. I had been shooting with two officers of the 69th—Boyle and Madden. We had wounded a very large gaur, and in following him up we started a young bull, and as he went away with his tail in the air I brought him down. Just then a herd of buffaloes put in an appearance, and off we went in chase, but soon lost them. After hunting about for some time—I was ahead of my comrades—I saw a very large bull buffalo about fifty yards off, unconcernedly browsing. I beckoned to those behind to hurry up, and when they came up we all opened fire. The bull was hit, but he turned and ran through a belt of forest. Whilst my companions followed him, I jumped off to load, as I was on a pad and it was raining. Whilst ramming in my bullets I heard the other two crying: 'Come here! come here!' As soon as I was loaded I remounted and followed; I found the bull had charged, and had all but floored one of the elephants, and neither it nor its comrade would budge an inch except to retreat. I was on a very slow female, but she was very steady, too apathetic to move if she could help it. I soon got within fifty yards or so, and opened fire; ball after ball went into the bull's ribs, but he took no notice. At last he entered a very heavy patch of grass, and there waited for me.

As we approached, when not more than twenty yards separated us, I could just see his form; I stood up on the pad—a very dangerous thing to do—and fired down on the enemy; he came round like a shot. I had just time to throw myself down in a sitting posture on the pad when he closed. In vain I told the mahout to drive his animal into the open: she would not budge an inch, but stood there roaring every time the bull drove his horns into her. He was fully six feet high, only a foot less than my elephant, and at one time he came close in front and looked up in my face. I touched his forehead with the muzzle of my ten-bore rifle and pulled the trigger; alas! it missed fire, a thing it had never done since it came into my possession. The elephant was being cruelly punished; neither of my friends could come to my assistance, because they could not induce their animals to move in my direction. At last, after five minutes of severe mauling, we got the elephant into the open, badly wounded, with some dozen deep stabs in her quarter and about her shoulders. I got on to another elephant, went back, drove the bull out and laid him low; he had some thirty-five bullets in him.

His horns were not very long, but twenty-seven inches in circumference at the base; and in bulk I never saw his superior.

Buffaloes seldom charge in a body, though individuals do so frequently when wounded. I was looking about one day for a wounded tigress in some marshy ground near the Kullung River, when two bulls jumped up and charged straight at me—they must have been twins, I never saw two so alike. I waited till they were within ten yards, and gave them a right and left, threw down that rifle and picked up another (a breech-loader this time), and firing right down, I dropped one dead, but the other struck my elephant, which, however, did not run away; the bull backed, and was about to rush forward again, when I seized another weapon and gave him two more pills. This seemed to sicken him, and he retired and lay down beside his dead comrade. I reloaded all the guns before resuming the offensive; he only shook his head as the shots struck him, but did not move or attempt to get away. At last, with a convulsive struggle and straightening of the limbs, he gave up the ghost.

Readers of the 'Reliques of English Poetry,' by Bishop Percy, may remember how he described the behaviour of the Dragon of Wantley, just prior to breathing his last. The symptoms of a large animal stricken to death are there most accurately described. The verses, however, are too graphic in detail to be repeated here, and I must refer the curious reader to the poem itself.

CHAPTER IX.

INDIAN RHINOCEROS.

Erroneous ideas as to the impenetrability of a rhinoceros' hide—Generally harmless, but dangerous when wounded—Herd with elephant and buffalo—Meet them first in Burma, then in Assam—Elephants indispensable—Difficulty of obtaining them—My first Indian rhinoceros—Make a sad mess of others—Rhinoceros-shooting in cold weather—Size of horns—Their value—A savage charge—Just in time—Charged by two rhinoceroses.

THE resisting power of the skin of rhinoceros against powder and ball has been much exaggerated. The hide on the living animal offers no greater, if as much, resistance as does that of a buffalo; a heavy charge of powder and a hardened projectile are required, not to penetrate the outer cuticle, but to go through the mass of animal matter lying between the skin and the vital organs. I have seen an ordinary shikar knife driven to the hilt by a blow behind the shoulder; and have killed, and seen them killed, by a lucky shot behind the ear from a smooth-bore loaded with a spherical ball and three drachms of powder. But for all that, let the rhinoceros-hunter have good weapons and plenty of them, for though, if left alone, these beasts are perfectly harmless, yet when wounded they are very savage, charge home and inflict fearful wounds, not with their horns, like their African congeners, but with a sharp tusk, not as long as a boar's, but far more massive and equally keen. With one blow they will cut an elephant's leg to the bone, and when they fight amongst themselves they score one another all over.

Elephants and buffaloes at certain seasons become very dangerous, lying in wait and charging without provocation man or beast, but I never knew, or heard, of a rhinoceros in India doing so. They are found in the remotest jungles, far away from the haunts of man, and consequently inflict little or no injury; but should anyone, attracted by the richness of the soil, cultivate a patch of ground within reasonable distance of their haunts, and they find it out, they will soon invade it. The African *boreli* often charges on getting the scent of a human being, but the Indian rhinoceros takes no heed. He herds in company with elephants and buffaloes; there is no rivalry between them; there is sufficient food and to spare for them all, and they graze near each other without quarrelling. I have seen buffaloes and rhinoceroses wallowing in the same pool. Mounted on an elephant it is not difficult to get near them, if your beast will only approach them, but, somehow, tame elephants have the greatest dread of the rhinoceros, and if they get its wind or hear the peculiar cry it makes, ten to one they make a bolt to the rear.

The great ambition of my youth was to slay an elephant. When I had accomplished that, I longed to undertake a campaign against the rhinoceros. There are plenty in Burma, but it is almost impossible to get at them, as they take up their abode in such a boggy country that elephants cannot travel over it. To follow them on foot is equally impossible; to pot them at night is not sport. I had helped to kill the two-horned variety in this way near Cape Negrais, in Burma, but never meant to repeat the experiment.

Running home on short leave, after eighteen years' uninterrupted residence in India, I found amongst the passengers a very nice fellow, who had been an assistant in a tea-garden in Koliabar, and thinking that some day I would take leave and visit Assam on a shooting trip, I got him to give me all the information he could, little imagining that about that very time I had been transferred to that province, and that I should remain in it over seven years.

I will here relate some instances of the killing of these beasts, but not in consecutive order nor in great detail; in truth, there is not much sport in the slaying of these inoffensive pachyderms. I killed forty-four to my own gun, and must have helped to kill, or been present at the death of, fully sixty more. I shot them in various parts of the country. At one time I had the districts of Nowgong, Tezpore, Goalpara, and the Cossyah and Jyntiah hills under me, and these beasts were fairly distributed over them all. Along the foot of the Terai was the best place, but none of the others were bad. The lesser rhinoceros, which is perhaps a foot less in height than the larger, is found more in the *churs** of the Brahmapootra and towards the Garrow Hills. It differs from the other in the arrangement of the folds, but the horn is often longer

---

* *Churs*—islands in a river.

than in the other variety. The habits of both are similar.

Loquaghat, opposite Tezpore, was a favourite locality for them, and Sir Charles Reid, of Delhi fame, shot two there with me, with one ball each, with a small-bore rifle. I killed many there afterwards. Once in the Dooars with Bowie, of the Police, one very cold misty day, either in December or January, when the whole valley was wrapped up in heavy fog, we had been hunting these pachyderms. I had killed two, to the great disgust of my comrade, who was a jealous sportsman, and rather a disagreeable fellow to be out with. There was a low depression. Bowie was on his elephant, standing on a natural *bund*,* and I had beaten through the long grass without seeing anything, though I knew there ought to be a rhinoceros there. We had been enveloped in this mist, but it was clearing away. Without the slightest warning I heard a movement in the grass, and close to me appeared the form of a rhinoceros; he was in heavy grass, and did not present a vulnerable spot for a certain shot, but Bowie and I fired almost together. There was a squeal and a headlong charge at me; my elephant Lutchmee, generally fairly stanch, took to her heels. I made the rhinoceros shake his head at the visitations he received from my heavy weapons, and he then went for B., whose elephant did not wait for the onslaught, but bolted through a tangled brake, upsetting B.'s guns, and all but causing the howdah to be dragged off by the pendent vines. She did not stop until she got to the bed of a considerable stream,

* *Bund*—corresponding to our word 'dam.'

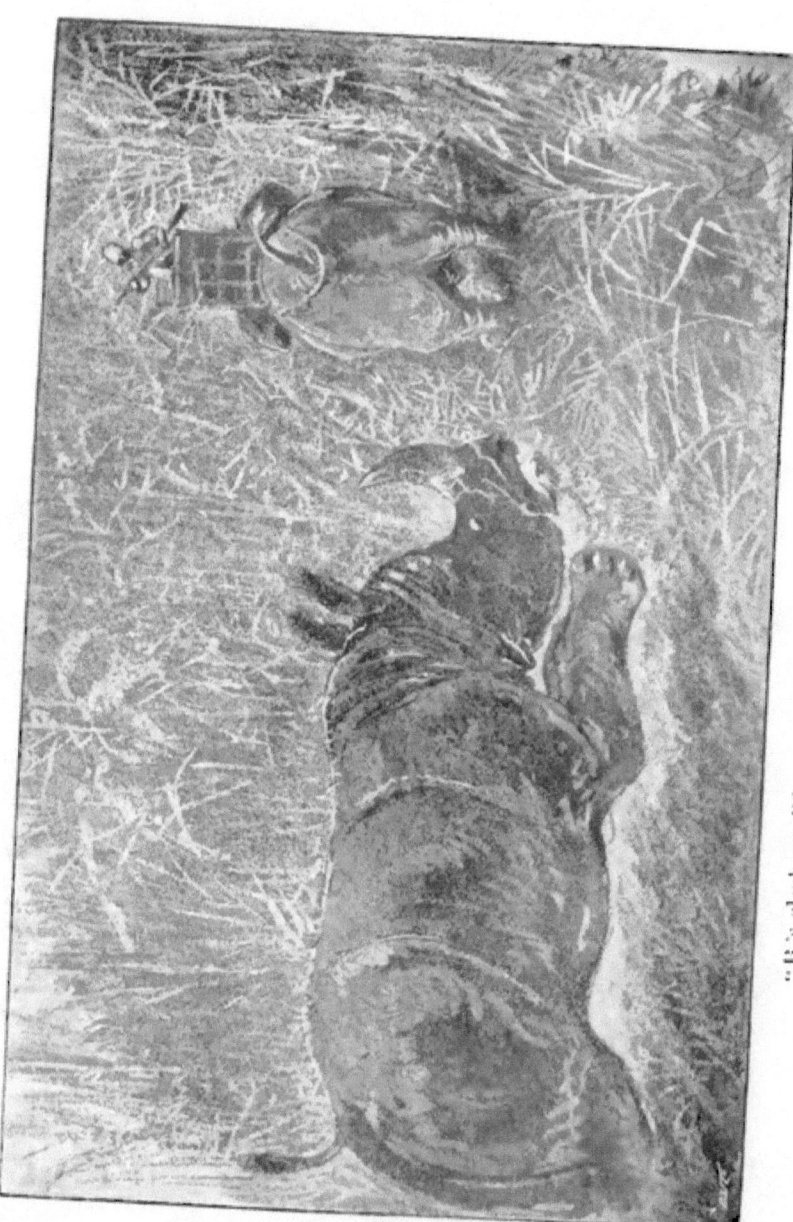

"B.'s elephant did not wait, but bolted through the long grass."

whence she was taken, with great difficulty, back to camp. I got Lutchmee turned round, and went back; but the rhinoceros, though bleeding, had gone fully two miles before I came upon him. Here he essayed to fight again, though he would have had no chance if my elephant had remained steady; but she was very fractious that day, and it was only by taking snap-shots that I mortally wounded the foe at last. He turned and ran into heavy grass, and his stertorous and peculiar breathing (which, when the animal is *in articulo mortis*, once heard, can never be mistaken or forgotten) soon proclaimed that all was over. I took off the horn, which was a good one, about ten inches long, and, as a sop to my companion, I allowed him to have it, for I really did not care for them as trophies at all, and had already several far finer. It was not till long afterwards that I took to selling the small horns, and thereby recouping myself all expenses, which were rather heavy. Many of these trips, with three or four guests, cost me as much as £100, and I was then not as rich as I had been before, or even then I should not have resorted to selling; but the Assamese put a fictitious value on these trophies, which are to us of no value. They will give as much as 45 rupees a *seer*[*] for a fair horn, and many weigh close on three *seers*.

On another occasion Barry, a tea-planter, and I were in the Dooars. I wounded a very large male, but in following him up I found that the right barrel of my No. 10 breech-loading rifle, for which I had paid £64, kept missing fire; I put in several shots with the left,

[*] A *seer* is equivalent to 2 lbs.

but the brute would not drop. I was getting very angry; I had over and over again killed them with one shot each, but this one declined to die. At last he went a short way into a very heavy patch of grass, and when I got near, out he came for me, his mouth wide open, the upper lip curled back, and uttering the cry elephants so much dread. I tried the right barrel once more; it missed again; the left failed to stop him. My elephant wheeled round, and went off at her best pace; but fast as she ran, her pursuer was gaining. I dropped the breech-loader, and seized my trusty two-groove muzzle-loader; leaning over the back seat, I took a snap-shot downwards. To shoot otherwise was impossible at the racing speed we were going at, and only a man long accustomed to an elephant's back could have fired at all; but I had almost lived on elephants, had acquired the necessary swaying of the body to balance myself, and could generally hit a moderate-sized mark at short distances without requiring my beast to halt. As the mouth of the rhinoceros was not a foot from my beast's quarter, I was afraid she would be cut and ruined for life; but my aim was true. I caught my pursuer just at the junction of the head and neck, and over he went, squealing fearfully; he tossed his mighty head about, but otherwise he was paralyzed. As soon as we had pacified Lutchmee, we got her back, and a shot behind the ear did for my foe. On examining my rifle, I found the nipple had got partially unscrewed, so the striker could not give the necessary blow to the cap of the cartridge to explode it; it was put to rights in a moment, but ever afterwards I took a nipple-wrench as well as a turnscrew in the howdah with me.

Near Doobrie, on the left bank, I fairly ran a lesser rhinoceros down on Lutchmee, and killed it in two shots.

On one occasion, when in company with another officer of the Police, near the Manass, two rhinoceroses charged me out of the dry bed of a rivulet. I must have interrupted them in some love scene at a critical moment. I had not fired at them—indeed, did not know they were there—when they came at me open-mouthed. I dropped them both, right and left, dead. These were as pretty a couple of shots as I ever made.

CHAPTER X.

SPORT IN THE NORTHERN DISTRICTS, MADRAS PRESIDENCY.

Discovery of the Bison Hill—The islands of the Godavery—Abundance of feathered game—Linga Reddie, the freebooter—A stiff climb—Lovely scenery—Abundance of game—Dreary life at a single station—Tatapoodi—Cossipooram—Ascend the ghauts—Change of flora and climate—Galicondah—Heavy rain—Go after gaur—Go to a distant jungle—Disgraceful shooting—Indian and Burmese gaur compared—Kill a tiger.

VERY many years ago, Colonel Cotton, R.E., and others under him, ascended a steep hill, overlooking a gorge of the Godavery, about forty miles above Rajahmundry. They found that the plateau was a favourite resort of numerous herds of gaur, commonly called by Indian sportsmen the bison. It ever afterwards went by the name of the Bison Hill. In the early fifties, when I was but a youngster, Joe Cotton, of the Civil Service, at that time Judge of Rajahmundry, Dansey, of our 30th, and I, hired a paddle-boat from the Anicut works, Dowlaishwarum, and determined to try our luck. These boats were very small; we were packed like sardines, and our rate of progress was but slow. Leaving Rajahmundry about three o'clock in the afternoon, by daybreak we found ourselves about twenty miles up the river amidst a lot of *lunkas* or *churs* (islands), and halting at a village to purchase milk, eggs, and other comestibles, a native offered to show us several bears. Although our time was limited, as we had to be back on the fourth day, we could not resist the temptation, so, enlisting quite a small army of beaters, we proceeded to beat several of the smaller islands. We were well posted, and it was agreed that we were to fire at nothing save bears. Directly the beaters commenced their infernal din, myriads of jungle fowl (*Gallus ferrugineus*) and peafowl flew over our heads in a continuous stream. I have never seen so many game birds in my life in the air at once as on that occasion. I am sure that no preserve in England could have shown a greater head of winged game. The sight to a young sportsman like myself was most tantalizing; it was with difficulty I refrained from letting fly at the rocketers overhead, all well within shot. Various spotted deer, too, broke close by, but not a bear showed itself.

We beat five or six *lunkas*, each one swarming with game, and I am sure I am within the mark when I say that we saw fully a thousand jungle fowl and several hundred pea-fowl—many of the cocks with tails close on six feet long—and perhaps a score of spotted deer—many of them noble bucks; yet none of us fired a shot. We neither saw any bears nor any signs of them; I am under the impression none existed on the *churs*, and that the natives only held them out as an inducement, thinking that doubtless, when we did not find bears, we should fire at anything, and reward them by giving them some of the game in addition to their pay. About twelve we breakfasted, and then decided to fire at anything, bird or beast, that showed itself. But, incredible as it may appear, we beat several islands without putting up a feather, nor did we get a shot until close upon four o'clock, when Cotton broke the leg of a spotted doe, which took to the water and was captured. This was the only result; we had wasted valuable time, so, thoroughly disgusted, we resumed our journey, and reached Linga Reddie's village, situated at the foot of the Bison Hill, just before daybreak.

Linga Reddie in those days was a sort of Rob Roy, or freebooter, nominally subject to us, but in reality independent. He broke out into open hostility during the troubles of 1857-58, was caught, and, I believe, hanged, and since then there have been many troubles in the Rampa country; but at the time of our visit Linga was very civil. Cotton was a *burra sahib* not to be sneezed at, so the chief gave us guides to take us to the hunting-grounds, and procured for us ample supplies. We started soon after sunrise, and after a terrible climb of four hours, reached the plateau. The hill is about two thousand three hundred feet above the sea-level. There are various hills, all very similar, being nearly flat on the top. The formation is laterite, and anything moving over it causes a reverberation, which can be heard a long way off. Generally the hillsides are perpendicular, steep as a wall for thirty, forty, or fifty feet, with a slope or shoulder at long intervals, leading to a valley below, while another similar path connects it with another hill presenting much the same appearance. The valleys are covered with forests, but the plateaux are only partially wooded, and partly covered with long grass, with here and there clumps of bamboos. Some portions of the scenery on these hills are lovely: undulating ground, covered with a rich grass about three feet high, studded with self-planted trees, either singly or in groups, rivalling any device of a modern landscape gardener; while some two thousand feet down below the Godavery rolls on through a narrow gorge, said by the natives to be unfathomable. On this plateau, in the early morning, gaur and various deer can be seen feeding about. Tigers, bears, panthers, and wild-hogs also exist.

On reaching the top we agreed to separate. There were two guides; Cotton was to have one, Dansey the other. I, as the youngest, had my choice of accompanying one or the other, and I elected to go with Cotton. The whole hill-top resembled a farm-yard; its surface was covered with the droppings of the numerous gaur. Getting into a dense wood, we wandered round and round and saw nothing. We had got hold of a coolie who did not know the ground. Dansey was more fortunate; his man took him over the open. He saw many gaur, wounded several, but secured only one—a cow. We could not on this occasion remain any longer, so, after taking the head and skin of the gaur, we walked down to the boats, embarked, and after dinner went down the stream, reaching Rajahmundry next day. So ended my first, but by no means last, visit to Bison Hill.

Shortly afterwards I obtained two months' leave, and determined to visit Daraconda, in the hilly districts of the Northern Sircars. Tom Prendergast was in those days collector of the district, one of the finest fellows who ever lived, who has but lately joined the majority. He had been very kind to me, and, as I was fond of sport, told me to apply to him whenever I wanted *purwannahs** to help me along. So I wrote to him, telling him of my wishes and intentions, and anticipated a budget of stamped orders on various officials to give me help. My disappointment may be imagined when I got back a letter, not only refusing to help me to visit those localities, but saying that he would throw every hindrance in my way. He stated that he accompanied a field force there some years ago; that very many of the party died, everyone suffered from jungle fever, some were invalided, and others, like himself, only recovered after years of suffering. 'If you want to commit suicide,' he added, 'or die, you had better go to Burma, but you shan't go to Daraconda if I can prevent you.'

I little anticipated then that within a few months I should be sent to Burma, and live there for thirteen years, and that eventually, when past middle age, I should wander over the very district to which Tom Prendergast would not allow me to go when I was little more than a boy.

During thirteen years' residence in Burma and seven in Assam, with an occasional visit to the Neilgherries, Wynaad and Ana Mullies, I had exceptional opportunities of indulging in the very best of sport. I had acquired experience, and possessed a capital battery.

* *Purwannahs*—official orders from either a collector or other official on the native officials of his district.

Leading an active life all these years, I had suffered little in health, and, though no longer young, I was just as fond of sport as I had been five-and-twenty years before.

In 1876 I was stationed at that dreary place, Vizianagram. It is only about eight miles from the sea, but as it is situated in a hollow surrounded by bare, rocky hills, it is at all times very hot and sultry. There was very little to amuse one in the station, thanks to the introduction of the irregular system into the Madras Army; for the officers of the regiment had been reduced from thirty to six, not one of whom even possessed a fowling-piece. We had no swimming-bath, no billiard-table. The Rajah was a splendid specimen of a man, and excelled in most things; but at that time he was ailing, and died some time afterwards. Life there, to one like myself, was dreary to a degree, so I took the first opportunity of obtaining leave, and, though the season was most inclement, on July 8 I was off on a ten days' trip into the adjacent hills. I had my camp pitched at Tatapoodi, fifteen miles distant. There used to be gaur at the foot of these hills some twenty years ago, but they had long been driven away. Swamp deer (*Rucervus duvaucelli*) also had once existed here, but the last of its race had been killed some ten years ago, and now only spotted deer and small game were to be found.

On July 9 I started for the hills; I sent the servants round by the road, but, expecting to find spotted deer, took an unfrequented pass through the hills. I heard a few peacocks and saw one sand-grouse, but nothing else, whilst my servants came across several herds of spotted deer returning from their nightly raids on the native cultivation. I was too early for them. I reached Cossipooram at 7.30 a.m., but my baggage cart did not arrive until 9 a.m. It took us some time to get coolies, for the cart could go no further, and I finally made a start at noon. The first portion of the road is pretty good, winding about amongst cultivation. The ascent then commences. Some years before there had existed a good, well-made road up this ghaut, but it had become nearly obliterated in many parts, and in some places it was so bad as scarcely to be passable even for my pony. This animal, which had been lent to me by H.H. the Maharajah, was such a screw that I was glad to get off its back and trust to my own legs. I had been, and was still, suffering from severe diarrhœa, and I was not in a condition to undergo much fatigue; but the higher I ascended, the pleasanter became the climate.

The flora changed from that of the plains to what I had been accustomed to in the Cossyah and Jynteah Hills, which have an elevation of between 4,500 and 6,500 feet, whereas I was, at the most, then only about 1,200 feet. I noticed the same terrestrial orchids, flowering shrubs, and trees with which I had become familiar in the hilly country beyond the Ganges. At first they were scattered here and there, but the higher I ascended the more plentiful they became, and on looking back the plains of Vizianagram, with tanks and *bheels* dotted about, reminded me somewhat of the plains of Sylhet as viewed from Cherra Poonjee. My destination was a deserted coffee plantation, called Annatagherry; but as it was getting dark I halted on the top of the first considerable range, at a small village called Railwal. My aneroid barometer showed an elevation of 2,400 feet above Vizianagram. I pitched my *bechoba* tent, but did not put up the *kanats*, or slides, and I awoke in the night feeling bitterly cold. Fortunately, I had brought with me a large blanket to sleep upon, in lieu of a mattress. This I cut into two, covering myself with one and sleeping on the other. Thus within twelve hours' easy journey of Vizianagram there was a delicious climate, necessitating blankets over one; whilst in that vile hole the heat was so great that sleep was all but impossible even under a punkah.

This portion of the hills is very pretty; it is but slightly undulating, with patches of different kinds of cultivation, in various stages of ripeness, which add a peculiar beauty to the surrounding higher hills and dense forests. At this elevation, too, the water, which is abundant and rippling from many a spring, is deliciously cool.

Next morning I was up at 3.30, and got under way by 5 a.m. The road, with the exception of a bit here and there, is very fair, showing engineering skill in its formation. What a pity it has been allowed to fall into such a state of disrepair! for if these hills were easily accessible, they would be such a boon as a place of resort during the hot months for those grilling a few miles off. I reached Annatagherry at seven, and pitched my camp in a nice open plain, a few hundred feet square, on the banks of a mountain stream, at an elevation of 2,800 feet. Immediately to the front and to the right were far higher hills, partially covered with coffee bushes painfully struggling for existence with the fast-growing second growth of jungle, which is always far worse than the first, originally cleared away when the coffee plantations had been made. Walter Fane, of the Civil Service, and some others, had formed about seven extensive gardens, where the coffee did very well, but labour was difficult to get. Coolies imported from the plains died off, and gradually the gardens were abandoned. I found them fast relapsing into jungle, and I expect by this time there is not a trace left of the cultivation on which so much money was spent.

Here the climate was really lovely, cooler and pleasanter than at Shillong, in the Cossyah Hills, at the same season. This time I took care to put up the *kanats*, and made myself comfortable. My servants were well supplied with *kumlies*, or native blankets, and were in a shed expressly built for them. Villagers had been warned of our coming, so supplies were soon brought in, and we were told some shikaries were out tracking. Six miles beyond where we were encamped is Galicondah (Hill of Storms), 3,500 feet high. It arises abruptly in a valley, through which nightly wind rushes down in a perfect tornado, to take the place of the exhausted air of the plains, and all who sleep within its influence are sure to contract a deadly jungle fever. Many years ago it was tried as a sanatorium, but it failed for the reasons above stated. It was also extensively cultivated with coffee, and there was then still existing a considerable garden in some sort of working order; but it was left entirely in the hands of natives, who took but little care of it, and seldom put a hoe to the ground, so very many plants have died out, and more have run into jungle. Annatagherry, though much lower, is away from the influence of this pestilential wind, and, I believe, is perfectly free from fever other than that which anyone is liable to get from a sudden chill, or from not taking ordinary care of himself.

Soon after pitching camp heavy rain set in, and continued for several hours. The trackers returned about twelve, and reported having marked down a gaur some two miles off. So about two I started, feeling very weak and out of sorts. We had a good deal of going up and down hills, the highest point reached being 3,300 feet. The coffee we passed through had not been pruned, nor the ground hoed, or the jungles cleared away, excepting a bit here and there, just to satisfy the Maharajah's agent when he visited the spot, which he did about once a year. The coffee seemed to have had once a vigorous growth, but the ground showed no signs of a rich soil, as it was covered with stones and rocks, and looked very indifferent. The hillsides were covered with thorny creepers and bushes, and as the ground was covered with loose stones, differing in size from an ordinary football to a marble, noiseless stalking was all but impossible.

We went fully two miles over hill and dale, and as we were descending into a densely-wooded valley, halfway up the side of the opposite hill, under the shade of a few scraggy trees, a gaur appeared, chewing the cud and lazily flapping off the flies with his tail. We were fully six hundred yards off; the wind was blowing from him to us, and as he did not move, we hoped we had been unseen and unheard, so we went right-about, intending to make a long détour to enable us to get within shot under cover of some bushes. However, we had not gone far when the gaur slowly began to ascend the hill. I wanted to retrace our steps, and endeavour to get ahead of him, but nothing I could say would induce the shikarie to carry out my views; he insisted on following in the beast's wake. I knew it was folly to do so, for we must then give him our wind; but as this was the first time I had been out with these men, I let them have their own way; and, though I knew it was a useless fag, I followed the brute up and down hill for two hours. I only got a sight of him for a second, for he was on the *qui vive*, went off at a trot, and I never saw him again. I was dead beat, and glad to get back to camp. A good hot bath soon restored me. Notwithstanding my blanket, I was very cold all night. Next day I was up and dressed by 4.30, but the shikaries, or guides, did not come till 5.30. We went over much the same ground as yesterday, but did not see a living thing. I returned to camp, and sent men out to track; these returned about 3.30 p.m. with fresh droppings of sambur and gaur, and reported having marked down a herd into some jungle near a village called Soba.

An hour later, just as I had bathed and made myself comfortable, a villager rushed in, saying that a gaur was feeding in a clearance amongst the coffee, not half a mile off. So I donned my shooting garments, and went for him. There he was, sure enough, feeding quietly; so, leaving some of the people who had followed me to watch him, I took one man to carry a spare rifle, and made a long circuit to get above him, and to approach him over the crest of the hill under cover of some bushes. This took me nearly an hour to do, and when I reached the place where he ought to have been he was gone. I took up his tracks, but as he had gone down hill and wind and through the most tangled places, I did not follow long, and went home.

I started next day with one guide at 5 a.m., leaving the other to follow with the beaters, for finding stalking did not answer, I determined to try a beat, though, as a rule, I do not believe in that mode of sport. It disturbs the country, and the chances are the game goes away by any pass rather than the one you are posted at, or it breaks back. I had a good six-mile walk, and descended fully five hundred feet. The country, though not so pleasant to live in, looked more favourable for sport. The beaters did not arrive till 8 o'clock. I was posted halfway up the side of a hill, and men were sent to guard other exits. The coolies entered a densely wooded ravine, and beat towards us. After an hour's din we heard a rustling, and looking over the bushes which we had erected as a screen, we saw three gaur within twenty yards of us, crowding together, hesitating whether to advance or retreat. I took a careful shot at the breast of the nearest; on receiving the ball it fell on to the one next to it, which exposed its shoulder and received the contents of my left barrel, a shell. The two floundered about and seemed about to fall, when they recovered sufficiently to run down the hill. I took the express, and again hit one, but whether it was the sound one or one of those already wounded I don't know. The three broke back, two of them apparently very groggy. As the beat continued, a gaur ran along the foot of the hill. I tried to cut him off, but failed, and he got away without a shot.

As the coolies objected to enter the patch of jungle in which the wounded gaur had taken refuge, I went down and took up the tracks, along which the blood lay in pools. I even picked up a bit of liver, as I believe; but the bison charged back through the line of beaters, and got into very heavy jungle. We had to advance through this very cautiously, for a wounded gaur is a formidable brute, and can charge viciously; but these, being too badly hit to be dangerous, allowed us to pass, and then broke away. I was too weak to follow them up, so sent the shikaries to mark them down. The beaters refused to enter the jungle, as they were afraid of the wounded beasts; and, to make a long story short, I lost the game for the day, though two were brought to bag afterwards, being found dead by the villagers. How I failed to kill all three, and with one ball each, I don't know, for I had splendid shots within twenty yards. I was perfectly cool, but I fancy my shaky state of health made my shooting very inaccurate. It commenced to rain heavily, and I was glad to crawl home, much disgusted with myself.

Although there are no painted partridges in the plains about Vizianagram, in these hills they were very plentiful, and the country reminded me very much of that about Nongpoh, on the way to Shillong.

I started next day in the pouring rain for Soba, to hunt up the wounded bison. We found the trail easily enough, and at one time I could hear a beast moving about with difficulty within fifty yards of me, but could not get a sight, owing to the density of the jungle. Presently it lay down, and I was going to crawl in after it, when one of the beaters ran back and told me there was a large herd of gaur close by, and if I stationed myself higher up the river, they would beat the game towards me. So, thinking the wounded one would remain where it was, off I went. In the first beat the coolies failed to move the herd. I then shifted my quarters, but that didn't answer, and for two hours I was running backwards and forwards endeavouring to guard three passes, until I was nearly dead. At last, losing patience, I went straight into the jungle where they were, and just as I got to an open spot a good-sized young gaur ran out and stopped for a moment. I fired a shell into its shoulder, low down. On receiving it she ran back; but a herd of eight broke. They were so mixed up—cows, calves, and one bull—that it was impossible to pick out one worth shooting at until they were some way off. I then picked out the bull, and firing well forward, my ball struck the ground close in front of him, and as he swerved he all but fell. The herd got into the forest, and I saw them no more. The wounded one brought up the rear at a considerable distance, and, after staggering about a bit, fell down and expired.

After trying two more fruitless beats, I went after the wounded one of the previous day; but the rush of the herd and my shots had disturbed it, and its tracks were overrun by those of the others, so I lost both them and him for the time being. I then went back to examine the dead gaur; it proved to be a cow about four years old, and certainly the smallest I had ever killed. Those in Burma were perfect monsters in comparison, and I noticed marked differences between them; the nose of this one was not nearly so arched, the head far shorter, the dorsal ridge not so prominent, and not extending so far back—in fact, it ended nearly in the middle of the back, whereas in those in the primeval forests of Burma the ridge reaches to within a span of the hip-joint. It was altogether a prettier, but far smaller, animal.

Some years ago I wrote on the subject of there being two varieties of gaur* distributed over the forests of India, Assam, Burma, and Malaya, and Mr. Carter ('Smooth-bore') says that although I was the first person who mentioned the existence of two varieties to him, he was sceptical until, visiting the Calcutta Museum, he asked Dr. Anderson, the curator, what he thought about it. 'Why, of course,' said that gentleman, 'Pollok is quite right. Come with me, and I will show you skulls of the two,' and he did, to 'Smooth-bore's' satisfaction.

At one time gaur must have been common all over India and Ceylon; at present they are extinct in the latter country, but are found here and there all over India proper and the trans-Gangetic provinces, down

---

* Lately a planter in Travancore wrote that there were two distinct varieties of gaur, one called *katu madoo*, and the other *katerimg*; one with a well-developed dewlap, and the other having little or none.

to the extremity of the Malayan Peninsula, but they do not extend to the neighbouring islands. On the west coast of India, gaur are found all along the Syhadi range on the western ghauts, both in the forests at the foot of the hills and in the upland forests and woody country beyond the crest of the ghauts. They are found on certain hills near Vellore, and are plentiful on the Anamullies, Neilgherries, Wynaad, Coorg, the Bahabooden Hills, the Mahableswar Hills; in the jungles on the Taptee River and its neighbourhood, north of the Nurbudda, on the Vindhean Hills; in the Pulneys, Dindigul, Shandamungalum range, the Shevaroys, and on the borders of Mysore, near Warungul, in the eastern ghauts, from the Rampa country to near Cuttack, Midnapore, and Rungpore; in Central India, especially in the Satpura range; in the Himalayan Terai; in the Darjeeling Terai, from Sikhim to Rohilkund; in the Bhootan Hills and Dooars; in the hill ranges bordering the Brahmapootra, and other localities extending to the Irrawadie and beyond to the frontiers of China; throughout Assam, Sylhet, Cachar, Chittagong, Arrakan, and Burma. Nowhere are they finer and in greater numbers than in the last-named country, where I have shot them fully twenty-one hands in height, fair measurement. On one occasion I saw a herd of about sixty, consisting of immense bulls, graceful cows and pretty little calves of various ages.

As my leave was now all but expired, I sent on my camp, telling my people to halt at the foot of the hills; and starting about half an hour before dawn, I strolled into the jungle, telling my shikarie to follow with the extra rifle. I did not anticipate getting anything, but about two miles inland, on the left of the descent down the ghauts, I had noticed a nice rivulet, which ran down a steep incline, on the borders of which I noticed numerous foot-marks of sambur, and I determined to go there on the chance of getting a shot. Just as daybreak made objects a little visible, I reached the stream, and soon heard a sambur belling. The wind was favourable, and the brushwood just sufficiently high to make stalking possible without being so thick as to obstruct my passage. I looked to see whether the shikarie was in sight: not that it mattered much, for I had plenty of cartridges with me, and the only game I expected to see was either a sambur, a chital, or a four-horned antelope.

I judged from the peculiar bell of the sambur that it was a cry of fear, and thought he might have seen a leopard or a wild-dog, traces of which I had seen in this neighbourhood some time back. The river was not deep, but very swift, and running down an incline; it caused a considerable noise, for it dashed over stones, rocks, fallen débris and the like, so my approach was not noticed as I drew nearer and nearer; the light became better, and at last I got a glimpse of a fine pair of antlers, which were thrown back, and the bellowing was incessant. Although the head and neck were visible, the body was obscured by some long grass, and I was just going to fire at the neck near the head, when, not ten paces from me, I heard a slight noise like that made by the twitching of a feline tail. I immediately looked in that direction, and partially hidden, but still visible, I could make out the form of a crouching tiger. The beast had seen me, and when our eyes met it attempted to spring across the stream, but my right barrel caught it fairly, a little in front of the ear, and over it went with a splash' into the water; as the deer rushed forward I gave him the left barrel, but he stumbled only, and, recovering himself, bounded magnificently across the river and rushed down hill. The tiger was borne down by the current, rolling over and over, and I yelled out for the shikarie to come up sharp, as I did not want to wade into the water and get wet. There was no reply for a minute; then there was a shot some way off in the jungle, in the direction taken by the sambur. I again called out—following the course of the stream. Presently the body of the tiger was caught in some creepers and anchored there. I now fired off a shot, and in a few minutes the shikarie came up. I pointed out the slain, and bid him drag it ashore. He had little on besides a *lungooty*, a slip of cloth between his legs, tucked into a band across his waist; as he waded in, he called out that he had shot the sambur, which had rushed almost on to the top of him. We dragged the body on to the beach; I sent the shikarie back to the camp, telling the people to remain there for the day, to send men at once for taking off the pelts of the victims, and to secure sufficient meat for our followers and the marrow bones for myself. I then made two forced marches and got back to the cantonment, shooting a spotted deer on the way.

CHAPTER XI.

SPORT IN THE HILLY DISTRICTS, NORTHERN CIRCAS, MADRAS PRESIDENCY.

Start for Daraconda—Brinjarie hunters—Salt-licks—Scene at daylight—Variety and abundance of game—Bear-shooting—A hunting chita—Porcupines—Firing the grass—On the tableland—Tiger, bears and deer—Buffaloes and swamp-deer—Four tigers—A mixed bag on Christmas Day—Camp in the forest—Twenty-one days' sport—Return to the coast.

IN 1878 I took a coasting steamer to Cocanada, thence by boat through the canals to Rajahmundry, where I only stayed a day or two, then dâked out to Jugumpeta. I had letters, from a native of influence, to the headman there, and he procured for me ten Brinjarie packbullocks, who were to proceed with me on a three months' tour, and then go on to Kamptie, whilst I returned across the Godavery to Warungul, thence to Secunderabad and to Bombay to embark. I bought a fair *tattoo*, or native pony, really good of its kind, for 125 rupees. I had, of course, my own saddle, bridle, etc. My battery consisted of two twelve-bore double rifles, an express ·577 and a smooth-bore, all of them having been made to order for me by a leading Birmingham maker. My retinue consisted of a cook, a dressing-boy, a maty-boy and a *kalashi*, or tent-pitcher. I had a *bechoba* tent, with an inner fly, which I had added myself, and a *rowty* for the servants. I had a camp cot and table and two chairs. I took with me only flannel underclothing, and not much of that, as it could be washed daily if necessary. I took two strong suits of native-made cloth, dyed brown, four pairs of strong English shooting boots, thick woollen socks, and a good helmet. Three bullocks carried all my personal impedimenta, five carried provisions, and two were set apart for the servants and Brinjaries.

We started for Rampa on November 18, and reached it late at night after a long, weary march. I killed a couple of pea-fowl and a partridge on the way, and allowed the Brinjaries to hunt, as we were far from where I wished to hunt myself. They brought in a spotted doe and a small buck, a portion of which I purchased for a few charges of powder.

From Rampa we went to Sunampadu; thence to Maradupali, Edkur, and Ukalur, passing over most difficult country, and shooting but little game by the way. At Ukalur I was told gaur and sambur were plentiful on the hills; swamp-deer and buffaloes in the marshes to the south-east, where several small rivers met. Very few indeed of the inhabitants had ever seen a European, and I was stared at most of the day; but my Brinjarie fellows were well known, and of great assistance to me, for by their influence I obtained guides to show me the neighbouring jungles. Supplies were very difficult to get; there was but a little coarse rice, and fowls and eggs were decidedly a rarity, and the nearest village was twenty miles off. However, I had brought a good supply with me, having purchased all I could get from the few villages we had passed through, and as I had knocked over pea-fowl and jungle-fowl daily, I had not drawn upon my own supplies. The Brinjaries had also killed something for their dogs every day, which sufficed for them and my retinue.

Two of the Brinjaries offered to act as gun-carriers, and I gladly availed myself of their services. Our first hunt commenced on December 2. It was decidedly chilly in the early morning; I had to be up and away an hour before daybreak, for the ground where we expected to find sambur and gaur was fully five miles away over very rough ground, and in order to find the finest animals we had to be at our posts by daylight. In the forests it was pitch-dark, and we stumbled over many roots and out-lying rocks. The Brinjaries knew the ground, but two villagers also accompanied us.

In all these hills there are salt-licks, the favourite resort of all kinds of game, and we came upon the first at dawn. The men hid themselves after stationing me beside a huge tree. The so-called salt-lick consisted of a depression, perhaps thirty yards long by ten broad, heavily fringed with jungle. It was swampy, and consisted of a whitish earth, strongly impregnated with salt. I was about the middle, and could easily command both ends. The bed of the hollow was about ten feet below where I sat, so nothing could get at me direct, and my flanks were protected by buttresses, whilst the trunk of the tree, some five feet in diameter, covered my rear. My men were ensconced in various shrubs of no great height, but of dense foliage. As the light became clearer, several splendid peacocks strutted out into the clearance, drinking from a little pool, and then scratching up the ground at the edge in search of grubs, ants, or anything that they could find. Then followed several peahens, and one old cock displayed his tail-feathers, erecting them into a huge fan for their special admiration.

Presently several jungle-fowl and cocks came on the scene. Close on sunrise I heard the belling of several sambur, and a few timid does made their appearance, and after a while a magnificent stag stepped into the arena. He was only about fifteen paces from me, and I could have killed him at any moment; but it was very interesting watching the various game as it appeared, heeding no danger, and utterly unconscious that their arch enemy, man, was so close to them. For fully a quarter of an hour nothing else appeared; then a *sounder** of hog, consisting of one huge boar and several sows, entered the marsh, and wallowed in a miry bit. In about five minutes more there was a distant low, and a herd of five or six gaur, all cows, accompanied by several calves, entered the clearing, and, standing up to their knees in the soft, yielding soil, began to eat the earth. These were at one end, the sambur at the other, and the pigs at the middle, right opposite to me. It was as pretty a scene as one could wish to contemplate, and I was in no hurry to disturb it. It was very chilly, and my position was a cramped one, as I dare not stir hand or foot; but I waited patiently, in hopes that something nobler would turn up—nor had I to wait long. Without giving the

* Sounder—a herd of wild pigs.

least warning, an immense bull gaur stood at the edge, peering about suspiciously; but, finding everything serene, he took heart of grace, and boldly splashed into the opening.

My three rifles, fully cocked, were at hand, and I must own I was not as eager to slay as usual, for it was very like murder, firing at such a colossal beast within ten paces, and from such a coign of vantage; for, even if he wished it, he could not possibly do me any injury. The deer had fed round, and the stag was within six or seven paces of the bull. Taking the express, I dropped the bull in his tracks, and severely wounded the stag. For a few seconds there was a perfect babel of frightened beasts fleeing for their lives, and almost tumbling one over the other. The peacocks flew away, uttering their most discordant screams; the pigs grunted, and, with the jungle fowl, scampered away, all except the boar, who stood at the edge champing his tusks, as much as to say, 'I wish I could see you; I'd teach you to disturb my morning meal!' It was a tempting shot, and I coveted his ivories; so, taking up one of the twelve-bores, I put a ball through his head, and he subsided without a groan. The gaur was dead, but the stag had disappeared; so as soon as my followers made their appearance, I bid the coolies, or villagers, cut off the bison's head, which they refused to do, saying it was sacred. But the Brinjaries had no such compunctions, and one of them said he knew some Dangurs—men of low caste—who would be glad of the meat, and help him to skin the animal; so I sent him and one of the villagers back to fetch them. I examined the bull;

he was very massive, and about eighteen hands high, with shortish, very thick horns, but of the same description as those I had killed in these hills before. The Brinjarie and villager, each carrying one of my twelve-bores, and I with the express, took up the slots of the sambur. There was not much blood; but he had not followed the does, and had gone through short scrub. At first it was easy enough following him, but after a while I found it necessary to enlist the services of the villager as a tracker. Our progress was very slow, but the man followed the trail like a bloodhound.

We were going along a track evidently used by wild beasts, and, on turning rather a sharp corner, the man doubled abruptly back, stooping low, with every sign of fear, and passed me at a run; the whole thing did not occupy a minute. I advanced very cautiously, with the express fully cocked. The Brinjarie stuck to me like a man. I had gone but a few paces, when I came upon the sambur lying in the embrace of a huge tiger. The brute had his fore-feet round the deer's neck, whilst his mouth was fastened on the neck. I could hear him gurgling down the blood. His head was away from me, and distant about five or six paces. I put up the rifle, and, aiming for the junction of the head and neck, fired. There was scarcely a movement—the head, perhaps, sank an inch or two lower; then slowly the drops of blood began to ooze down his neck from a small hole at the back of his head.

The noble beast was stone-dead.

The villager now came up, and wanted to pull out

the tiger's whiskers, and was much disgusted at my preventing him, as he said it was a necessary operation, otherwise the tiger's spirit would haunt us. It was as much as our united strength could do to separate the two animals which lay dead, but we managed to drag away the royal beast, who proved on measurement to be nine feet seven inches in length; but his tail was very short, being only two feet nine inches long. He was massive and very fat. The sambur, too, was a prize, as he had a splendid head, only inferior to one or two in the possession of that veteran sportsman, Douglas Hamilton, who in his day probably killed more game than any man in the Madras Presidency, except, perhaps, Nightingale and Mitchell, and certainly had the finest sambur heads in his collection at Ooty I ever saw. I sent the villager back to get help, while the Brinjarie and I flayed the two animals, and before we had quite finished our task, six or eight wild-looking fellows came up; these took the small breastbone of the tiger as a charm, and some of his fat, which they said was a cure for rheumatism if well rubbed in.

The men told me about two miles further there were some bear-dens, and if I liked they would smoke the bears out. But I proposed going there later in the day to sit over the caves, as I wanted to see the tiger's skin well pegged down; besides, I knew if my back was turned for a minute the beast's whiskers would disappear, so I accompanied the men with the spoils of the chase back to camp. On the way I heard a *muntjack* (small deer) barking, and going in that direction, I saw him in a state of excitement, and should have peered about for its cause; but as the little animal's horns were rather good of their kind, I foolishly fired at him, and on the report a beautiful leopard bounded away. I only saw his spotted hide for an instant, and took a snap-shot, but unfortunately missed, my ball crashing into a tree just above where he had disappeared. The Brinjarie took up the deer, and we got back to camp about half-past ten.

Whilst I had my bath, all hands were busy preparing bamboo pegs, and after breakfast I superintended the stretching out of the pelts. The tiger's skin, when pegged out, measured close upon thirteen feet. The sambur's and the gaur's and other heads were boiled in earthenware pots, care being taken that the horns were not submerged. This process loosens the teeth, but renders the skulls beautifully white and free from all offensive smells. There was ample meat for everybody; the people pretty well gorged themselves, and when I proposed to start for the caves, none of them seemed willing to move.

The dens were a long way off, so, taking my express and accompanied by a Brinjarie with the shot gun, I went through patches of cultivation. I soon changed the rifle for the smooth-bore, and had capital sport, for jungle fowl, partridge and spur fowl were plentiful, lay well, and gave easy shots. I went back with seven brace and a half of sorts. At night I had the skins covered over with brambles, and huge fires lit to keep off hyenas and jackals. I was up and away with my followers at 4 a.m. It was so dark we took torches to show the way. We did not follow the path of the previous day, but took a short-cut, which was infinitely worse. We went up hill and down dale, through nasty-looking ravines, crossed several small streams, and eventually climbed up a very rocky hill almost destitute of vegetation.

It was still dark when we got there, but the morning star was well up, and by the time I was posted, dawn began to appear. There are but few inhabitants in these parts, so the wild beasts remain out rather late, as they are never disturbed; it must have been fully seven before I saw anything. Then two bears went into a cave out of shot. I saw two or three others wandering about, which disappeared, but nothing came to my cave until past eight.

The men told me it was the largest den, and that there was a whole family of bears who lived in it, the male being particularly vicious, and that several villagers had been chased by him. They had posted me there as they wanted him killed; the others, they said, did them no harm. It was getting late, and I was thinking of trying to smoke out some of the bears I had seen, but the men begged me to remain a little longer, to which I consented.

Close upon 9 a.m. I saw five bears coming my way. I was lying on the top of the cave, over the entrance. There were huge rocks and granite slabs about. The bears seemed in no hurry; they stopped here and there turning over stones, and devouring various beetles which they found underneath. At last on the top of the crest appeared the ugly mug of the old bear. I gave him a shot, and he fell on the top of a large female, and immediately pitched into her, and they rolled downhill. The other female, followed by two cubs, made for the entrance at a gallop, but I killed her with a ball through the head, and the little ones nestled up close to her. Descending, I went down to the scene of the conflict, the Brinjarie following close on my heels, and it was lucky he did so, for directly the combatants heard us they charged viciously. I gave each a shot, but they would have been on me had not the man put the spare rifle into my hand. I dropped the express, and firing from the hip, the ball went into the open jaws of the male and out through the back of his head, making him drop at once. The female stood up and struck at my face with her muscular arms, but, dodging the blow, I fired into her chest, the muzzle actually touching her when I pulled the trigger. The ball went right through her, breaking her back, and she rolled down the hill, uttering most dismal moans, and biting her paws through and through. I had to go down to give her her quietus.

On returning to the cave, we determined to catch the cubs, and found the villagers' *kumblies* (native blankets) most useful, for the little brutes scratched and fought like fiends. The two natives suffered somewhat, but in the end we secured the two youngsters, who were as large as good-sized spaniels. We left two men to skin the slain, one in charge of the cubs, and with two Brinjarie and three natives I tried to smoke out the two bears I had seen enter in the early morning; but there were two many passages, and after wasting two or three hours in futile attempts we had to desist. We tried several other dens, but only succeeded in driving a hyæna out of one of them, which I shot. I then sent the villagers to help the others, and to carry the spoils to the village, and, accompanied by the Brinjaries, I walked along the summit of the hill.

I had gone some way, when one of the men touched me, and pointed to a rock, saying in Telegoo, 'China puli.' I looked, but could see nothing. I wanted to advance, but the man held me back, and still pointed, and seemed astonished that I could not see what was so plain to him. At last the very slightest movement on the part of the beast revealed him to me. It was a *Felis jubata*, or hunting chita, lying flat on a rock watching something below. It was the first at which I had ever had a chance, for though they are not at all rare, being distributed over considerable portions of India, I had never come across one in the jungles. This one was only about forty paces off, so I had no great fear of failing to bag him. I changed the charge in the express, substituting the shell for the solid conical, and firing behind the shoulder, he fell over the rock, and we found him stone-dead. His full length, tail included, was a little over seven feet. I was very well pleased at getting this specimen for my collection. It did not take us long to flay him and to cut off his head, and by the time we had finished it was getting towards mid-day. We walked back to the village. We saw some doe sambur, but, as there was plenty of meat in camp, did not fire at them.

I did not go out in the afternoon, but superintended the pegging out of the skins, and had a rude cage made for the bears. Milk was not very plentiful, but we got just sufficient to keep the little ones alive, and they gave us great trouble in feeding them. They only survived three days; then they managed to get out somehow, and were killed by the Brinjarie dogs.

I had various luck here, killing three bull gaur, five sambur, one leopard, two four-horned antelope, and then on December 10 I went in light marching order to the Pendakoonda range. These hills are about 4,500 feet high, with tableland at the top. It took me three days to get there, through the most abominable country I ever scrambled over in my life. We followed the partially-dry bed of a watercourse which led to the range. We saw much game, or, rather, heard it, for moving about was not easy work, and the noise we made effectually drove away all the animals; but by halting and going some way up the rivulet, and stationing myself behind rocks, I did get several shots towards evening, when the deer came down to drink. In this ignoble manner I killed four sambur, three of them being does and only one a stag. I also got two peacocks and a porcupine, the latter being very good eating if properly cooked.

On December 14, after one of the most fatiguing climbs I ever had in my life, I reached the plateau. The grass was very high, but I tried my old dodge of a bamboo ladder, and by planting it against trees saw much game. One old gaur gave me much trouble; he was badly hit—would run and hide, and then charge out fiercely. I must have fired fifteen or twenty shots at him before I laid him low, and many were the narrow escapes we had from this savage old bull. After the first day I determined to try and burn the long grass; there had been no rain for a considerable time, and though there were heavy dews at night, the heat in the day was considerable. There was no scarcity of old rotten wood and bamboos about, and we collected a lot and made heaps of them here and there, and about 1 p.m. on December 16 we fired them simultaneously. At first the grass would not burn, but as it dried it caught fire, which rapidly spread about 4 p.m.

It was a grand sight; the whole surface was alight, the bamboos bursting with reports like pistol-shots. It continued the whole night and next day. Within thirty-six hours fully as many miles in length, and perhaps a mile in breadth, had been burnt. The valleys were all but untouched, and for three days I wandered about in the most lovely forests I ever saw; the sun was scarcely ever visible. The conflagration had disturbed the game, but I got two gaur and one sambur.

On December 21 we moved camp, following the plateau, which lay in a north-westerly direction. The fire had done its work, and the surface was nearly bare, only a clump of grass here and there having escaped. Marks of game were plentiful; their slots were scattered over the ashes. We started very early, taking our *chagul* (leathern bottles) filled with water, for streamlets were only met with here and there, far apart, and some way down the hillsides. We saw many *langoors* (monkeys) busy turning over the stones in search of beetles; they swore at us in their own language for disturbing them. Our progress was very slow, for all our traps had to be carried by men, and there were no paths other than those made by wild beasts. We did not come to our halting-place until close upon 5 p.m., and all I had shot were three spur fowl. We had gone some fifteen to eighteen miles over an uninterrupted plateau, nearly flat, with but very slight, long undulations. The men had an ample supply of rice and dried meat with them.

The next day I stirred camp at 3 a.m., and we got off an hour before dawn. I went ahead with the two Brinjarie gun-carriers, and bid my men make as little noise as possible, for these were virginal hunting-grounds. Even the villagers had never been over them. They only knew that three days' journey in this direction we should come to a small village, which was connected with theirs by a narrow path through winding valleys. I had only one servant with me. My whole camp, with the exception of what I had with me, I had sent on from Ukalur to Nulkamindi, with directions to the Brinjaries to burn the jungles on the top of the plateau. These plateaux are all connected, and run nearly parallel to one another, and after the jungles have been burnt you can travel over tableland for sixty or seventy miles. Nulkamindi is at one extremity, and Daraconda at the other. The valley and swampy plains swarm with game; but we were at the wrong season. Towards the end of March, April and May are the best months for sport, and then the jungles have been burnt and the young grass sprung up.

Marching along in the dark, we disturbed several deer and porcupines, but only got a glimpse of the latter. These porcupines are a great nuisance; they burrow under the loose stones; if you step upon one of these stones it tips up and catches you a crack across your shins, and you don't bless the fretful creatures, the cause of your agony. It was just dawn; objects were still indistinct, when I saw something black moving along across us at about twenty or thirty paces. I stopped to get a better look, when one of the Brinjaries said, 'Pedda puli,' which means tiger. I had heard of, and indeed seen, black panthers, but did not believe in the existence of a black tiger; but in the dusk this animal had the shape of a tiger, and was certainly black. It was moving along leisurely, and, aiming as well as I could, I let fly. There was a bound and a roar; I took a second and snap-shot, with what result I could not tell, as the next moment the object disappeared down the hillside.

I immediately called a halt, determined to search for the creature, as a black tiger was not to be met with every day. As soon as it was light enough I took up the trail. The beast had bounded along, digging his claws into the ground, a sure sign of its being hit, and in a passion. Over the crest there was a little grass and short jungle, so I had to advance very cautiously, for in such a place a tiger is a very dangerous animal, as it can hide where one would think there was not sufficient cover for a hare. I traced him step by step down hill for a quarter of a mile; then I could see some grass moving backwards and forwards, and knew that the tiger was at bay.

My bamboo ladder, which a man carried behind me, came in very handily. I bid the men make themselves scarce, whilst I climbed up the nearest tree. I could not see the animal, but fired several random shots into the grass. After every shot the movement ceased for a moment, then the tail was swayed about as usual. I did not want to waste ammunition, but how to get at the animal I did not know. I then tried a shell, and this, bursting close by, made the tiger move. I got a momentary glimpse and fired; the thud told me I had hit, and the brute left me in no doubt, as, before I could reload, he charged and clawed at the trunk of the tree. He was so immediately below me that I could not fire; but one of the Brinjaries had the sense to throw his puggaree from a tree close by towards the tiger, which immediately rushed at it, and I bowled him over with two shots. My disgust may be imagined when I found him to be but an ordinary tiger; but he had been rolling in the burnt grass, and in the dim light looked black. He was a fair-sized animal, nine feet four inches in length, and massive. We lost no time in skinning him, and then resumed our march.

When we got back to the plateau, we saw by the footmarks that our people had gone on, and we hurried after them; but they had a good two hours' start, so we did not overtake them until past two o'clock, and camped soon after. Our people had seen several gaur and sambur, and certainly their spoor was plentiful. These animals eat the ashes when they cannot get at the white earth which they are so fond of. During the night two bears were busy digging out a white ants' nest. I was half asleep in my tent, when I heard their inhalations as they sucked up the white ants. Looking through the window of my tent, there were the bruins, sure enough, busily engaged. I seized the rifle, and gave them a right and left. They both ran off; but I saw one fall, and heard the other floundering about in some bushes. The camp was alarmed, and it was three o'clock. I bid the boy get tea, and whilst it was being prepared, I went towards where the bear had fallen; he was not quite dead, but seemed paralyzed, so I put him out of his pain. I had a long march before me. I had only that day's rations for my men, and I wanted to kill some game before reaching the village; so I did not wait for morning, but, leaving one of the Brinjaries and a villager behind, I told them I thought they would find the other bear dead about a hundred yards down the slope at daylight. But when they joined me, they declared they could not find it—I doubt whether they had looked for it: for though I had left one of my rifles with them, they were not accustomed to firearms, and, though undoubtedly plucky, had no confidence in their own shooting, and were not likely to run into danger without their dogs being close by.

I started at 4 a.m. with the other Brinjarie, and certainly I had a glorious day's sport. Gaur so far away were worthless, unless carrying unusual heads, especially as my coolies would not eat the flesh; so though I saw several old bulls, I did not fire at them. About half an hour after dawn, I heard most unusual sounds; and hurrying forward, on turning round a clump of bamboos I saw two splendid stags engaged in mortal combat, whilst some six or seven does were looking on in a most unconcerned manner. The two were well matched, and although I was within fifty yards of them, I hid myself to see the dénouement without having been perceived by any of the denizens so near. The two stags were wild with fury, their nostrils dilated, their eyes flashing fire, and first one, then the other, drove its antagonist backwards. For at least ten minutes no real harm was done; there was a great deal of butting and thrusting, but beyond a score or two upon their hides where the hair had been torn away by the sharp-pointed antlers, no blood had been drawn. The two were well blown, and their panting sides showed that the fight could not last much longer, and that one or the other must soon give way. Their horns were interlaced, and for a minute or two there was scarcely a movement; they were evidently taking breath. The one nearest me gradually drew back very quietly, until one of the tips of his horns touched the extremity of his adversary's basal antlers; then suddenly lowering his head, and dodging a vicious prod made at him, he threw himself with a scream upon the other. A few rapid passes were made—so rapid that I could not follow the movements for a minute or two, and then both were bleeding : the one furthest from me from a prod in the shoulder, and the other from a thrust in the chest. They had evidently got their second wind. They separated, and then rushed one upon the other. The horns seemed inextricably interlaced, and both fell over upon their sides. The one furthest from me first recovered his legs, and as the other was rising rushed upon him, drove his horns well into his side, and then, borne forward by the impetus of his rush, turned a complete somersault, and lay there unable to rise. My Brinjarie ran forward, and in a second the poor stags were dead. The does scampered away as soon as they saw the man. One head measured forty-two inches, and the other forty-four. The ones I had secured the first day were an inch or two longer, but not so massive. The heads were soon severed, some meat cut off and given to the coolies when they came up, and we resumed our journey.

In about an hour the plateau began to slope downwards; there was more grass about, for the fire had been very partial here, and clumps of bamboos were scattered about. The aneroid showed that we were 3,900 feet above the sea—600 feet lower than the highest point of the plateau. I was skirting a bamboo clump, and came upon a bull gaur face to face. Had he charged, I should have been in an awkward fix; but, fortunately, he wheeled round, exposing his shoulder, and I gave him the contents of both my barrels. He ran off; but I heard him fall, and found him on his back, his legs up in the air, resting against a clump of immense female bamboos, stone-dead. The coolies, who were close by, said the village we were bound for was not far distant, and that the people there ate bison or any flesh, having no caste; so we hurried forward. In another hour we had descended nearly a thousand feet, and there for the first time we came upon some spotted deer.

There must have been some twenty or thirty does and several bucks; they jumped out of a patch of grass about three feet high, ran some fifty yards, and then faced round staring at us. I secured a buck and a doe. Hanging them up to the bamboos, we went on, and reached the village—Peddachurla, elevation 2,200 feet—about eleven o'clock. Some dozen men started at once for the meat of the gaur, and to bring in the spotted deer. Whilst breakfast was being prepared, I had a talk with some of the villagers, the Brinjarie acting as interpreter. They said game was plentiful. They had two old muskets in the village, but no powder or lead. They killed various animals with cross-bows and arrows, and by means of pit-falls, which they set in pathways made by wild beasts. They said that, if I liked to stop a few days, they would show me buffaloes, gaur, and two or three kinds of deer. I got rice for the people here; but my own supplies were running short, so I said I could only remain two days with them, as it would take us at least five days' hard marching to reach my camp at Mulkamindi, but promised them some powder, lead, and shot if they showed me good sport. As an earnest, I gave one of the village shikaries a few charges, and he went away well pleased, reappearing at 3 p.m. to show the way. He took us downhill, and through some horrid jungles to a flat, marshy valley covered with long grass fully ten feet high. My bamboo ladder was all but useless, for there were but a very few trees scattered about, and a long way apart. We had to move along narrow paths made by wild animals. The man told us that buffaloes were fairly plentiful, and I soon saw from their spread-eagle footmarks that the *bubali* were here. Now, I had seen a great deal of buffaloes and their ways, and had shot very many of them in Assam and Burma, and knew that there was not a more savage beast, or one more difficult to kill, in the world than one of the *arni*, and I did not at all like the prospect of meeting one on foot in the sort of jungle we were in. It would have been an admirable plain for work on elephants; but the grass towered over our heads, and we could not see beyond a yard or two at the most. However, as the native with his old Tower musket walked on at his ease, I, who was well armed and used to all sports, did not like to lag behind; but, at the same time, I devoutly wished that we might not see any buffaloes on such ground.

As we advanced, the grass became higher and more dense; then suddenly before us appeared a vast marsh, covered with aquatic plants and short grass, with here and there clear water spaces, which were literally covered with wild-duck. Peering about, the man pointed to a spot about a quarter of a mile away, and there a herd of buffaloes were feeding; they were within fifty yards of the belt of long reeds with one solitary tree. Leaving the Brinjaries here, and telling them to scramble up into some of the stunted trees, I gave the villager an extra rifle to carry, and drawing back into the long grass, we made for the solitary tree, which was our landmark, and was to be our coign of vantage, by tortuous wild-beast paths. It took us more than half an hour to get there. The tree was easy to climb, and soon I was up in the topmost branches, with my sable companion beside me. The buffaloes were seven in number, not counting the calves. There was one old bull with thick massive horns. The villager was anxious to try the powder I had given him, so I took the extra rifle from him and hung it by its sling to a broken branch close to me, and, pointing out a large cow, told him to fire at it whilst I fired at the bull; they were only about thirty paces away, and presented an easy shot. The native took some time to aim, and as soon as I saw he was ready I fired at the bull. The shikarie's gun went off with a bang like a 24-pounder, and he was almost thrown from his perch; but his cow dropped dead, whilst my bull only fell on his knees, then recovered, and would doubtless have got off had not my second shot caught him in the neck and rolled him over. The remainder of the herd ran some fifty or sixty yards, then halted for a second, and with the extra gun I broke the fore-leg of another, and with three more shots killed it.

It was getting on for evening, so, having secured the tongues only of two, we hurried home, as it was not a nice country to wander over in the dark, intending to return for the head of the bull on the morrow; as it was, we did not get to the village till an hour after dark. I was up and away before dawn, and, sending some men to the dead buffaloes, I skirted the marsh and got a little beyond it; the grass was not so high there, and the walking much better. We were trudging along, when close to us some deer, which we did not see, bounded away. We went along as silently as we could, and presently came on a herd of swamp-deer feeding on aquatic plants, up to their bellies in water. One of my principal objects in coming to these regions was to ascertain whether this deer did exist here, as reported by the villagers, and sure enough there they were. I shot a stag, a noble brute with eighteen points, but missed another with the second barrel. Within the next two hours I put up several more, and killed another stag and two does.

We then went round to the first marsh, and found

our men perched up in the trees. On asking the reason, they told us they could not approach the buffaloes, as there were several tigers tearing at the bull when they came. I soon joined them, but could not see the ghost of a tiger. The men said they had retired into a patch of grass close by, and if I waited quietly some of them would be sure to come out into the space to drink.

The hind-quarter of the buffalo had certainly been well eaten, and as I intended to move on the morrow, I thought I might as well try and get a shot at the tigers. I had some biscuits and potted meat with me, and a flask of wine, so I took it easy. Further up the marsh several buffaloes showed themselves from time to time, but were far out of shot. The sky was clear and the sun very hot, and I was getting tired of being perched up there, and wanted to go home; but the people begged me to remain a little longer. I was getting scorched myself, and the patient natives, eating only a little parched rice, looked like so many statues. At last a man touched me, and pointed in the direction of the buffalo. There was nothing visible but the swollen body, but on looking about I saw just the slightest movement in the grass. There was a little clear water about twenty yards beyond, and it was evident that some animal was making for it. In about five minutes a tiger walked into it and lay down; then followed a tigress, which commenced to drink. After a slight interval two three-parts-grown tigresses showed themselves, but kept apart from the others. These three presented easy shots; but the tiger, by far the largest, had only his head above water. The men urged me to fire, and I was sorely tempted to do so, but determined to give them a little more grace. After slaking their thirst, the three came to the buffalo and commenced to tear at the flesh. The male probably thought they were eating more than their share, for he, too, got up, and, dripping wet as he was, commenced his repast.

The tigress and tiger were close together, almost touching. I had some of my Assam cartridges left for the twelve-bore; they each had six drachms of powder and a steel-tipped conical; so, changing the express for the larger weapon, I waited until the two heads were close together, and firing at the junction of the neck and head, I rolled over the two with one shot. It passed clean through both, and my left barrel caught one of the youngsters in the stern, as she bounded away, and disabled her. The tigress was stone-dead; the tiger showed some signs of life, so I put an express bullet into his head, and then, dismounting, I had no difficulty in killing the third, for she was unable to move, the conical having entered high up the buttock, traversed the body, and gone out by the chest, smashing the fore-quarter to atoms. Thus both the hind and fore quarters on the same side were crippled, and all she could do was to flounder about in the mud.

We removed the three dead bodies to a dry spot, cut off the buffalo's head, and went back to the village, all but the native shikarie, who said he would sit up, as the fourth tigress was sure to return. I certainly thought he was a fool for his pains, but he knew the animals better than I did, for she came back just at sunset, and he shot her dead with one ball, and reached camp in triumph at about eight o'clock. The truth is, the wild beasts are so seldom disturbed here that they do not know what fear is, and do things in this remote locality which they would not dream of doing in a more populous district. The people begged me to remain another day, and as my time was my own, I consented, provided they would take me to some fresh ground, for I did not care for shooting buffaloes in such a country on foot. We were busy till late, staking out the skins, and I found that the whiskers of two had been removed. I threatened to withhold the *bucksheesh*, but of course only said this to frighten them; the poor ignorant brutes knew no better, and it is an article of faith with them always to deprive a tiger's skin of its hirsute adornments, otherwise they firmly believe that something dreadful will happen to them.

Next morning, Christmas Day, I was up and away at about 3.30 a.m. We went back over the route we had come by for about two hours. Then we found the plateau had a branch which went to the west, and by following it the men said we should reach the Godavery a little above Buddrachellum, without having to ascend or descend above one hundred feet or so. They said it was a *maidan** the whole way, but the elevation was 2,375 feet. There was still a great deal of grass, for the fire had burnt the crop there but very slightly. I fancy it had reached this after heavy dew had fallen, so had not had much effect. In parts the grass was very heavy, in others only about three feet in height. The natives, who turned out in numbers, sent me ahead, and then silently walked through the long patches, hitting

* Plain.

the trunks of the trees with their *dahs*.* It was an admirable way of beating, and I should be afraid to say the number of beasts I saw. I had a long day's work. We had some fifteen beats, and went probably twenty miles on end. I got two gaur, five sambur, three four-horned antelope, one spotted buck, and one doe. I saw a leopard too, but he was far too quick, and directly he perceived I had seen him, he sneaked behind a bush, and though I ran forward to cut him off, I never saw him again. I might have doubled my bag, but I chose only exceptionally fine beasts, and only shot the doe for the pot. When we ceased shooting it was too late to return to the village, so we cleared away a spot in a heavy bamboo tope, and the men rigged up a shed in no time. I had no servant with me; but the savages cut up the meat in thin squares, and, sprinkling it with salt, strung it upon long bamboo skewers and roasted it over the hot embers. They also cooked some young bamboo shoots, and when eaten hot they are excellent. I had a few biscuits left, and a little wine, so did not do so badly, after all; my servant, knowing it to be our great day, was going to prepare a great feast, but it would keep till next day.

The natives lit huge fires, for it was very cold. I had no wraps, and I must own I did not sleep much that night. Taking only the Brinjaries and one villager to show the way, I started at 3 a.m., reached the camp at 11 a.m., and, after a good breakfast, took a long sleep. The villagers returned in the evening laden with meat. I had my traps packed up, ready for a

* *Dahs*—large two-handed knives, used for felling trees, etc.

move in the morning. The people were really sorry that I was going. I was the first sahib who had ever stopped at their village; but I told them I must be moving, and that I was bound for Daraconda viâ Nulkamindi. 'But why go to Nulkamindi,' they said, 'to get to Daraconda? We can take you a short-cut to the plateau which will save you thirty or forty miles.' 'But all my traps are there,' I said. Four of the villagers offered to go off at once, marching day and night, and would bring my traps after me, and probably be on the appointed spot on the plateau as soon as myself; their only reward was to be two canisters of powder, some shot, and lead. The people here are not afraid of tigers (there are no man-eaters); but they do dread bears, and at night move about with torches.

We did not get away ourselves until daybreak, and then were followed by fully twenty adults, and some six or seven youngish women, who were very useful in bringing water, etc. We went across paths only known to these people, I going ahead with a couple of men to shoot game, of which there was plenty. In three long days' marches I reached Guntira, having shot one buffalo, three gaur, and two sambur *en route*. Here I halted for a day, for I was worn out; my pony was with my camp at Nulkamindi. Many of the men and women had gone back laden with meat, and there were only some six or seven left when we started from the plateau; but several of the men and women from the new village also joined my camp. For the next four days we had a good deal of climbing. At first we went along undulating ridges, then descended into-a densely wooded valley, up a steep hill on to another plateau, and along it for some twenty miles, then down again, and at last reached the tableland, which is, on an average, 4,200 feet above the sea-level, and which extends uninterruptedly for fully seventy miles in a north-westerly direction, with connecting spurs, with others running parallel. The rainfall is considerable, and there are many watercourses separating the various plateaux. I was glad to see that the grass had been burnt some days, for the new grass had commenced to spring up.

During those three days I had shot three marsh-deer, two sambur, and four gaur. I had seen bears, but had not got a shot. Tigers' pugs* were frequent, but I did not see the animals themselves. We moved on to a watering-place some five miles above where we had struck the plateau, and at least two miles before I got there I saw signs that people were about, and I guessed that my camp had arrived, which proved to be the case. They had been there nearly three days; they had stockaded the pony, as they said tigers and panthers abounded. Lower down the Brinjaries had used their dogs, and had killed several deer, and had seen much game. They had procured sufficient rice to last us a month by going long distances from village to village, exchanging salt for grain. I was pretty well tired, and rested for two days, shooting only pea-fowl and spur-fowl for the pot. At night many gaur came to drink, and one or two passed right through my camp.

All the villagers had left us, carrying off an ample

* *Pugs*—footmarks.

supply of *biltong*, except two men and three women, who proposed to go with us to Daraconda, and on to Buddrachellum, should I decide on going that way. I need not give the results of each day's journeyings. For twenty-one days I wandered over a lovely country, finding game everywhere, and killing fifteen gaur, two buffaloes (on the last day, close to Daraconda), seven sambur, one barking deer, and three or four four-horned antelope; these were killed for the pot only. At last, after wanting to visit these localities for twenty-five years, I had accomplished my purpose. The country lower down was far better for game than Daraconda itself, but I had had enough of sport for the time. I went out twice near Daraconda, and killed three buffaloes, four marsh-deer, and one sambur, and then, dismissing the villagers with a good gratuity each, I altered my plans, and went back.

I had kept only six of the best gaur-heads, three buffalo-heads, four sambur, and four marsh-deer, two barking deer, three four-horned antelope, and all the tiger, and bear, panther, and leopard skins and heads. I allowed the Brinjaries to hunt every day after leaving Daraconda; they used to pick out a small hill, place men, with a couple of dogs each, at intervals, and then slip three or four couples. These soon started game, and as it attempted to break other dogs were let loose, and in a short time deer of all kinds were run down and killed.

I was nearly four months in these hills, which have such a deadly repute. I only took ordinary care of myself. I lived as well as I could, but could not afford to carry sufficient beer for the trip with me. I had two three-dozen cases with me on starting, and I treated myself to a bottle now and then after extra fatigue; but I had sufficient sherry to afford to drink two or three glasses a day when I could not afford to drink beer. I might have killed much more game, but too much slaughter palls upon one. I picked out the animals best worth killing, and as I had many mouths to feed, not a scrap of meat was thrown away. The Brinjaries finally left me with the remoter villagers at Antarla, and I trust they all got back safe to their homes.

CHAPTER XII.

MAN-EATERS AND BUFFALOES.

Go to Bustar—How to live well in the jungles—Bengal humps—My shikaries—Toddy—Escape of the man-eater—Nine people killed—Move camp—Sand-grouse—Miseries of night-watching—Shoot a tiger—Another beat—A woman killed—The man-eater killed by buffaloes—Spotted deer—A panther—Bears—Fail to bag one out of eight—Jungle fowl—Dummape—Abandon carts—Share ponies—A hunt with dogs described—A tigress—Teak forests—Mahseer-fishing in the Godavery—Sironcha—Large game in Bustar—Vicious charge of buffaloes—Shots at a sambur and tiger—Encounter between buffalo and tiger—Salt-licks—A mad gaur converted into beef—Send for camp—Two bears with sore heads—Brinjari dogs—Four-horned antelope—Camp at last—Cause of delay—A bullock killed—I am tossed—Carried to the coast.

I HAD long intended taking a trip into the Bustar country, and a friend advised me to go there viâ Rajahmundry, and through a part of the Nizam's country to Sironcha, as he said there was good shooting *en route*, and the country was not so unhealthy as it was in the northern circars; so I sent on my camp ahead, and leaving Cocanada at 2 a.m., I reached my camp at Pedda Pungadie, on the right bank of the river Godavery, at 9 p.m. I lost no time in throwing off my dust-stained garments, and poured over me the contents of a lot of earthenware pots filled with deliciously cool water. These *chatties** are porous when new; if filled overnight, their contents cool rapidly, owing to evaporation, and nothing refreshes one in the East so much as a bath, especially after a long ride or *dâk* journey. I was soon arrayed in light, airy costume, and whilst partaking of the meal prepared for me, I called for the shikaries, who had been sent on a fortnight ahead, and asked what *kubbur* they had to impart.

Now let me give the reader an idea of what constitutes a dinner in India, as prepared by an ordinary Madras cook, as exemplified in my case. First there was mulligatawny soup, then a fish with anchovy sauce and oysters (tinned, of course), a capon and a Bengal hump, chicken cutlets, curry and rice, *poppadums* (thin wafers, only prepared in the East; very delicious if properly made), cheese and rusks. Now, a properly-cured hump off a good Brahminee bull is unequalled, but it is difficult to get; ordinary ones are common enough, for all the cattle in the East are humped, but there is as much difference between them and a real high hump off a sacred bull as there is between chalk and cheese. Wilson, in the palmy days of his hotel in Calcutta, was the only man who could be depended upon to supply them, as he had a large farm of his own, and reared these cattle expressly for this greatest of all delicacies, but now they are not easy to get. Brahmins especially, and all Hindoos, object not only to ordinary cattle being killed, but more particularly to the slaughter of these bulls, which in parts of Northern India roam about at will and are never molested, even

* *Chatties*—earthenware pots.

if they commit great damages. In the Mutiny we had a rare time, for then, somehow, these bulls came frequently to grief, and their humps, tongues and marrow bones formed a common article of food among the troops.

But to return to my tale. The head shikarie was Elapah, a tall, thin Hindoo, very wiry, and far tougher than he looked. He bore the marks of several encounters with wild beasts; he had been nearly scalped by a bear and ripped by a boar. He was no longer young, but a man thoroughly to be depended upon under any circumstances. As a gun-carrier he was all but unrivalled, and as a tracker he had few equals. He had been in my employ for very many years. Before he took service with me he had been a professional slayer of tigers and other of the *feræ naturæ* for whose destruction Government give a reward, but as I gave him a wage of 15 rupees a month, shikar clothes, when he condescended to wear them, besides the greater part of all sums I received for dangerous animals destroyed, he was content to play second fiddle, and to help me to kill, instead of slaying beasts himself. For a wonder, he never drank to excess, but had no objection to a tot of grog, and if we came to a tope of date or Palmyra palms on a grilling hot day, he would be up a tree like a squirrel, bring down the pot containing the toddy, and, after his master had taken all he required, help himself liberally to the remainder. Now, this toddy, when unfermented, is not only most palatable and refreshing, but most wholesome; but there is toddy *and* toddy. You never get it alike from any two trees. I do not think I ever got what I call delicious palm wine above twenty times in my life, and twice out of the lot was in Africa. Generally it is only so-so, better than nothing on a hot day; but a draught from a really good tree is a drink for the gods.

Ramiah, the second shikarie, was a head shorter than Elapah, but very strongly built, and better for small game than for big. He was always in scrapes, for he not only drank, but was a great admirer of the fair sex, and was constantly running after them, irrespective as to whether they were already appropriated or not. If their lords and masters objected, he generally thrashed them, for he was not only very muscular, but a dab with his fists, having in his younger days been attached to a European regiment, and taught the noble art of self-defence.

Such were the two men who came in, and bidding them squat down, I asked Elapah the news.

He said that owing to the *chota bursôt* (small rains) having partially failed, and the intense heat of the weather, there was a great scarcity of water, that the pools were few and far between, and that many of them were filled rather with liquid mud than water; consequently deer were plentiful only in certain localities in the vicinity of three of the principal tanks, or *bheels*. In the smaller tanks large sounders of hog were wont to wallow nightly, but they had not been able to examine the neighbouring jungles thoroughly, because of a man-eating tiger which was the scourge of the country. Seven men, he said, had been killed in the last fortnight, and they had been solicited by the villagers to sit up for and to attempt to destroy this animal, but that, being my servants and expecting me daily, they had declined.

'A man-eater!' I exclaimed; 'when was it last heard of?'

'It killed a young woman only two days ago, about two *coss* (four miles) from this, as she was collecting withered sticks for firewood, but it has not been heard of since.'

'Well,' said I, 'before going on to the Nizam's country I will remain here for a few days, and see if I can't bag the beast. But it is late; be off to bed, and in the morning I'll go with you to the village to ascertain if there be any fresh intelligence.'

I was up next morning at 5 a.m. After the usual bath and *chota hazarie*, which in my case never exceeded a cup of coffee, I mounted my *pegu*—Burmese or Shan pony. Handing a couple of rifles to the two attendants, and slinging my own smooth-bore over my shoulders, we started for Ananteepore, the hamlet in question. We got there soon after daybreak, but could obtain no news of the game I was in search of. After a long palaver, three of the villagers accompanied me, and led me through a nice tree forest, where they said spotted deer were fairly plentiful, but we must have gone fully four or five miles without seeing a living thing, with the exception of a few squirrels. We then came to an open glade, in the centre of which there was a fair-sized tank. I got off the pony and carefully examined the margin of the bed, which contained very good water. The marks of spotted deer were plentiful, with a few of sambur and pig, and innumerable traces of pea-fowl, jungle-fowl, and sand-grouse, while at its further extremity there were the pugs of a large tiger, which the people declared were those of the man-eater. This trail we followed up, and marked him into a dense thicket in the midst of the forest. Presuming that he would lie up there during the heat of the day, the shikaries and I remained on guard, and sent the villagers to collect coolies, with orders to bring them back as soon as possible; but the hamlets were small, scattered, and far apart, and the inhabitants few, so I knew that a considerable time must elapse before the requisite number of men could be collected.

I sent my pony with them to be picketed in the nearest village, and to await my return. I was not altogether a stranger to these jungles; I had hunted here years before, and had met with some success by sitting up at the pools; but since the completion of the Anicut the country had much changed: the various irrigation channels had made a howling wilderness into something resembling civilization. However beneficial this might be to the revenue or to the people, it was not a blessing to the sportsman, and I greatly preferred the former state of things.

I always take something to eat and drink with me when I start on an expedition; all I required was prepared overnight, and put into a haversack, which Ramiah had to carry. So I took a snack about eleven, and washed it down with a pint of pale ale. In the meanwhile my two attendants carefully and noiselessly scrutinized the country round the brake into which we had traced the feline; there was no doubt that it had entered the patch and had not left it, so, hoping for the best, I chose three trees, one for myself and two others for the shikaries, so as to guard every outlet. My object was to rid the country of its scourge. Sport I could get in plenty elsewhere.

But what a weary time we had of it! Hour after hour passed, yet no beaters. The men with me had brought a little parched rice, and munched it as they sat like a couple of statues on their perches, but their *chagul* (a leather bag) of water was soon exhausted, for the heat was most oppressive, without a breath of wind. The men were afraid to go singly to the tank for a fresh supply, and I did not like the two to vacate their posts, for fear that during their absence our prey might sneak away, for a tiger, especially a man-eater, is most cunning, and will crawl away unseen in a most marvellous manner. At last the *patel* (head man) of the nearest village appeared with about twenty men, five of them carrying tom-toms, and two *cholera* horns. No time was lost in arranging them, and at a given signal the most discordant noises burst forth. For a proper beat, we ought to have at least fifty men; but we had to do the best we could with the few at our command. I had armed the shikaries, one with my twelve-bore rifle, and the other with my smooth-bore, which, being cylindrical, carried ball fairly well, whilst I myself retained my pet .577 express. The beat did not last long, and ended without a sign of the tiger having been seen. I got down, and walked into the thicket, and carefully examined it. Sure enough, under a bush, there was the impression of a beast having reclined—the grass was pressed flat; but there was not the ghost of a sign how it had escaped.

As it was then close on half-past five, and daylight ceases in the East at 6.30, we commenced to retrace our footsteps. I told the *patel*, if he got any news of the tiger, to let me know at once; and on reaching the first village I mounted my pony, and got back to my camp about 7 p.m.

I could not have been asleep more than a couple of hours, when I was awakened by most discordant noises, and the light of many torches, and, hurrying out, found a posse of some dozen men, and nearly as many women, the latter chanting their dismal cries for the dead. On inquiring what had happened, I was told that, a couple of hours after my departure from the village, the *patel* had wandered just outside the hamlet, and had never been seen again. On being missed, he was searched for, and shreds of scanty clothing with which he had been attired were found fixed to thorns here and there, proving that he had been dragged away. There was little or no blood to be seen. The people were afraid to penetrate far, and had at once organized a party to communicate the sad intelligence to me. As nothing could be done until daylight, I told the people to come again at 4 a.m., and in the meanwhile to find shelter in the village, and not to venture out until I could accompany them, and that I would endeavour to avenge the death of their head man, whom they seemed to have respected.

Although I was up and dressed a little after four, none of the people turned up till past five. The early hours of the morning are the favourite time for man-eaters to seize their prey. So great was the fear entertained by the people, that, though they had ventured through the four or five miles of forest and jungle which lay between their village and my camp during their excitement in the middle of the night, they were afraid to start back, even in my company, before daylight. We had no difficulty in tracing the unfortunate man, and we found his remains within a mile of where he had been seized and carried off. The tiger, after sneaking away during our hunt for him, must have lain in wait in a small clump of bushes within a couple of hundred yards of the village, and revenged himself on the leader of the gang which had attempted to help us to destroy him. The remains of the village official were removed to be cremated, and we took up the pugs, and followed them as far as a neighbouring tank, where the tiger had slaked his thirst, and on to the skirts of the jungle beyond; but there all traces were lost. The shikaries and people were of opinion that he would now go further inland, and advised me to move my camp to a village called Settapilly, and there wait further events. Sending orders for my people to move as proposed, I searched about the jungle with Elapah, shooting a spotted deer, a couple of jungle-fowl, and a peacock with a tail close on six feet long, and got to Settapilly long before the arrival of my traps.

In the evening I sat in a *mart* (a circular pit) close to the edge of a small tank, and shot several sandgrouse when they came for their evening drink, but retired to my tent at dark, and went to bed early. The night passed quietly enough, and, mounting my pony at daylight, I went off to a jungle, distant about eight miles, trying for sambur, but had no luck, and got back at twelve. I was lying down on my cot reading the last *Field*, when my boy told me there were some villagers who wished to see me. My tent was pitched under a splendid tamarind-tree, and I was soon outside, seated on a camp-stool, and listening to their tale. They came from a village about three miles to the north of my last camp, to report that a girl who was collecting firewood had been seized and carried off by a tiger at eight o'clock that morning. What to do I knew not. The brute seldom returned to a kill; he preferred fresh meat, and was here, there, and everywhere. If I went back, he would probably kill someone at or near Settapilly, and I should have to tramp back. If I stopped where I was, I might lose a chance of a shot; but, after due consideration, I came to the conclusion that the day was too far advanced for me to go to such a distance, and that I had better remain where I was in the hope of hearing of the beast at closer quarters. On further cross-questioning, I ascertained that the body of the girl had been recovered and removed, and, as it had been untouched, it seemed as if the poor wench had been killed more out of devilry than for the purpose of satisfying the cravings of hunger. The men went back much dissatisfied because I would not accompany them, as they said they had sent to all the neighbouring villages for coolies to collect for beating the jungle where the man-eater was supposed to be; but I told them to have patience, and I would rid them of their enemy, if I devoted the whole of my leave for that purpose.

I amused myself shooting small game, and for two

days I heard nothing of the man-eater, and was thinking of moving on, when it was reported that two people had been killed far apart, but only about four miles from my camp. What was I to think? Were there two tigers preying on man, or could the same animal have slain two men two or three miles apart within an hour or two? I was soon on my pony investigating the cause of death. We found the first body almost intact, only a mouthful or so having been taken out of the buttock; but this was accounted for by the beast having been disturbed by a party of travellers. We then went to the second kill, and found it had been dragged into the jungle, and nearly demolished. We traced the fell destroyer a long way, but eventually lost all traces, and returned to camp, fully convinced that both men had been destroyed by the same beast. As I did not think the tiger would remain in that neighbourhood after killing two men there, and after such a heavy meal, I thought he would lie up nearer water, so I moved further inland to a small group of huts. They could scarcely be said to form a village, and its name, if it had one, I have forgotten; but the camping-ground was good, and there was a small tank in the jungle, which was heavy, about three miles off, where it was said tigers, bears, and deer came to drink at night. So I thought I would take my chance of getting a shot at something or other whilst waiting for news of the man-eater, or perchance the beast itself might put in an appearance.

I had a pit constructed, and went down to it about an hour before sunset. In remote and isolated places, especially where there is a scarcity of water, wild beasts often come to drink just before dark; it is well, therefore, to be early, so as not to throw a chance away. I took Ramiah with me to sit up, and three villagers to return with the syce and pony, for there was no knowing where the dreaded man-eater might be. Elapah I sent to a village further off to obtain news. I had been ensconced in my pit about a quarter of an hour, when I heard the bell of a sambur; but only a brocket and a couple of hinds came to drink, which I let alone.

Although I detest night-shooting, I resort to it occasionally, and the most interesting times to me are just at sunset and at dawn, for then every variety of bird-life, especially, comes to the water to slake its thirst, and can then be closely watched. After the sambur had departed, some spotted deer appeared on the scene, and the whirr of wings, particularly of the sand-grouse, was incessant. There are three varieties of these birds in India; the largest and commonest fly in flocks. Water seems an essential to them; but it is difficult to understand how they get on in Africa, where they are called Namaqua partridges, and are often found in the centre of vast saharas or sandy deserts far from any known water. The other varieties in the East are found only in threes or fours, and the very smallest, generally called painted sand-grouse, from their beautiful plumage, consort in pairs only; they are in size equal to a Californian quail. On this occasion sand-grouse, pea-fowl, jungle-fowl, spur-fowl, and a few common red-legged partridges, appeared, some settling near the water's edge only a few yards from my hiding-place. About three-quarters of an hour after sunset, just as objects were becoming almost indistinguishable, a sounder of pig came down, and whilst some wallowed in a shallow and miry part of the tank, others dug up roots with their snouts along the margin, and kept up a constant grunting and squealing. I was sorry, and at the same time glad, to hear the din they created—sorry, because it showed that they were in the habit of feeding there undisturbed and unmolested by either tigers or leopards; and, on second thought, glad because their grunting might attract some midnight marauder.

The moon rose about half-past seven, and it was only a day or two past the full. At first the shadows cast by its slanting rays deepened the gloom, but as it got higher these gradually faded away, and about ten I could have almost read a book by its light. There was not a cloud about; yet it is almost impossible to distinguish the fore-sight of a rifle by moonlight. I had tried many dodges to overcome this difficulty, but none had answered. I was now, for the first time, trying luminous paint, and congratulated myself on the result, for I was enabled to cover several of the pigs as they wandered about, sometimes coming within a yard or two of my *cache*, and at others disappearing in the far distance. About twelve I wrapped myself up in my *kumblie* (native blanket), bade the shikarie keep a bright look-out, and, with a clod of earth for a pillow, I was soon fast asleep. But such slumber is always fitful; mosquitoes revel on the sleeper, and their buzzing is far more irritating to one than their bite. You dare not make a noise by slapping at them; the pit is but shallow, and any sudden movement of arm or body might reveal your presence to some beast hovering about the outskirts of the surrounding jungle; for before venturing into the open, every animal scans the space in front carefully, and the least noise or movement on the part of the hunter would frighten it away. Those who live in the jungles, and are given to sport, sleep but lightly, and the moment they are awakened they are on the alert, and have their wits about them. There is no yawning or stretching of limbs; as the eyes open the hand silently grasps the rifle, the body is carefully raised, and the hunter, who was unconscious but a moment before, is wide awake now and ready for action.

About three o'clock Ramiah touched me, and just then the moon was somewhat obscured by a passing cloud; but peering about, I saw a bear some way off, too far for a certain shot at night, so I waited my time. After drinking, he commenced to turn up with his paws clods of earth and the few stones scattered about—in search of beetles, I believe. To my left there was a white-ants' nest, which attracted the attention of the bear: he shambled towards it, uttering a peculiar cry as he did so, and soon he was joined by a comrade. The two between them soon began to demolish the cone to get at the nest containing the larvæ, which I knew it would take them some time to get at, for it is always at the very base of the ant-hill in a series of cells, and although the newly-built portion is easily crumbled away, the older gets baked by the sun, and is as hard to break through as a brick wall. There was no hurry, the bears were not likely to leave until they had got at the hidden delicacies, and, telling the man to wake me again, I turned round, and should have been asleep in another moment but for a touch from my attendant. Looking up, I saw him intently gazing in a direction diametrically opposite to where the bears were at work. At first I could distinguish nothing. I flatter myself I have very good eyesight, but natives are phenomenally acute in their vision, and although in broad daylight I would not have owned much inferiority, yet at night I was nowhere in comparison, so it took me some little time to distinguish what he was staring at. The two bruins still continued their work of destruction; the shikarie bent his head towards my ear, and whispered 'Bagh!' (tiger). I silently cocked both barrels, hoping and praying it might be the man-eater, and afraid to breathe almost; the next few moments seemed an eternity, they appeared to pass so slowly.

I hate suspense, and if it is continued any time I get quite nervous through excitement. If this had been an ordinary tiger I should not have been so anxious, but—why, I do not know—I jumped at the conclusion that it must be the man-eater, and was doubly anxious to slay him. I had been lucky enough to kill over two score of tigers, but very few given to homicidal propensities.

In less than five minutes, which I could have sworn were an hour, I saw the outline of a magnificent tiger stealthily creeping along towards the water. The bears must have scented him—they could not have seen him, for their bodies were half buried in the centre of the ant-hill; I could hear them sucking in the succulent morsels, and lapping up the ants' eggs with their long tongues. Suddenly they desisted, and, with a grunt of disgust and despair, scampered away towards the jungle. The tiger took no notice of them, but taking advantage of a place less muddy than the rest, went up to the tank and began to lap the water right in front of me, and not twenty yards off. I have noticed that there has been considerable discussion as to whether a tiger laps like a dog or a cat, or whether he sucks in water with his lips without a movement of the tongue. All I can say is, that I have seen over a dozen tigers drinking, and that certainly they lapped.

The broad side of the tiger was towards me. Resting the rifle on the earthen rampart in front, I took a careful aim and fired. There was a splash and a series of half-growls, half-roars, for he had fallen into the water, and whilst struggling and endeavouring to get on his legs, he was being half suffocated. He managed to get to the edge, and there he lay lashing himself with his tail, and uttering roar after roar.

I soon perceived that his back was broken, and that he was helpless. I would willingly have put him out of his pain, but shooting at night is very uncertain, and I did not want to spoil his skin. I did not like to go up to him to administer the *coup de grace*, for one never knows what a wounded tiger can do with a last expiring effort, and, as it was then close upon five o'clock, I waited for the first glimpse of daylight before I fired again. I could not account for the bad, at the same time lucky, shot I had made. My rifle had a very low trajectory. I had fired at the point of the elbow, but it must have carried very high to have broken the tiger's back; but this was soon accounted for, for I found one of the flaps of the back sight had accidentally been raised.

The tiger's moans, groans, and roars were dreadful and incessant, and I was only too glad when I could see sufficiently distinctly to put a ball through his head.

Ramiah and I with great difficulty managed to drag him out of the water, and after washing off the mud which clung to him, we found that he had a most lovely coat, and was a beast of the largest size.

About half-past six my syce, with the pony and half a dozen villagers, turned up. I told them that I had at last destroyed the man-eater, but on examining the defunct animal, one of the villagers shook his head and said: 'That, sahib, is not the *adme-kha-na-wallah* [man-eater]; this is far too large, and he has evidently been feeding on a sambur, for here are some of the hairs sticking to his mouth, but the man-eater kills and eats only us.'

On cutting open the beast to enable us to remove the body more easily, we found inside him pieces of fresh venison with the hide adhering, proving that he had but lately killed and eaten a deer. Any tiger is better than none, and I still hoped against hope that this might yet prove the beast I had been after all these days. But I was soon convinced such was not the case, for that very afternoon, as I was superintending the pegging out and curing of the skin by having ashes of burnt bamboos well rubbed into it, four men from Ananteepore, distant fully fifteen miles off, came reporting that at five o'clock that morning a *tappal runner* (postman) had been carried off by a tiger. It was evident the brute kept near the river, and never wandered far inland; so, leaving Elapah, who had just returned without any news of importance, and two men in charge of the tiger's skin, and forbidding them to allow the whiskers to be burnt or singed off, as natives are so fond of doing, I took a short cut, and got back to my former encampment at dusk. There was no news next day, and as the beast seldom killed twice running in the same locality, I moved back to Chotamundry.

The next day I was told the tiger had attempted to carry off a herdsman tending buffaloes on the sands of the Godavery, but had been driven off by the cattle, who had charged and chased him for a considerable distance. For two more days we heard nothing of him. Then it was reported he had killed a boy some seven miles south, and had been traced and surrounded. I lost no time, you may be sure, and in a couple of hours I was in a *machan*,* and fifty men in a line beating towards me. They formed a half moon, and I saw no means by which the beast could get away without exposing himself; but I was not half acquainted with the resources of the animal I was after. The very thicket he was in was known; the people were exasperated, had collected in great force from every village within a radius of twenty miles, and as they kept well together, the din they made with shouting and yelling, and beating tom-toms and blowing cholera horns, was terrific. I had my eyes on the thicket. I was not twenty yards off it, with my rifle on full cock, expecting every moment that the quarry

* Platform built on a tree.

would break. The line was within forty, then thirty, then twenty yards; yet not a movement betrayed that there was any living thing within the bushes. The coolies halted for a moment, redoubling their diabolical noises, and then, thinking that perhaps the beast had decamped, with a sudden impulse, and in a compact body, close together, almost touching, they rushed at the spot to which he had been traced. When they were almost into it, there was a roar, a striped body sprang at the nearest man, and in spite of a heavy blow from his victim, and numerous whacks from the heavy *latties* carried by the men nearest at hand, he bore the man to the ground, gave him one dreadful crunch, which nearly sickened me, and then disappeared.

I was helpless. I could not fire, for the men clustered almost round the beast in their excitement, and the man-eater of Chotamundry had again escaped.

One would imagine that after his narrow escape the brute would have been quiet for a few days, or have gone far away, but the very next day he killed a man. I was out after other game, and was not far from where the murder took place, and as the body had been untouched, I persuaded the villagers to let it remain, and sat over it. The man killed did not belong to that village, otherwise they would not have given the requisite permission, for these men, greatly disliking anyone using a dead body as a lure, always remove it at once and burn it. However, the man-eater did not put in another appearance here, but killed a woman near the river bank some two miles higher up. I had tried to circumvent him in every way for the past ten days. My leave was dwindling away; I had a long journey before me if my original intentions were to be carried out, and in hunting this man-eater I was losing all sport; yet I did not like to go away and leave this creature to prey on the poor unarmed people.

As soon as I returned to the village from my night's vigil, I went off to view the body. It was scarcely cold. For some reason or another the tiger had not completed his work; the girl had bled to death from the wound he had given her. It was not then eight o'clock. For two consecutive days the beast had been interrupted in his meals; I thought he must be hungry, and that he was probably lying near, and, if not disturbed, would return to make a repast off the body. It was with the greatest difficulty I could persuade the people to go away for a while, and leave me alone with the corpse. I hid myself in a crevice, well sheltered by thorny bushes, and within fifteen yards of the body. There were a few other bushes scattered about. I had not lain there long when, taking my eyes off the corpse for a moment, attracted by a noise I had heard in another direction, I found, when I looked again, that the body was gone. The brute had taken advantage of that momentary inattention on my part to snatch his victim away. Although alone, and at a disadvantage in such ground, consisting as it did of inequalities and heavy bush, I hurried forward, determined to 'do or die.' The ground was so dry I could trace no footsteps, and the body had not been dragged along, or some mark must have been left. The beast must have carried the woman in his mouth, much as a cat does a mouse, and have turned down a dry watercourse, of which there were very many about. So, although I ran along some way, I failed to find a trail; but just ahead of me I saw a herd of buffaloes, headed by a very large bull. The tiger was not likely to have gone towards them, for these animals, when together, act in concert, and do not fear a tiger.

I got hold of the *gwalas* (herdsmen), and promised them 20 rupees if they would drive their herd as I should indicate. The men took the cattle right across the place where the girl's body had lain, and no sooner did the bull smell the blood and the scent of the tiger, than with a bellow, lowering his head, he galloped forward, followed by the cows and young bulls, tracing the scent much as a pack of dogs might have done. I ran my best, hoping to get a shot, but the ground was covered with trailing vines, over which I kept stumbling, and finally came a cropper. By the time I got on to my feet again, the buffaloes had overtaken the tiger; the bull rushed at him, and I saw a brindled mass thrown high up. It had barely reached the earth again, when it was again sent flying. The tiger roared, clawed, and bit, but he had fully twenty beasts on him; I could not put in a shot; if I had rushed in amidst the infuriated herd, I stood more than a chance of being hoisted myself. The cattle formed a phalanx round the tiger, and what with tossing, prodding, and kneading, they soon deprived the scourge of the country of its life. The buffaloes were in such a state of excitement that even their attendants hesitated to go in to drive them off; the bull in particular would not leave his prey: when driven off, he would make a détour, return to the charge, with eyes flaring almost out of

"I saw a brindled mass thrown high up."

his head, nostrils blowing like a grampus, and furiously assail the dead body again. I promised the men ten rupees more to get him away, as I did not wish to have the skin ruined. They succeeded at last in doing so, and as soon as the coast was clear, I found the tiger stone-dead, beaten, or rather kneaded, into a jelly.

Considering the length of the horns, the pointed tips, and the vast strength wielded by a buffalo, I was surprised at the little damage done. There were a few prods, but only one serious one—in the chest, which had gone in a good foot or more; otherwise the tiger met its death more by being pounded than by stabbing. The body of the girl lay close by, unmutilated by the tiger, but somewhat trampled upon by the herd. The brave old bull showed some ugly scratches, and his nostrils had been nearly torn in two; one cow had a severe bite near the shoulder, and she it was, I fancy, who had thrust her horn so deeply into the chest. Three or four had been scratched, but not seriously. The young bulls had behaved gallantly, and taken their share in the affray; none had suffered, to speak of, but they were so many that the tiger had no chance of fastening on one, for they were all on him together. Thus, after all my trouble, the famous man-eater escaped my rifle, but met a deserved death from the horns and hoofs of a herd of buffaloes.

I got 100 rupees reward for the death of this beast, which I distributed amongst those who had lost relations. The *gwalas* got their 30 rupees, and were glad their animals had been blooded, because in future they would be less afraid of tigers when herding their cattle. I remained three days longer; but confidence had been restored, the people went about as usual, no more deaths took place, so, feeling sure that the dreaded man-eater was no more, I resumed my journey towards the hilly district of Bustar.

The road, not of the best, and out of repair, was passable for country carts as far as Dummapet. There I should have to hire pack bullocks to carry my goods. I was told there were generally Brinjaries there who would let out cattle and accompany me wherever I wished to go. I was not far from Tallapudi, and by making a forced march I got to Golpalpuran late next day. In the evening I visited a tank, and bagged sufficient rock-pigeons and sand-grouse for the pot. There were numerous traces of spotted deer and pig about.

Starting two hours before daylight, I got to Koyelagudem, eight miles, soon after 7 a.m., and, under the guidance of a local shikarie, scoured the jungles for the greater part of the morning, but saw nothing worth shooting. During the heat of the day I rested under the grateful shade of a banyan-tree, on the bank of the Bayana River, and in its waters I managed to cool a bottle of Bass. After the mid-day lunch I took a nap, and about three we set out again, keeping for some time along the banks of the river, where, to my surprise, I saw the two varieties of Indian jungle-fowl— *Gallus Sonnerati* and *ferrugineus*, the latter being the bird so common throughout India, Burma, and Assam; the former found oftener in Mysore and South-western India. I would not then fire at these beauties, although I did want to collect the hackles of some of them, because I saw there were spotted deer about, and meat was badly wanted. After following the stream for two or three miles, the man led me away from it, through heavy jungle, and eventually brought me to an open glade, and bid me be very wary, as it was a certain find for the speckled beauties.

After searching about carefully, at last I espied the tips of a fine pair of antlers, though no part of their owner was visible; but, from the position of the horns, the animal must have been staring in my direction. Knowing that I had been discovered, I did not attempt to get any nearer—the distance was probably one hundred and twenty yards. The stag was standing in a patch of grass surrounded by low jungle, and between me and him there were a lot of stalks through which I should have to fire, and I was more than half afraid that, before reaching the deer, the bullet would strike some of them, and be deflected. Taking a careful aim, two and a half feet below the only mark visible, I gently pressed the trigger. I saw three or four stalks fall asunder, but the deer never moved! I quickly put in the left; the *chital* gave a bound, and ran straight towards me. I reloaded as fast as I could, but before he had gone twenty yards he commenced to rear and plunge, sure signs of a wound in the lungs, and in less than two minutes rolled over dead.

The shikarie and I went leisurely towards him, and when within two yards of him I saw the eyes of a panther, which was standing just beyond the carcass. My attendant was stooping down, and had not seen it, so he was startled by my firing close past him, and greatly surprised to find a splendid leopard dead. I had aimed straight between the eyes; but the beast was crouching, his head had been lower than his withers, the bullet went a trifle high, caught him in the spine, and dropped him dead. He measured seven feet three inches. We had not time to skin him, so, after having gralloched the two, we slung them on a stout bamboo, and between us carried them by short-cuts to the camp, where we arrived at 7.30 p.m. My shoulder, unused to the exertion, was not only swollen, but was perfectly raw; whilst my attendant, a far frailer man than myself, and with no covering, had not a mark to show.

I had the two beasts skinned, and their pelts pegged out to dry, and determined to halt there for a day, for every bone in my body ached from the unusual experience I had undergone. My boy tied a plantain leaf over the sore, and when I awoke the next morning, I felt so much better that I consented to visit some hills about five miles off, where bears were said to be very numerous. These beasts are nocturnal feeders, retire to their dens soon after daybreak, and remain there sleeping till close on sunset, when they sally forth again. So, taking it easy, I read until 4 p.m., when I set out with a local shikarie, Elapah and Ramiah, together with a couple of men to act as torch-bearers, for I knew we should not be back till long after dark.

Reaching our destination half an hour before sunset, we carefully, silently, and quickly examined the locality, for we had no time to spare. There were many caves, and, judging by the marks, every one of them was tenanted. So, choosing a central rock somewhat higher than its fellows, I took up my position. I kept the two shikaries with me, but sent the rest some distance off, but within call. Hardly had we settled down, when sundry growlings and grunts denoted that Master Bruin and his family had awoke from their siesta, and were probably yawning and stretching themselves. Within five minutes, two large and one small bear emerged from a den some way off, and began to turn over stones, searching for beetles, etc. These were a little too far off for a certain shot, and as I could hear others right under us, I would not fire. But those I was waiting for did not come out as soon as I had anticipated, and before they did appear, the first three had wandered away some distance. A fourth bear now put in an appearance, and I was just going to fire at him, when two others emerged from a cave not fifteen yards from me, and presented the easiest of shots. I gave them a right and left, and, seeing them roll over, seized another weapon, and poured its contents into the third.

When the smoke cleared away, all three bears were rolling over each other, and fighting with the utmost fury. Although it was not quite dark, yet it was dusky; I could see a struggling mass of black fur, and I quickly poured in four barrels, and beheld the first three animals, and two new ones, all hurrying back to their dens. I fired at the new-comers without partiality or favour, but whether I hit I do not know. There was a perfect pandemonium—all eight bears were engaged in a general scrimmage; I again emptied my battery into them, and before I could reload, every beast had got back within shelter, where they continued their moaning and groaning. By this time it was quite dark, so I gave the caves a wide berth, descended the hillock on the opposite side, lit the torches, and got home by 8 p.m., expecting to find several dead in the morning.

I was up again next day at 4 a.m., and on the rocks by 5.30, and sat there till past seven; but we heard no noises, nor did any bears appear. We then descended from our coign of vantage, and carefully examined the ground. There was plenty of blood scattered about, but the whole of the bears had departed. Thinking there must be some dead inside the dens, I had them carefully examined, but not one did we find. How I made such a mess of this affair has always been a puzzle to me. I was perfectly cool, in a safe position, and well armed; yet I failed, after some fifteen shots, in bagging even one bear out of eight at close quarters. My shoulder was sore, it is true; but that would not account for such execrable shooting. I then went back to the river Bayana, and bagged three brace of *Gallus Sonnerati*, and one of the other variety, which were all carefully skinned when I got back to camp.

The next day we started at daylight. The road was so bad we could not get under way earlier; but we reached Jangamreddigudum at 9 a.m., breakfasted and rested under shade till 2 p.m., when we inspanned again, and got to Rantagudum, nine miles, a little before sunset. This was the last halting-stage within our territory; the next march would take us into the dominions of his Highness the Nizam.

By starting early, and making a forced march, we got to Dummapet at twelve—a good-sized place, with plenty of supplies available. Here I had to dismiss the carts, and to engage bullocks. I found the headman very civil, and on notifying to him my wants, he promised to procure all I required. About four he returned with five or six Brinjaries, who agreed to accompany me, wherever I chose to go, for six weeks. They demanded eight rupees a month for each bullock, and for themselves, four men, fifteen rupees each, and I was to give them all surplus meat not required for the use of myself and servants, and permission to hunt if we ran short.

These men are allied to the gipsies. Before the introduction of railways, they were the principal carriers throughout the length and breadth of the land, and have been, and are still, noted for their honesty and trustworthiness. Their occupation is gone, to a great extent; but even now, in more remote places where the iron horse has not penetrated, the merchants would fare badly were it not for these useful people. The men are a sturdy race. In comparison with their women, they are almost ugly. But the females of these nomads are probably the most comely and well-made of the Indian races; as a rule, when young, they are unrivalled in form and features. But for their dusky complexions, many would be reckoned beauties in either Europe or America. Wonderfully well made as are the Hindoo, Mussulmanic and Burmese women, the Brinjarie, when young, surpass them, if that be possible. Moreover, these women remain chaste in a country where most of their sex are frail. The great drawback to them is that, whereas the Burmese women are superlatively cleanly in their persons, as the Hindoos are also in a slightly less degree, these gipsies, when married, do not follow the example set them by their Arian sisters. A young girl may be cleanly enough; but when she marries she dons her bridal raiment and lives in it day and night until it no longer suffices for purposes of decency. She then washes and changes her clothes, perhaps for the first time since her nuptials, and puts on raiment which she continues to wear for years. Thus, three or four dresses suffice for a woman during her lifetime, and a married gipsy of a few years' standing is never an inviting object to look upon.

From Dummapet to Sironcha eight bullocks sufficed, for provisions could be purchased on the journey; but beyond that I should require a lot more, as no supplies were procurable between Dummapet and Jaggadur; but the head Brinjarie told me he could get them from his brother when he reached the Godavery. These grain-carriers are noted sportsmen—poachers in their way, but very successful hunters, all the same. They have a fierce breed of large hounds, which they would not part with in my day.

My camp now consisted of two boys, a cook and his wife, a water-carrier, two shikaries, four male and six female Brinjaries, a syce, grass-cutter and my *pegu* pony. A word about these ponies will not be amiss. They are called Burmese, but are bred and reared by the Shans, who live on the confines of China. For their size—they vary from twelve and a half to thirteen and a half hands high—they are the finest nags in the world. There is a strong dash of the Arab in their blood, Shan traders having in years gone by purchased, whenever they could, pure Arab stallions from officers resident in Moulmein. No dealer ever brings down either an entire pony or a mare (unless she be barren) for sale. For polo they are unrivalled; they have the best of tempers, a fair turn of speed, and can jump like deer.

I halted a couple of days at Dummapet, resuming my march on April 20. Nine miles beyond Dummapet we got into rough and hilly country. The Brinjaries proposed a hunt with their hounds, to which I in no way objected. Telling the boys to camp at Kapee-Gaugawaram, then six miles distant, we turned off into the forest, leaving a couple of spare bullocks under charge of two of the oldest women to remain there till required to carry on the spoils of the chase. The paths wound round the hills, and in a couple of hours we arrived where the men proposed to hunt. Elapah carried the ·577 rifle, and I was armed with the 'Paradox.' These men have firearms, but are often out of powder, and they trust to their dogs and knives to procure them all the meat they require. I was stationed on a commanding position, more as a spectator than as an actor. The men separated, going about one hundred yards or so apart, each accompanied by two hounds in a leash. When the furthest point had been reached, the hunter let his dogs loose, and followed them as closely as he could, knife in hand, very much in the style described by that prince of travellers and sportsmen, Sir Samuel Baker, when he was a young man in Ceylon. These hounds soon struck off a scent, and ran it, giving tongue only now and then. They had either been well taught or their instinct was uncommonly good, for they endeavoured to drive the game towards the next relays of dogs, who again took up the running; thus, in a very short space of time, six powerful dogs, followed closely by their masters, brought an animal to bay, and whilst the dogs attacked in front, a man crawled up and drove his dagger in behind the shoulder.

In about two hours we had three does and one stag, which we thought ample for our wants, for game abounded everywhere; we had only to hunt it to secure all the meat we wanted. Whilst one of the men went back to bring up the spare cattle, we had one more beat. This time a sounder of pig, headed by a huge gray boar, broke. Now these gipsies particularly affect the flesh of the swine. The boar disdained to run far, and was soon, with his wives, brought to bay. As the men were afraid he would kill or rip up some of their dogs, they asked me to slay him. No man has greater respect for a wild boar than I have, provided he lives on the borders of a ridable country, where he can show sport to mounted men; but here, in this interminable jungle and an amphitheatre of hills, hogs were of no account for hunting, so I shot him to please the men and murdered a fat sow for myself. Venison, especially of the axis deer, is not to be despised, and would be better if it could be kept a day or two, but a long course of venison palls, so I thought a nice pork chop would be a desirable change. The bullocks arrived, and were duly laden, and the game killed was as much as they could carry.

Leaving the gipsies to bring in the spoils, the

shikaries and I walked on ahead. I found my pony waiting for me; I got on him and rode on without delay, getting to our camp at 5 p.m. I found the village very insignificant, and no supplies procurable, but as the next stage was only six miles distant I halted there till past 2 p.m., to enable the men to jerk a good deal of the meat. We reached Gopalraopet in good time before dark, and moved on to Naganienpalli the next day. This is a good-sized village, and nearly opposite to Bhadrachellum, a large town. Having plenty of meat, I only shot a few jungle-fowl. On the 23rd I reached Ashwapur, a small village, and the Brinjaries asked permission to hunt, which I readily accorded, and in the evening they brought home two spotted does. On the 24th we marched for Managur; we had to cross six unbridged nullahs, with steep banks and muddy bottoms. About half-way we saw the fresh pugs of a tiger, and tracked her to her lair in the bed of a dry ravine. Out of this she was soon turned by my men and their hounds; she passed me close, and as she endeavoured to sneak along, I killed her with a couple of shots. To my great regret, I found she would have been a mother within a month or six weeks—but the deed was done, and could not be helped.

We came upon teak forests here, and on the 25th reached Karpairawarum, having been considerably delayed by having to cross four unbridged nullahs. On the 26th we got to Rajupet. The Brinjaries killed a couple of sows and a doe chital on the march. On the 27th we camped at Mangapet, the country open and villages numerous. I laid in a stock of fowls and eggs, and advanced next day to Nagaram, the country being good, and the road running along the right bank of the Godavery.

On April 29 I reached Pargrapur, where is no village, but as game was reported to be plentiful, I determined to halt there. Early next morning I went out stalking under a guide from a neighbouring village. We saw numerous marks, but had no great luck, and as I had promised, if unsuccessful, to be back early to enable the gipsies to hunt, I turned homewards about nine. When passing a ravine, densely covered with grass and jungle, I heard a peculiar noise, something like that made by telegraph wires on a windy day. I paused for a moment to listen, and the shikarie, pointing downwards, said, ' A bear asleep sucking his paws.' There was little or no undergrowth on the edges of the crevice; peeping down, I thought I could distinguish a dark object curled up amidst a lot of dry fallen leaves and withered grass. Telling the man to stand close by with the ·577, I let fly the right barrel of the ' Paradox.' The next instant, the bear, after one heartrending yell, came at me open-mouthed; the bank was very steep, but he scrambled up, and when he was within a couple of feet of the muzzle of the gun, I discharged the contents of the left barrel down his throat. He gave one gurgling sound and fell backwards, dead. On examining the body, I found the roof of the head all but blown off, so destructive is a charge of buckshot, driven by four drachms of powder at close quarters. I then hastened home, and sent back the shikarie with men to bring in the slain. When it arrived, I found it had been mutilated. The penis and sheath had been cut off. It is well known that this portion of a bear differs from that of all other animals. It is not altogether gristle, but a portion of it is bone, which natives greatly prize, as they think if they pulverize it, and partake of it, it will rejuvenate them, and give them renewed vigour, which they have lost either through old age or excess.

This portion of the beast was, of course, useless to any sensible person; but if you allow an inch, natives will take an ell; they will singe off the whiskers of a tiger or leopard, which ruins the appearance of the pelt as an ornament, so I told the Brinjaries I would stop their hunting if the missing portion was not given up. It was found in the possession of an old villager who had lately taken to himself a young wife, but although I could not help laughing at the anxiety displayed on his countenance, I made him burn it before all the people. In the evening the gipsies returned, bringing a pig and a fine sambur, and said they had seen the pugs of a tiger and of two leopards.

On May 3 I reached Chinnur. My tent was pitched on the bank of the Godavery, a fine clear stream. Towards evening I got into a light 'dug-out,' and trolled for mahseer. My bait was a large spoon; it was almost immediately taken, and the fish went off with a rush, taking fully fifty yards of line, and when I checked him, he threw himself clean out of the water, exhibiting grand proportions, with enormous scales varying in hue from gold to silver, and as tough as tin. My tackle was Farlow's best, new and strong, so I gave him the butt; he came back to me at such a rate that it was as much as I could do to wind up fast enough to keep the line at all taut. When he got within twenty yards of me, he altered his direction, and took a header for the bank; fortunately there were no snags, weeds, or rushes, and I soon drew him back into mid-stream. Seeing a shelving sandy beach a little lower down the stream, I told the men to take me there and fasten the boat ashore; I landed and played the fish, which was still full of fight, and two or three times he tried to break the tackle by springing into the air, more like a salmon than the barbel which he really was. It was getting dark; I retreated until I was no longer visible from the water's edge and gradually drew my victim into shallow water. As the back fin became visible, one of the boatmen crept in behind, and inserting his fingers into the gills, cast him ashore, high and dry, and a few knocks on the head with a large stone soon deprived the mahseer of life.

I then fished on for another hour and a half, and caught three more fish, weighing nine, fourteen, and seven pounds, till a monster took away the whole of my cast of treble gut, spoon and hooks, and as it was getting dark I left off. I kept the smallest fish for my own eating, and gave the rest to my followers. On May 4 we moved to Dewalwara, eleven miles, in the morning, and crossed over the river in the afternoon to Sironcha, and I put up in a bungalow just then unoccupied. The officer commanding offered to give me a room, but I preferred being independent. Here I found a lot of papers and letters awaiting me, and I was very busy the next two days in answering correspondence and seeing to the arrangements for my further progress across an unknown country. I was assured that only lightly-laden cattle could travel over these hills, so ordered extra bullocks. I also found here my stores of wines, beer, and preserved provisions waiting for me, which I had to open and repack into bundles suitable for transport by cattle instead of in carts.

The officer in command of the detachment thought I was mad to go into such a country without being forced to do so; but then he was no sportsman. I cannot help thinking that a man who cares nothing for sport is unfitted for service in the East. During peace, unless one is fond of outdoor amusements, time hangs heavily on one's hands. In out-of-the-way places, like Sironcha, there is no literature to be had. The ordinary routine of military duty in garrison does not occupy one above an hour morning and evening. What can a man find to beguile time if he cares nothing for the sports of the field? He probably passes more than half the day in sleep, and when called upon to serve on a campaign, is unable to undergo the necessary hardships and exposure, and has to be invalided, thus proving a hard bargain to his employers. Now, in most single stations, particularly at Sironcha, game is plentiful, and shooting or fishing affords a pleasant recreation to the solitary European condemned to reside there alone for six months or more on end, with nobody to associate with. I tried to persuade my acquaintance to take even to fishing, and offered to give him tackle; but he said he could not swim, and was not going to trust himself in a cockle-shell for the pleasure of catching a fish which he could buy for a few pence in the bazaar. As for shooting, he did not even possess a gun. His was a hopeless case, and, I fear, not a solitary one, for very many of those who obtain commissions under the new rules are bookworms, and but poor at that; for the more a man is crammed, the sooner he forgets in after-life all that has been driven into him in his youth with the view of passing a certain examination.

I engaged a couple of extra shikaries. I had to send Ramiah back, as his propensity for running after the fair sex had already caused several rows, and however virtuous the Brinjaries may be as far as Europeans are concerned, it was more than half suspected that my follower had found favour in the eyes of one of the gipsies, and if the intimacy was found out there would be murder, for these men know no law but *lex talionis*, and would not have hesitated to put a knife into Master Ramiah's carcass.

Although I had never been in the Bustar country, I have hunted in the districts somewhat south, near Daraconda, and have had famous sport. In these hilly regions buffaloes, gaur, sambur, chital, four-horned antelope, barking deer, bears, tigers, and leopards abound.

On May 7 I made a forced march to Assarelli, twenty miles. I had a train of thirty cattle, fourteen Brinjari men and women, my own servants, and three shikaries. Next day I sent on the greater part of my camp to Madnair, thirty-six miles, and taking a week's supplies, I went north-east about fifteen miles, and encamped on the Indravati river. Two of the gipsies, three of their women, and eight hounds, accompanied me. We camped in an open space in a bamboo forest, and cutting down a lot of canes, we soon improvised a *chevaux de frise* round us to keep off wild beasts, which were said to be rather numerous. We were getting short of meat for the dogs, as the biltong was almost exhausted. We heard tigers calling, this being the time the females were generally in season, but none came our way.

We were up and away before daybreak. The Brinjaries followed with their dogs in leashes, and we made for certain salt licks, which were said to be found about three or four miles away. The country was very hilly and densely wooded, with fearful thorny undergrowth. Had it not been for the paths made by wild beasts, we should not have been able to move at all.

Unfortunately I had broken my barometer, so could not tell the elevation of the country; but the hills range from 2,000 to 5,000 feet, and with even higher peaks. The Bustar country is a mass of hills upon hills, for the most part unexplored. There are a few stations which have been fixed by members of the great trigonometrical survey, and during disturbances a few civil officers, accompanied by small forces of military and police, have penetrated here and there by the few native paths which exist; but so bad is the repute of this district for fever, that no one ever ventures into it unless forced to do so on duty. I believe I was the first to enter it of my own free will, and I did it for the sake of sport only, and because I did not fear jungle fever, having suffered from it severely many years before, and been free of it ever since. I had become 'salted,' as they say in South Africa. We moved in single file. I led the way with my ·577, of which the cartridges carried six drachms of powder and a hardened solid projectile; then followed Elapah with a twelve-bore double rifle, also heavily loaded, and a local man brought up the rear with the 'Paradox.' The gipsies with their hounds kept well behind; their orders were to loosen the dogs only in case of a scrimmage.

We had gone fully three miles; we had not heard a sound; not even a tree-cricket chirped—it was a silence that could be felt. At last a faint glimmer of a reddish tint became visible over the tops of the hills to the east, and we hailed the approach of morn with delight, for the gloom of the forest was depressing. Ever on the *qui vive*, I heard a slight movement in the bed of the river, which lay about a hundred and fifty yards to our right. Holding up my arm—a gesture taken up by each follower in succession—we halted. Hearing the noise repeated, I cautiously advanced, followed by the shikaries. We were in a bamboo forest, free of undergrowth; the fallen leaves had rotted and formed a rich mould over which we could advance silently, the little noise we occasionally made by stepping on to a broken twig being drowned in the ripple of the stream. I kept a large clump of bamboos between me and the spot I was making for, whence I thought the noise had come. I did not hurry, as I wanted a little more light for correct shooting. The noise, I guessed, proceeded most probably from some buffaloes lying down in the river. When I reached my objective point I found I was too far below, for I could see some buffaloes in the water up the stream some way from where we were; so retracing our steps, we made for another clump nearer the game.

By the time I got there objects had become more visible, and I found myself within ten yards of four buffaloes. I took a careful aim at the bull, and fired at the junction of the ear and head. He fell over; the cows sprang up, and I gave them three shots; two were hit, but got to the main bank and rushed into the jungle.

Leaving a Brinjarie and one of the shikaries to decapitate the bull, as he was a very big one, and had a good spread of horns, I followed up the others; not that I wanted them particularly, but I make a point of killing all wounded animals if possible. It is incumbent on every sportsman to inflict as little pain as possible on the game he hunts. These buffaloes are not to be compared to those in Burma or Assam either in size or ferocity, yet they are nasty customers. They are probably the descendants of tame cattle run loose, and become feral in time. We found blood on two spoors; the third apparently had gone away unwounded. The tracking was easy enough at first, but when we came to a dry rivulet, up the bed of which they had gone, following them was not pleasant. The channel was very narrow, full of boulders of rocks, loose stones, and thorny bushes, which were bespattered with blood. On either side the banks were high, sloping up, and forming the bases of two hills, which ran parallel to one another. It was about as nasty a place as ever I saw.

I told two men to get on to the banks, where they would be safe, and to go ahead, and as soon as they saw the quarry to give warning by striking the trunk of a tree. As each man had a couple of hounds, I told them if the *bubali* charged to lay on their dogs, but not otherwise. I cursed my folly for having fired at the cows at all. I got covered with blood, and my advance was necessarily slow, but I came upon the beasts sooner than I expected. Their wounds had probably stiffened, and hearing us approach, they made up their minds to die fighting. I heard a warning tap given by one of the men, and put my rifle on full cock only just in time, for one of the beasts with a snort was down upon me. I fired into her face when the horns were all but round me, and threw myself aside, just escaping being trampled upon, for the second charged close behind the first. Whilst on the ground I put in the second barrel, and had the pleasure of hearing one of them topple over amongst the loose rocks. Two of the dogs had followed these, and two took after the third, which went on up the nullah. Unfortunately we followed this one, and after half an hour heard it at bay; but before I could get within shot, the beast sent the dogs flying, and went off full score again. As both these hounds were hurt, and we ascertained we had been following the unwounded one, we gave up the chase.

The wounded dogs were carefully attended to, and we retraced our steps. The men tore out the liver of the cow just killed, and fed their hounds on it.

Leaving them to flay the beast, and promising to send back more men to help in transporting the meat (to be jerked), I wended my way homewards. When I got to within a mile of camp I heard the bell of a spotted deer, some way to our right, and knowing that these deer are silent during the day unless frightened by some beast of prey, I hastened towards the sound. The jungle varied a good deal—here and there teak, then bamboo, now and then magnificent mango-trees, and the mohwa-tree with the blossom lying thick on the ground. In this jungle I came across a circular pond of clear water, a portion near the edges being covered with aquatic plants, whilst in the centre was a patch of long grass and reeds. On the further side stood a noble spotted stag gazing at the clump of grass, and now and then uttering a peculiar cry which is generally called belling. I ought to have recognised the fact that there must be something there that attracted his attention, but, like an ass, without thinking, I fired at his chest. On receiving the bullet he spun round and went off at his best pace, whilst a splendid tiger bounded out of that very bit of grass and dashed through the water, giving me the easiest of shots, yet, disgraceful to say, in my anxiety to bag, I fired in too great a hurry, a little too far forward, and missed him clean. He did not even favour me with a growl, and before I could seize my other gun or reload, he was gone. Whilst inwardly abusing myself, my shikarie informed me that he had heard the deer fall against a tree; we took up the trail, and found him stone dead. His head was well worth preserving, the length of the horns being over thirty-one inches, thick in proportion and with a splendid burr. Cutting off the head, I gave it to Elapah to carry, whilst I slung the extra rifle over my own shoulder. We reached camp without further adventures. Elapah and two Brinjaries went back for the meat of the deer and his marrow-bones, whilst the others went for the beef to be jerked for the use of the dogs, and the tongues, which are capital eating, for my own use.

The men made two trips, and the last time they did not return till very late, and reported that they had heard the noise of some beasts fighting in the direction taken by the wounded buffalo, and thought she had been attacked by a tiger. Telling them to be ready for a start an hour before daybreak, I retired to rest. The dogs were very restless all night, barking and moving about. I got up twice, but could see nothing outside our fence, but one of the men on watch told me he had seen a couple of bears prowling about, and he thought that hyænas or leopards had also been present, attracted by the meat in camp. We were well on the way by a little past five, and when we approached the carcass of the first cow, something bounded off it, but it was too dark to distinguish what it was. Proceeding a little further, we halted until daybreak, and then the men led the way towards where they had heard the disturbance the previous evening. In half an hour we came upon the spot, where there had evidently been a great struggle. The ground was torn up, the bushes beaten down and covered with blood, and we had not to go far to ascertain the cause. We soon came upon the second cow, not dead, but hamstrung. The poor creature tried to get up to do battle with us, and I put a ball through her head to put her out of pain. A little further on, as I approached a bush, there was a growl, and, with a roar, out came an immense tiger at us, meaning mischief; but his rate of progress was slow, and he dragged one hind-leg behind him. I gave him the left barrel, but failed to stop him. Elapah, as usual, stuck to me well, and handed the other gun quickly. I fired the right barrel when the brute was only two or three yards off; then, jumping on one side, I gave him the contents of the left barrel in the shoulder at less than a yard distant, and he collapsed all in a heap. Although game to fight us, he had had enough of the buffalo, though if he had renewed the attack she must have fallen an easy victim. In the affray she had driven her horn right through the tiger's thigh high up, and I very much doubt whether the animal would have got over the wound, for many die from less severe inflictions owing to mortification. She had driven her left horn up to the hilt, and it was covered with blood and pieces of flesh and skin. The men declared it was the same tiger that I had missed yesterday.

Leaving a couple of men to take off the skin and to cut off the tiger's head, I went on. The amount of climbing up and going down hills I underwent the next two hours was a very severe experience. When at length I reached the plateau, I was dead beat, so sat down and fortified the inner man. The men became very impatient at my resting, and pointed to a long row of trees, which they said fringed a nearly dry watercourse, where the white clay, of which all animals are so fond, was to be found. They declared that, unless we made haste, we should arrive too late, as directly the sun was well over the horizon these animals retired to their lairs in such dense brambly thickets that there was no getting at them. As soon as I recovered my wind, we went on, and got to the desired locality about 8 a.m., and as there were no human beings but ourselves within a radius of twenty miles, I did not think the wild cattle would be so shy and retire thus early. But it turned out that I was wrong. Footmarks were plentiful, and we saw more than one place where the earth had just been gnawed or scooped out, forming shallow caves in the sides of the nullah, but there was not the ghost of a gaur anywhere. I was in no hurry. I had ample provender with me to last through the day; I knew from their footmarks that these beasts were numerous, and if not there they would be found elsewhere. So on we went, following the course of the stream; in places it narrowed considerably, in others it spread out more like a marsh than a river's bed. These depressions were covered with grass, bushes, here and there a tope of trees, and every now and then huge blocks of stone. It was just the sort of place for animals to retire to during the heat of the day, as there was in places sufficient foliage to afford them shelter.

What I wanted was to get, if possible, a solitary bull, to compare him with his brethren in Burma. The shikarie touched me, and pointed to what I may almost call an island, about sixty yards away, and whispered 'Jungly gooroo' (Wild cattle), but I could see nothing. It turned out that he had seen the tips of the horns of some cows, which, with their calves, were lying down chewing the cud; but as I was looking for an animal six feet high, it is no wonder that I failed to see the objects pointed at. Determined to come to close quarters, I began to descend the bank by an existing path. Whilst so doing, I inadvertently stepped upon a loose stone lying under some fallen leaves, which gave way beneath me, and I all but fell. The noise disturbed the herd, which bounded up and scampered away, their stampede frightening a herd of sambur, which also went off full score, a fine stag bringing up the rear. My men wanted me to fire, but as there was plenty of meat in camp, I refused.

The sun was well up now, so, leaving the nullah, I struck across the tableland to another and further belt of forest, which formed, the men told me, the extremity of that plateau, beyond which was a deep dip which I should have to negotiate before I could ascend to the next. As there was water and shade in that valley, I made for it, intending to have my breakfast there and to rest under the trees, and try my luck later on. We got to a lovely glen, which the sun never penetrated, and, strange to say, amongst the giant wild mango-trees, I came across a dwarfed one that had not only a few of the fruit ripe, but quite edible. Elapah was soon on the branches picking out the best. I lay down on a shelving bank, and whilst my bottles of Bass were cooling, my tiffin-basket was spread out before me. I soon made a hearty meal, and, pending the return of Elapah, who had gone with the Brinjaries to look for spoor, was lying alone, sucking a mango, when I heard the dogs giving tongue not very far off, and evidently chasing some animal through the glen in my direction. I jumped up, seized the nearest weapon, which turned out to be the double twelve, and got behind a large trunk of a tree. There was a great rattling and scattering of stones along the hollow, and a huge gaur tore down upon me. My tiffin-basket attracted his attention. Lowering his head, he rushed at it, and, as he tossed it, the pepper and salt went full into his eyes and up his nose, and for a second or two I could not fire for laughing at the extraordinary antics of the bull. That he was partially blinded there could be no doubt, for, in his struggles to rid himself of the condiments, he butted several trees with great force.

As soon as I could steady myself, I gave him the contents of both barrels, but they seemed to have little effect on him. The four hounds were tearing at his heels, and he was kicking, pawing, and plunging like an Australian buck-jumper. In reloading, I got hold of the wrong cartridges, and whilst I was fumbling about for stray ones in my pockets, the bull partially recovered his eyesight, and came at me. I jumped behind a tree, and the bull struck it such a blow with his massive forehead that I wonder he was not stunned: the tree had far too great a girth even to be shaken. He then tried to get round, and I dodged him, and one of the largest hounds sprang and pinned him by the nose. How he did bellow, to be sure! But the mighty beast, with a toss of his head, sent the dog flying through the air, leaving a portion of the cartilage of his nostrils in the tenacious jaws of the hound. Just then I found one solitary cartridge, and, with the muzzle all but touching him, I fired behind the shoulder, which sickened him, and he sought refuge in flight.

But the good hounds stuck to him. I ran to where the express was lying, picked it up, and had no difficulty in giving the great bull his quietus. The whole scene did not last five minutes, though it has taken some time to tell. When it was all over, my followers appeared on the scene; but during the scrimmage they had judiciously taken up positions behind trees.

On examining the prize, he turned out to be as fine a bull as is generally found in India, but far inferior to those I have shot in Burma. As nearly as I could tell, he measured nineteen and a half hands high, and, judging from the ridges on the base of the horns, he must have been at least thirty years of age. Across the water, an old bull of his age would have been a hand or more higher, and would have had a far finer head; but the tips of the horns of this one had worn down. He was by far the finest I ever got in India proper. The men told me they had wandered some way up the valley in search of mohwa-trees, and had come upon the gaur unexpectedly, and, with a view of driving him towards me, they had set the hounds on him. I told them their doing so was contrary to orders, for the baying of a hound disturbs the country for miles around, and I had over and over again told them only to loosen the dogs in the event of a mêlée. However, the beast was bagged, and the damage done, so it was no use saying much.

Having come so far, I thought I might as well have a look at the tableland beyond. It was no easy task for my followers, heavily laden as they were, and climbing up from the valley was very fatiguing; but when we reached the top, the view fully repaid us for all our trouble. The surface was nearly flat, with undulations so slight as scarcely to be perceptible: fully ten or twelve miles long by five or six broad, with clumps of trees dotted here and there. There is seldom water on the top; of course, in the valleys which separate these plateaux there is almost always a little water in the dry season, whilst in the monsoon they are raging torrents. Sometimes a tiny stream of water trickles down the hillside from a natural spring.

But on this tableland there was a slight depression in which there was still some water left, and the numerous marks showed that it was the resort nightly of all kinds of game. I was so taken with the place that I determined to halt for a few days. Choosing a suitable locality under some clumps of bamboos, some of them nearly a foot in diameter, I told two of the men to go back, and to bring my camp there. From the top of this plateau I could see a mass of mountains to the north, east, and south. To the south-west the country was equally hilly, but here and there I could get a glimpse of the Godavery, which at that distance looked more like a silver thread than a mighty river.

We were on one of the highest of the hills. I could only see three others, two to the north and one to the south, that were higher than ours. As the men collected the thorny brushwood, for which they had to go some distance, I arranged it round us in a circular form, and soon had a respectable defence against intrusive beasts. I expected my people up before dark, and as they did not appear, I made a kabob out of some of the beef, and found it not at all bad. A pint of beer, which had been put into the running stream, had escaped when the rest of the contents of my tiffin-basket had been scattered. Elapah had a little salt, so I did not do badly. The men found lower down the seed from a bamboo clump which had flowered and would soon die. They collected this, and boiled it as we do rice, and I found it very palatable, and, with plenty of meat, they were quite content. As no camp had arrived by 10 p.m. I gave it up, lit a good fire, and was soon fast asleep. It was very cold. We were at least 5,000 feet high. There were no mosquitoes, however, which was a blessing. At two I awoke, told the men to go to sleep, and took my turn at watching, piling on the fire-wood without stint to keep off the cold.

All was quiet until about 4 a.m., when I heard the distant lowing of cattle, and was not sure whether it was made by my pack-oxen or by gaur. There were buffaloes in the country, but they were not likely to climb up so high; but now and then an old bull does go up the highest hills, taking a short-cut to some favourite feeding-ground. I had once before come upon a bull on similar hills to these, far away from any known habitation of the *bubali* but on this occasion our visitors turned out to be a herd of gaur, consisting of cows, young bulls and calves. They passed close by and went to the water, and, after a good drink, continued their course along the *maidan*. Just before daybreak, two bears made the welkin ring with amorous parley, which I soon converted into active hostilities by giving each a bullet through its body, and, as usual, they set to and had a round or two with each other. When they perceived me, they made for me. The fence stopped them a bit, and the largest, the male, stood up. He seemed fully six feet high, and showed a set of formidable ivories and most muscular arms.

He was only about five feet off, and I poured a charge of buckshot out of the 'Paradox' into the horseshoe, and over he rolled right on to his mate. For a moment she was undecided whether to fall upon him tooth and nail, and was actually going for him, when, finding him motionless, I fancy she realized that her lord and master was dead, and determined to vent her rage upon me. She made a dash at our fence and broke through it; but just then the dogs were loosened, and fastened upon her quarter. She turned round, whirling her arms about like the sails of a windmill, but this was not the first bear these hounds had tackled, for they seemed quite at home, and avoided her blows with great agility. They were all so mixed I was afraid to fire, but Elapah threw a blazing log right into her face; with a deep groan of disgust at this unfair mode of fighting, she turned to fly, and in so doing exposed her broadside, and a right and left laid her low.

Leaving the bears where they lay, I consulted the men as to the non-arrival of our camp. Then, taking Elapah and going in the direction pointed out by the local shikarie, I took a stroll. I had not gone very far when, looking down the hillside, I saw a couple of four-horned antelope browsing on the bamboo-like grass. Being above them, and walking over the thick velvety turf in indiarubber soled shoes, I made no noise, and got quite close just as the two were feeding side by side, and a solid conical out of the express accounted for each of them.

By the time we had deported these to our temporary abode, Elapah said he heard voices, and in a quarter of an hour my boy appeared. I learnt I had to thank the two bears for preventing my camp reaching me the night before. The path my men and bullocks had to traverse was a mere track along the edge of a ravine, with a hill on one side and a deep hollow on the other, off which they could not get, and just in front of them were these two bears, billing and cooing in their fashion, probably spending their honeymoon, and do what my men would, the amorous couple would not give way. So the men had to halt where they were, and to light huge fires to keep them off. Great was their rejoicing when they saw the dead bodies of the two bears.

After a hasty meal I took two men and reconnoitred. It was a splendid game country, but I had only two months' leave, of which five weeks had expired, and I was a long way from my headquarters, so could not loiter long. To do this district properly at least three months were requisite. So I determined to get on and return another time. I saw much game, but it was in the open, and I could not get at it, so I only killed a sambur for the pot and got back to camp about an hour before dark. I found that one of our cattle having strayed had been pounced upon and killed by a tiger. The carcass was just down the hillside, not five hundred yards away. A *machan* had been prepared, and as there was no moon, in order to get an effective shot I must 'sit up' at once and trust to the brute putting in an appearance before dark. So telling my boy to delay dinner till eight, I went down and mounted into my perch.

I had not been there a quarter of an hour, when a stealthy pit-a-pat warned me of the approach of some soft-footed beast. There was just sufficient light to distinguish objects; the sun had not set, but we were in a valley, and the deep gloom of the forest helped to render objects obscure. A tigress trotted on one side, whilst a tiger appeared on the other. The two, if not lovers, were intimate acquaintances; the female was licking the face of the male, and neither seemed in a hurry to commence operations on the dead bullock. Every moment was to me precious. The shadows deepened. I was very hungry; so, taking the tigress between the shoulder-blades, I fired down upon her as she was almost beneath my *machan*, and then, rapidly shifting my aim, I knocked over the tiger. The first never uttered a sound; the second, on getting the bullet, roared blue murder, but Elapah quickly handed me the second rifle, and with it I gave him his quietus. Getting down, I climbed up the steep hillside, and was ready for my meal. This was the most wonderful luck I ever had in *machan*-shooting. I have been oftener unsuccessful than otherwise; but on this occasion I had bagged a couple of tigers within a quarter of an hour after sitting up.

After this my luck deserted me for some days. I saw game in plenty, and killed enough for all our wants, but got only a very few trophies worth carrying away. So I went on to Madnair on May 13. On the following day I moved to Pursagudem, a long, rough march of sixteen miles. I went off the beaten track, but only got one good sambur stag. Passing a small village, I met a native with a fresh leopard's skin. I gave him the Government reward, and took the pelt.

Next day, the 15th, I made a double march to Mingachilla, twenty miles distant, and only picked up a couple of pea-hens and a couple of jungle-fowls. On the 16th I reached Bhyramghur, thirteen miles, getting a barking deer on the way. On the 17th, letting the camp continue its route, I as usual went in search of game. The hills were very steep; we had left the tableland behind us. Coming to a stream called Daukani, which falls into the Indravati River, I was some way ahead, and had my rifle slung over my shoulder. Taking out my flask, containing Crabbie's ginger-wine, I put some into the cup, and stooped down to fill it up with water out of the clear running stream. I heard a shout, but before I could straighten myself, something rushed down the steep bank, tore through the water, lifted me high up, and tossed me with great violence on to the opposite bank, which, fortunately for myself, was fringed with heavy grass and clumps of bamboos. My rifle was sent flying. When I alighted on the ground, I attempted to get up, but could not. I was in no pain, only benumbed, and, although I could move my arms and legs, I could not move my body, so I lay still. The buffalo, a rogue, after playing at shuttlecock with me, made for my men; but these, as nimble as monkeys, were up trees in a moment. As soon as he was in a safe position, Elapah opened fire. He had my twelve-bore, and plenty of cartridges. The buffalo seemed impervious to pain, and paid no attention to his wounds, until a shot broke a fore-leg; he then bellowed for the first time, and at last the shikarie, with a good shot, killed the monster.

They lost no time in descending and picking me up. I was quite conscious, but paralyzed. My right thigh was double its usual size; from the groin to the knee there was a deep welt, the skin, though furrowed, being not much broken, only a little here and there, through which a little blood had oozed. My strong shooting-breeches were cut through, but the whole surface of the inside of the thigh was blackened. The brute had struck me with his full force in the abdomen; the concussion had jarred the spine, and rendered me incapable of any movement. The men improvised a litter, and, after recovering my valuable express rifle, carried me to the camp at Nilguda. All my followers behaved splendidly, sent word ahead for relays of coolies to be ready at each village, and, going day and night, carried me to Jagdalpur. There I found a native dresser, a hospital assistant, who, after examination, said no bones were broken, nor any permanent injury inflicted, but that I must lie up for three or four months. I underwent no medical treatment; in about two months the numbness began to wear off, and in three months I was able to get about again. I sent Elapah back afterwards to try and recover the head of the beast who had tossed me; but he said that when he got there the horns were worm-eaten, and not worth the removal. So I did not get a souvenir of the urus who had behaved in such an unfriendly manner to me.

Although, apparently, I got all right again, my back has never been as strong as before; now and then it almost gives way, and I am in agonies for hours. But many years have passed, and I am still alive and fairly well in health, and still able to undergo a day's fatigue in search of game.

CHAPTER XIII.

ADVICE TO SPORTSMEN GOING ABROAD.

Advantages of medical knowledge—Native idea of Europeans—Precautions against the sun—What to wear—Underclothes—Clothes—Boots—Socks, etc.—Shoes for stalking—Waterproofs—Sleeping on the ground—Fever—Trestle-cots—Mosquito-curtains—A list of articles to take—Tents—Natives—Men and women—Tree-leeches—What to wear to keep them out—Buying a gun—Selling it again—Gunpowder—To harden bullets—Best bullets for different game—What size shot to use—How to keep your health—Total abstinence—Stimulants—Night-shooting—How to make the fore-sight visible—How to obtain fire—How to make soap—Sanitary precautions and cleanliness.

IF a man wishes to become a second Livingstone, or to emulate the travels of Stanley, let him walk a hospital, and learn how to treat ordinary diseases, to amputate a limb, and to perform other simple operations, which can all be learnt in six months. He will find such knowledge far more useful to him than money. All natives, whether of Africa or Asia, firmly believe that a white man must be a medical man, and the more nauseous the medicine you give them, the better they are pleased or contented. I myself believe in going to the East when a man is still in his teens; very few public schoolboys, accustomed to cricket, football, and other field-sports, suffer from the sun if they take simple precautions. The first thing to think of is a suitable head-dress. I commenced my novitiate in India with a soft felt round wide-awake, with the addition of a turban wound round it, and felt no ill effects. But, doubtless, a good pith hat is an improvement. It can be purchased for a rupee, now worth 1s. 1d.; but it does not last any time. A heavy, soaking rain soon spoils its shape, and it becomes useless; but solar helmets can be purchased in England. They cost up to a guinea, but last for years, so are probably cheaper in the long-run. It is well to wear flannel next to the skin, for it absorbs perspiration, and prevents sudden chills. Unshrinkable flannel should be chosen. It is dear, but the material supplied by a good firm will last a long time, whilst the ordinary flannel, after a couple of washes, becomes so attenuated that it is useless for anybody but a child. I do not care for woollen socks. I prefer good merino, with double heels and toes, which can be bought for under 2s. each pair.

For India and Africa well-dressed deer-skin is the best material for clothing, as it is impervious to thorns, but failing that, Burbury's gabardine is probably the most suitable. Take a pair of the best binoculars with you; those of aluminium are the lightest and best, but rather expensive. Shirts of a mixture of silk and flannel are most comfortable. Good roomy knickerbockers are the best for breeches, and then you must encase your legs either in stout gaiters, which are a nuisance to button, or, what is decidedly better, a pair of 'Field' boots, originally made by Dean, of the Strand, but now for sale in every store. If you go to

Africa for an extended trip, take at least four pairs of these boots, and three pairs of stout shoes, besides slippers. The knickerbockers should be long in the leg so as to fasten close to the ankle-joint, and to fit the leg accurately. Of course, your dress must be similar in colour to the vegetation amongst which you intend to hunt. Three shades of khakie are sufficient —brown, light dirty brown, and light green. For the higher hills, which are covered with snow, white is the best. For stalking in forest, take shoes with serrated indiarubber soles; you will find them a great comfort, as they are nearly noiseless and damp-proof. Be sure that your boots and shoes fit you easily, for the feet swell in hot climes, and nothing is so unpleasant as a boot that pinches.

You can get very nice boots *to look at*, made in India, for a few rupees, but avoid them, as the leather is little better than brown paper. About Nagpore excellent sambur skin, well tanned, can be procured. This, when made up for riding-boots and gaiters, is capital. It is a pity it cannot be obtained in England. A waterproof coat and leggings, and a cap to fit on to the helmet, should also form part of one's kit for the tropics. Remember never to sit in damp clothes, or allow them to dry on you in the wind. Change if you can at once. If you cannot, then put on either a wrap or a waterproof. If you don't follow this advice you will get fever to a certainty. A little timely discomfort and precaution may avert serious consequences. Never sleep on the ground. Trestle-cots made by Edgington, of Duke Street, with an extra large waterproof sunshade, with a couple of mosquito-curtains, one net and one muslin, are out and out the best. Have a *razzie** to put under you, and an air-pillow for your head; but take a light hammock as well.

List of Articles Required for a Trip.

If you wish to be comfortable and enjoy sport you must live well, and had better be provided with all that is requisite:

6 flannel shirts, unshrinkable.
4 shirts of flannel and silk.
8 Indian gauze vests.
8 pairs good merino socks, with double heels and toes.
2 pairs knickerbocker stockings.
2 pairs long, closely-woven silk stockings, greenish tint.
6 pairs of pyjamas, and 6 night jackets, all very loose.
18 pocket-handkerchiefs.
1 leather suit complete, with plenty of pockets in the coat.
3 suits of gabardine,† one brown, one khakie, one green.
2 pairs light ordinary trousers.
2 double-breasted coats, light material.
2 pairs braces.
1 broad leather belt.
1 shikar belt, fitted by Thornhill.
2 helmets; Ellwood's for choice.
1 soft wide-awake.

* *Razzie*—a quilt lined with cotton.
† *Gabardine*—procurable from Burbury of Reading.

4 pairs Dean's field boots, rather large, as feet swell in the tropics.

2 pairs ankle-boots.

2 pairs leather gaiters up to the knee; 2 flints, and steel and tinder.

2 pairs easy slippers; 1 pair stout ditto.

3 pairs of shoes with indiarubber soles.

1 light waterproof-coat, leggings and cover for helmet.

A large, long-handled umbrella for use in howdahs.

1 canvas hold-all, containing combs, tooth-brushes, razors, a strop, soap, needles, thread, buttons, scissors, penknife, a knife with corkscrew.

12 towels—large; 4 large Turkish towels for scrubbing after bathing.

2 pairs bathing-drawers.

12 napkins; 2 tablecloths.

1 Berthon's collapsible indiarubber boat and oars.

6 inflated rubber supports for those unable to swim to cross rivers.

200 yards of thin but very strong cord.

6 balls of twine.

4 waterproof sheets with eyelets, from 8 feet to 12 feet square.

Pack-thread and sail-maker's needles.

Rockets and other fireworks.

A good magic-lantern with dissolving views to astonish natives.

If you can learn a few conjuring tricks so much the better.

A photographic apparatus and dry plates. Learn its use thoroughly.

A camera lucida for use, if unable to sketch from nature.

OUTFIT

1 good saddle with Ds, saddle-bags, holster-bags, cartridge-bags, a small chagul (a leather water-bottle), and a valise for putting behind saddle.

A good-sized chagul for yourself; 50 others for your followers. These can be procured from any firm of saddlers in Cawnpore. Water kept in these is always cool—they cost but little. Take also hobbles and knee-halters.

2 bridles and head-stall, with fringe coming over the eyes.

A good revolver.

6 spear-heads, laurel-leaf pattern.

6 skinning-knives.

A dozen bill-hooks.

6 felling axes (American bush-wood ones).

2 hand axes.

1 pair hunting-spurs.

1 case of carpenter's tools in box.

2 medicine-chests.

If you are subject to gout or acute rheumatism, take some bottles of Laville's mixture. It is a patent French medicine, and acts as a charm if taken when the first twinges are felt. A teaspoonful in a glass of any wine three times a day, but do not continue taking it too long.

Tents in accordance to your party—one for each.

Tents for your servants.

Enamelled drinking cups and glasses.

6 pocket filters.

Wine and some beer as a treat, occasionally whisky.

6 camp buckets. These are often made of stout canvas.

Camp tables and chairs.
Washing-stand and rubber basin.
An indiarubber bath.
A set of block-tin saucepans, to fit one inside the other.
1 frying-pan, removable handle.
4 block-tin pots on Warren's principle, to be clamped together. One pot rests within the other, there being a space for water between the two.
Tins of biscuits. Milk or water.
Tins of condensed milk.
Tins of cheese (cheddar).
An extra watch or two.
A clock with alarum.
Trestle-cot, sunshade and curtains, my pattern.
Lea and Perrin's Worcester sauce.
Tins of mushrooms, black Worcestershire being the best.
Tins of baking-powder.
Carving knives and forks.
Plated ware for table use.
Block-tin plates of various kinds ; teacups, etc.
A Carson's salting-machine.
A small meat-saw.
A pestle and mortar.
Tins of sultanas, raisins and currants.
Tins of sugar, tea and coffee, cloves, cardamoms, coriander seed, pepper, salt, almonds, saffron, turmeric, dried chillies, cinnamon, peppercorns, garlic, green ginger.
Barrie's Madras curry-paste. Mulligatawny paste, and lime pickle.

Tins of veal cutlets and tomato-sauce.
Wilson's Chicago beef.
Strasburg potted meats.
Oxford sausages in tins.
Bacon in square tins, thin, painted yellow—for breakfast, as prepared by Crosse and Blackwell. Reject all thick tins.
Small hams ready cooked, in tins.
Ox tongues.
Irish stew in tins.
Vegetables of sorts in tins.
Tins of oxtail-soup. Don't forget a tin-opener or two.
Lamps, candles, court-plaster, diachylon plaster.
Papier fayard is invaluable for cuts.
Holloway's pills and ointment.
Black draughts for natives.
Blue pills, mustard-plasters.
Take extra powder, shot and bullets, wads and caps.
The battery is mentioned elsewhere.

Each gun and rifle should have its waterproof case and sling. I consider hammerless weapons the best. A good shikar knife is essential. All rifles should have the lowest trajectory possible, and be finely sighted and well tested. Judging distances is very difficult; more animals are missed through mistakes in this respect than from any other cause. It is a difficult knack to acquire. Every rifle should carry point-blank up to two hundred yards, or as near that as possible. Have the sights of your rifles, after testing, screwed into the rib.

If you drink fresh toddy either from the date,

Palmyra or cocoanut, it is wholesome and refreshing. Avoid it when fermented.

If you run short of clothing made for you in England, you can get very fair shikar clothes from the Basil Mission in Cannanore, but they do not wear very well. The native tailors are very clever, and if supplied with a pattern will copy it exactly. A Mr. J. J. Meyrick, writing in the *Shooting Times*, recommends trousers of very finely woven English corduroy as impenetrable for the tree-leeches, and it also resists the barbs of the seed of spear-grass. This I have not tried, but *charsoottie*, which he recommends as almost, if not quite, impervious to both leeches and spear-grass, I *have* tried many times, and my experience of it is not the same as his. I have never found anything that could keep out the tree-leech for any length of time. He says also that he found if he saturated his socks with salt water, the leeches avoided them; but I have tried that and the crude petroleum. Both answered for a time, but in walking through grass reeking with dew the ingredients were washed out, and the leeches soon found their way in.

For guns and rifles I have already recommended a battery. There are so many makers of repute that it sounds invidious to recommend one in preference to another, yet it is only fair to speak of a firm that has served one well. There is scarcely a maker of note whose guns I have not had. In buying a gun remember you may wish to part with it again some day, and the name of a favourite maker carries great weight. It may cost you more in the first instance, but it will also realize more than a gun perhaps equally as good, but by a maker less known. In days gone by guns and rifles made by Sam Smith had a great name, especially in India, and realized their full value; but that renowned firm is no longer in existence. Purdey's are unrivalled for excellence, but the price is prohibitive. Old Joseph Lang is no longer in the land of the living, and his sons have parted with their business. Holland and Holland have made a great name for themselves. Of all the old firms, the weapons constructed by Westley Richards, Limited, fully keep up their reputation, and no one could do better than go to them for a battery and cartridges. Their guns are almost in the same favour in India as Sam Smith's were fifty years ago (and even longer), and their top lever snap action is certainly the best, Purdey's the second, and Greener's the third best in the world. Be measured for your weapons. No two men are built alike; the length and bend of stock that fits one will not suit another, and although in time a man given to shooting can learn to kill fairly well with any gun, he is heavily handicapped by having a gun that does not suit him. Discard black powder; rifleite and other nitro powders can be used in rifles as well as in guns. I must say that of all the nitros none is superior to Schultze's. I have used it since its introduction, and wish for nothing better; but it is not yet adapted for use in rifles. E. C. is almost as good; in fact, there is very little difference between the two for sporting purposes. Adopt the 'Field' loading. Have your cartridges for dangerous shooting loaded either by Eley Brothers or by your gunmaker. Take extra cartridges, powder, shot, bullets, wads and caps with you, but trust to the loaded cartridges principally. These should all be in airtight cases, not soldered down, each case to weigh not more than fifty pounds.

A solid leaden bullet is the best for the larger game. For pachyderms, such as elephants, rhinoceroses, hippopotami, and buffaloes, use hardened bullets. Quicksilver is the best to use for that purpose, but don't put in more than a twelfth-part, and don't keep it too long in the molten lead, as it quickly evaporates. This adds to the weight of the bullet, whilst a mixture of tin lessens it. If you add too much quicksilver the bullets become brittle, and fly to pieces on impact. For deer, use hollow expansive bullets fired out of an express. The most useful gauge is No. 12, because shells of that calibre can be got almost everywhere in our colonies. I myself, for small-game shooting, prefer a sixteen-bore top lever snap action. In France and abroad generally cartridges of this bore can be got now more easily than the larger, but in India and Africa it is different. For snipe and quail, when they lie well, I use No. 10 shot; if they are wild, No. 8; for hares and partridges, No. 6; for duck, guinea-fowl, and florikan, No. 4; for bustards and geese, No. 2; for woodcock and teal, No. 7. Most weapons shoot small shots better than big, but the shot must be in proportion to the size of the game fired at.

In India tents can be purchased which are more suitable for the climate than those made in England, because they resist the heat better. Those made at Jubbulpore are the best, but they are very heavy. As there are always topes of trees for pitching a tent under, I should advise the order being given to Edgington, who has had great experience, having supplied travellers and sportsmen for years past in Africa, and his are lighter and more waterproof than Indian ones.

Men in robust health prefer for bathing purposes the coldest water they can get, but if you are at all inclined to be unwell, or are getting on in life, use tepid water. A tub is a necessity in all hot climates, but it need not be overdone. Keep your head cool, your feet dry, and your bowels open, is a very good precept. I detest all medicines, though one is forced to take a dose now and then, but the less you take the better. Moderation in eating and drinking, with plenty of outdoor exercise, will keep most men in health. We read of nostrums that are supposed to cure every ill a man, woman or child is subject to; but common-sense will prove the absurdity of such a theory. We hear of pills worth a guinea a box which are retailed at a shilling. Does anybody suppose that these are better than the thousand similar nostrums advertised daily? A man has only to advertise. If his pills are but bread covered with a coating of some noxious drug, he will find fools to purchase them and to believe in their efficacy. Effervescing citrate of magnesia is a good mild aperient, not unpleasant to take.

I do not believe in blue ribbonism for the tropics; total abstinence is as bad as excessive drinking. No man can undergo excessive exercise day after day without stimulants of some kind. The water procurable is generally bad, and in it are germs of various diseases, the very worst being the guinea-worm. Beer, especially lager, is the best for the tropics, but it is too bulky to carry about. Whisky is the best and most wholesome of spirits. The Karens make excellent *shamsho* out of rice, which is just as pleasant and as wholesome as whisky.

For night shooting, if you must resort to that mode of slaying or trying to slay game, use luminous paint. I have tried every dodge, but none succeeded so well as the paint. Do what you will, even by the brightest of moonlight, the fore-sight if left alone is invisible, but by using the luminous paint you can see it. If you have a stock of fire-flies, and can stick one on the fore-sight with the tail end uppermost, gumming the beast on to its back, the flickering light will be a good guide; but when you want these insects you cannot always find them; they don't keep alive long in confinement, and once dead are useless. But night shooting under the most advantageous circumstances is most uncertain. The disadvantages are great; far more beasts are missed or wounded than killed, and you are very liable to contract fever. The mosquitoes devour you all night, and you dare not move a limb to drive them off. It is poor work at the best, but has to be resorted to at times as the only means, perhaps, of ridding the neighbourhood of a pest.

Take matches, but not too many, for fear of combustion. Take two kinds— one that will strike on anything, and the other that ignites on the box alone; this is to astonish the natives. If an African sees you ignite a match by rubbing it along your trousers, tell him it is *jado*, or magic. Give him one of the other kind, and when he finds he cannot ignite it, he will believe you to be a great magician; but, of course, this will not go down in India.

Take a very powerful magnifying-glass with you for obtaining fire where big game abounds in Africa and India; by focussing the rays of the sun, a piece of tinder can at once be set on fire. I have seen Burmese procure fire by friction, rubbing two pieces of bamboo together; but I never learnt how to do it myself, though I have tried often enough.

If you run out of soap, the following is the mode adopted by that great traveller and sportsman, the late Sir S. Baker, for manufacturing that most useful commodity:

'We had a large supply of various kinds of fat, including that of elephants, hippopotami, lions, and rhinoceros; but our stock of soap was exhausted, therefore I determined to convert a quantity of our grease into that very necessary article.

'Soap-boiling is not so easy as may be imagined; it requires not only much attention, but the quality is dependent upon the proper mixture of the alkalies. Sixty parts of potash and forty of lime are, I believe, the proportions for common soap. I had neither lime nor potash, but I shortly procured both. The *hegleck* tree (*Balanites Egyptiaca*) was extremely rich in potash; therefore I burned a large quantity, and made a strong ley with the ashes; this I concentrated by boiling. [If the *hegleck* tree, which bears a small fruit somewhat like a date, be not procurable, potash can be made from the stalks of the plantain: open it by layers, thoroughly dry it, then burn it, and boil the ashes.] Tinder can be made from inside the bark of the wild fig-tree, dried and pulverized. There was no limestone, but the river produced a plentiful supply of large oyster-shells that if burnt would yield excellent lime; accordingly I constructed a kiln, with the assistance of the white ants. The country was infested with these creatures, which had erected their dwellings in all directions. There were cones from six to ten feet high, formed of clay so thoroughly cemented by a glutinous preparation of the insects that it was harder than sun-baked bricks. [These ant-hills are plentiful all over Africa and India.] I selected an egg-shaped hill, and cut off the top, exactly as we take off the slice from an egg. My Tokroories then worked hard, and, with a hoe and their lances, they hollowed it out to the base, in spite of the attacks of the soldier ants, which punished the legs of the intruders considerably. I now made a draught-hole from the outside base, at right angles with the bottom of the hollow cone. [A similar kiln can be made in clayey soil on the side of a hill by scarping it, and otherwise doing as recommended by Sir Samuel.] My kiln was perfect; I loaded it with wood, upon which I piled about six bushels of oyster-shells, which I then covered with fuel, and kept it burning for twenty-four hours. [Any shells or coral will make excellent lime by burning.] I commenced my soap-boiling. We possessed an immense copper pot of Egyptian manufacture, in addition to a large copper basin called a "teske"; these would contain ten gallons. The ley having been boiled down to great strength, I added a quantity of lime and the necessary fat. It required two hours' boiling, combined with careful management of the fire, as it would frequently ascend like foam, and overflow the edges of the utensils. However, at length, having been constantly stirred, it turned to soap. Before it became cold, I formed it into cakes and balls with my hands, and the result of the manufacture was a weight of about forty pounds of most excellent soap of a very sporting description—*savon à la bête féroce*. We thus washed with rhinoceros soap; our lamp was trimmed with oil of lions; our butter for cooking purposes was the fat of hippopotami; while our pomade was made from the marrow of buffaloes and antelopes, scented with the blossoms of mimosas.'

If you run out of candles, procure beeswax, to be got everywhere in Africa and the wilds of India; make wicks out of cotton-threads or scrapings of cloth spun together. Suspend these from a height into hollow bamboos, the upper part being open, and a small aperture only in the joint below to keep the wick in the centre; pour in the melted wax, and you will have very serviceable candles. I have had these made for me by Karens in out-of-the-way parts of Burma when my servants have either forgotten to bring a sufficient supply with them or lost what they had.

If you wish to preserve your teeth, use daily a silver tongue-scraper. Clean your teeth morning and evening, using either camphorated chalk or the finest charcoal passed through fine muslin or a very fine sieve.

Accustom yourself to go to bed pretty early. All healthy men find a few hours' uninterrupted sleep ample, and they will feel fresher if they then get up on waking than if they turn over and sleep on for a couple of hours more. To enjoy life in the tropics, you should be up an hour before daybreak, and start for a ride or for a walk or stalk at the first glimpse of daylight. If you can get fresh toddy (juice of the palm), drink it early, daily. Never touch it after fermentation. Many of the Africans make a very good substitute for beer from plantains and other native produce, whilst, as I have said elsewhere, the *shamsho* made by the Karens and Shans from rice distilled is as palatable and as good as the best whisky. When hunting, vary your food as much as possible; eat vegetables when you can get them. Indians make delicious curries from vegetables alone. Do not be afraid of the sun, with a good covering to the head. Mansfield Parkins says that, during his seven years' wanderings in Abyssinia, he wore no covering to his head, excepting the scanty head of hair God had given him, and an occasional pat of butter when he could get it. That may do for the highlands of Ethiopia, but not for the plains of India or Africa.

APPENDIX.

SIMPLE RECIPES FOR USE IN TRAVELLING.

It is almost as easy to live comfortably as to rough it, and far more conducive to health. Most Indian cooks are adepts, but very few Africans can do more than spoil a roast or a boil: they can be taught, however, and it will repay the traveller to instruct those with him in the culinary art.

Do not go to second-rate firms for tinned goods. Messrs. Crosse and Blackwell are not only one of the oldest, but one of the best of the firms dealing wholesale in all provisions; and I can strongly recommend Messrs. Moir, of Aberdeen. In ordering hams and bacons from Messrs. Crosse and Blackwell, get small hams ready cooked and soldered down in tin, but ask the firm not to over-boil them, as is too often done. For bacon get their square yellow tins of breakfast bacon, the thin streaky belly parts and no other; their veal cutlets with tomato sauce are also very good. Wilson's Chicago compressed beef is also useful to fall back upon in an emergency, but tinned meats should be avoided as much as possible, and only resorted to when there is nothing fresh procurable. Take plenty of tinned vegetables. In India you can get plenty of native vegetables, in Africa scarcely any. Take only Patna rice; it is out and out the best. The only good currie-paste and mulligatawny paste is that made by Barrie and Co., of Madras, and sold by Messrs. Crosse and Blackwell. Bombay ducks are a relish; they only require to be toasted. Poppadums, pickles, and other Indian relishes, are sold by Messrs. Stembridge, of 33, Leicester Square, London. If in the East, it is better to buy the ingredients and let your cook prepare the condiments, by which means you will get a new curry daily instead of having to stick to one kind only.

Giblet Soup.

Scald and clean the giblets of a goose or a pair of ducks, stew them in water—a pint for each set—till they are quite tender, or with a neck of mutton, or a couple of pounds of gravy-beef, three onions, a bunch of sweet herbs and 4 pints of water. Stew them until the gizzards are quite tender, then remove and set aside; add more stock if necessary to the soup. Flavour with mushrooms, or Harvey or Worcester sauce, and a little butter rolled in arrowroot or flour to thicken it. The gizzards of all game-birds will answer.

Ox-tail Soup.

One tail is sufficient to make soup for four or five persons. Divide the tail at the joints, and soak them in warm water; if the bones are partially sawed across, they will give more strength to the soup. Put into a stewpan the slices of the tail, and fry them a little; then add a few cloves with a couple of large onions, a bunch of sweet herbs, some black pepper and a blade of mace. Cover the whole with water, and as it boils, keep removing the scum whilst any rises; then replace the cover close, and set the pot on the side of the fire to simmer gently for two or three hours until the meat is tender, when remove and cut into small pieces, laying them on one side. Strain the broth through a cloth or sieve, add a glass of wine with a couple of spoonfuls of mushroom-ketchup or Harvey sauce, or one of soy; return the meat into the soup to give it a boil up. If you wish the soup to be thick, take a couple of spoonfuls of the clear fat that has been removed, mix it into a paste with flour, and add the warm broth by degrees, stirring it quite smooth, and let it simmer for a short time; or add a little arrowroot with the wine and sauce. Have ready some nicely-cut carrots, turnips, and small onions (tinned ones will do), prepared and boiled previously, which add to the soup a minute or two before serving. Two or three slices of bacon or ham laid at the bottom of the stewpan with the meat will increase the flavour of the soup. The tail of any wild bull or deer will do.

Chicken Broth.

Clean and divide the chicken into quarters, after having removed the skin and rump. Add a blade of mace, a small onion sliced, and ten white peppercorns, with a quart of water. Simmer till the broth be sufficiently reduced and of a pleasant flavour; remove the fat as it rises; season with salt. A little chopped parsley may be added. This broth may also be made of snipe, quail, partridges.

Sauce for Game, Duck, Snipe, etc.

Take half a pint of clear gravy, cut into it the thin peel of a lime, a few leaves of basil or sage, with a small sliced onion. Let it boil until the gravy is flavoured, then strain it off. Add the juice of the lime, some cayenne pepper, a glass of red wine, pepper, and salt. Send it up hot. Savoury herbs must be taken; they can seldom be got in the wilds.

Steak-pie.

Cut the steak off a rump or any other good part of the beef (beat it with the rolling-pin), fat and lean together, about half an inch thick; put over it salt, pepper, and parboiled onions, minced or grated bread seasoned with pepper, salt, and pickled cucumber minced; roll it up or pack it neatly into the dish, or lay the beef in slices; add some spoonfuls of gravy and a teaspoonful of vinegar. Cover with a puff paste and bake it for an hour. In Devonshire slices of apple and onions are added, when it is called squab pie. The flesh of the sambur or of any deer will answer as well.

Marrow-bones.

Saw the bones even, so that they will stand steady; put a piece of paste over the ends, set them upright in a saucepan, and boil till they are done enough. A beef marrow-bone will require from an hour and a half to two hours. Serve fresh toasted bread with them. Bones from the gaur, wild cattle, buffalo and sambur, and most large deer, answer admirably.

PICKLE FOR BEEF, HAM OR TONGUE.

Boil together for twenty minutes 2 gallons of water, 3 pounds bay salt, 2 pounds common salt, 2 pounds coarse sugar, 2 ounces saltpetre, and 2 ounces black pepper, bruised and tied in a fold of muslin; clear off the scum thoroughly as it rises, pour the pickle into a tub or a deep earthen pan, and when it is quite cold lay in the meat, of which every part must be perfectly covered with it. Better use a Carson's syringe and saturate the meat.

SALTING.

Meat preserved with Carson's salting machine will keep in proportion to the strength of the brine with which it is impregnated. If it be required to keep for a month, use the recipe marked No. 1: if for two months, No. 2; if beyond that time, No. 3. Meat pickled with No. 1 will preserve the character of fresh meat, and No. 2 corned meat; so that by this instrument and process persons on a voyage may have provisions nearly fresh for a good length of time, as by forcing a little salt-and-water (for example) to the bone, particularly when there is a joint, and around the pope's eye in a leg of mutton, the other parts will remain sweet without salt for many weeks if hung in an airy place.

To making Pickle or Brine.

No. 1.—Take of common salt 5 pounds, molasses $\frac{1}{2}$ pound, water 1 gallon. Mix together, and allow it to stand quiet for half an hour (or longer); then pour or strain off the clear liquid, taking care that no particle of salt or other substance pass into the machine. This is very important, as such particles may stop the hole in the nipple; but should a particle of salt or fat get into it, if the nipple be placed in hot water the salt will be dissolved, and the fat can be blown out.

No. 2.—Take of common salt 6 pounds, saltpetre $\frac{1}{4}$ pound, molasses $\frac{1}{2}$ pound, water 1 gallon. Dissolve as above.

No. 3.—Take of common salt 7 pounds, nitre or saltpetre ¾ pound, water 1 gallon. Dissolve and use as No. 2.

No. 4.—Take of common salt 7 pounds, saltpetre ½ pound, coarse sugar ½ pound, water 1 gallon. To be used the same as No. 2. If the ham, tongue, bacon, etc., is to be cured or smoked, it is only necessary to add to each quart of the above pickle a tablespoonful or more of Hackin's essence of smoke.

Fried Liver and Bacon.

Cut the liver (any deer's liver will do) rather thin, but not too thin, so as to harden in the frying. Chop a quantity of parsley, season it with pepper, and lay it thick upon the liver. Cut slices of bacon and fry both together; add a little lemon pickle to the gravy, made by pouring the fat out of the pan, flouring, and adding boiling water.

Chops.

Cut your chops and trim them; dip them into hot melted butter or warm ghee. Cover with grated bread mixed with chopped parsley, a little sweet marjoram, salt and pepper; then dip the chops into the yolks of eggs beaten up, and sprinkle them with crumbs of bread. Fry them in butter, and serve with a thickened gravy. All deer and antelope give excellent chops.

Broiled Kidneys.

Cut the kidneys down the centre, and remove the skin that covers them; then keep the two sides open with a small skewer of wood. Dust them well with pepper and a little salt; dip them into melted butter. Broil the side that is cut open first; then turn them that they may retain their gravy. Have ready some chopped parsley mixed with fresh butter, lemon-juice, pepper and salt; put a little over each kidney, and serve on a hot dish.

Roast Fowl and any Game-bird of a Large Size.

Clean the fowl nicely; mix a little butter with lime-juice, pepper and salt, and put it into the inside. Cut off or turn up the rump. Fix it to the spit by skewers, and cover it with paper; when nearly done, unpaper, froth, and give it a nice brown. Fowls and all game-birds may be stuffed with a farce and larded, or the bodies filled with a ragout of mushrooms or oysters, served with bread, egg, or any other sauce. A large fowl will take from a half to three-quarters of an hour roasting.

Buttered Eggs.

Beat and strain ten or twelve eggs; put a piece of butter into a saucepan, and keep turning it one way till melted. Put in the beaten eggs, and stir them round with a silver spoon until they become quite thick. Serve them on a dish with buttered toast. They may be eaten with fish, fowl, or sausages.

Country Captain.

Cut a small or large fowl, or any other bird fit for the table, in pieces; shred an onion small, and fry it brown in butter. Sprinkle the fowl with fine salt and curry-powder, and fry it brown; then put it into a stewpan with a pint of soup. Stew it slowly down to a half, and serve it with rice.

Partridges and Francolins.

Both black and gray are best boiled; the former are in season from October until May, the latter from September to February. Clean the birds and truss them as chicken. Have ready a large vessel of boiling water, into which place the birds, keeping the water at a boil; they will be done in ten or twelve minutes. They are also very good stewed with some butter and a small quantity of water. Place them in a stewpan or conjurer over a brisk fire; look to them occasionally, and constantly turn, to prevent them being burnt in the bottom of the pan, and as soon as the gravy begins to ooze from the birds and mixes with the butter, they are done enough. Serve with bread sauce. Quail, snipe, rock or green pigeon, may be dressed in the same manner, only the two latter should first be skinned and dressed in vine leaves.

A Luxurious Quail Pie.

Take twelve quail, nicely pluck them, and 2 pounds of steak. Put a spoonful of pâte de foie gras inside each bird, and wrap it in a slice of thin bacon. Add a small tin of truffles, half a bottle of black Worcestershire mushrooms, six hard-boiled eggs, each cut in half, some Worcestershire sauce (Lea and Perrin's); fill in with rich stock. Cover with good crust, and bake slowly.

To dress Quails.

Pluck and draw your quail; cut a piece of lemon or lime the size of a dice and cover with a sprinkling of cayenne, then wrap the dice in a very thin slice of bacon. Have boiling water handy; take it off the fire, drop the quails into the water, leave them there three minutes; then take them out, insert in each the lemon wrapped in bacon; fry them nicely in breadcrumbs, and serve on hot buttered toast.

Partridge Pie.

Four young partridges, 1 pound rump steak, half a dozen oysters, a tin of Worcestershire black mushrooms, a cup of stock, proper seasoning; cover with good crust and bake.

Salad Sauce.

Take the yolks of two fresh eggs boiled hard, mash in a plate with a silver fork, then add a saltspoonful of salt, and two spoonfuls of mustard; rub the whole well together; add by degrees three spoonfuls of sweet oil or fresh cream, then two of good vinegar, stirring it well the whole time until quite smooth; a small spoonful of anchovy sauce is sometimes added, but is no improvement if the salad is to be eaten with cold meats, though it may be with fish, prawns, or lobsters.

Salmi of Game, Meat, etc.

Take a pound of any under-roasted meat, hare, turkey, game, goose, or duck, and cut it up into convenient pieces; put them into a saucepan; bruise the livers, and should it be snipe or woodcock, bruise the trail; squeeze over them the juice of two lemons and the rasped zest of one or two bitter oranges; season with salt and the finest spices in powder, cayenne, and mustard prepared with flavoured vinegar and a little white wine or claret; put the saucepan over a lamp or fire, and stir it constantly, that it may all be incorporated with the sauce. It must not boil, and should it attempt it, a stream of fine oil must be poured over to prevent it, or diminish the flame, or keep it up a little higher and stir it two or three times; it is then ready to be served, and must be eaten very hot.

To Grill Mushrooms.

Take those of middling size, skin and wash them very clean, if necessary strain and dry them in a cloth; put a little butter over the inside of each; sprinkle some salt and pepper, and grill or fry until tender. Mushrooms are very plentiful at times in certain seasons in India, in Burma, and Assam.

Mushroom Omelette.

Prepare and cook the mushrooms in butter, pepper, and salt, and mix into a plain omelette.

To devil Legs of Poultry or Game.

Score the legs of a roasted turkey, goose or fowl, or any game; sprinkle them well with cayenne, black pepper, and salt; broil them well and pour over the following sauce. Take three spoonfuls of gravy, one of butter rubbed in a little flour, one of lemon-juice, a glass of wine (port or white), a spoonful of mustard, some chilli vinegar or two or three chopped green chillies, a spoonful of mushroom catsup. Warm up, and serve in a boat.

Omelette.

Break four eggs into a dish, with a little pepper or chopped green chillies, a small quantity of fine salt, with a teaspoonful of milk or water, merely to dissolve it; beat the whole well to a froth, then put a tablespoonful of butter or ghee into a frying-pan; when it is hot, throw the mixture into the pan, holding it a little distance from the fire; keep shaking it, to prevent its burning and sticking to the bottom of the pan; it takes about five minutes to dress. Gather up one side with a knife, and roll it equally before you dish it. Chopped parsley, onions, minced ham, or kidneys, may be added, and a variety given by grated hung beef, dried tongue, anchovy paste sauce or chopped oysters.

Indian Ramekin.

Take equal quantities of flour, butter, and pounded or grated cheese, with an egg to each spoonful of the other ingredients. Mix all well together and bake in moulds or cases; serve with toast, made mustard, pepper and salt.

Macaroni au Gratin.

Break 4 ounces of macaroni into lengths of about a couple of inches; wash it in water, and then boil it in white broth or milk with a little salt until tender; rub up in a mortar 4 ounces of dry double Gloucester or Cheddar cheese, and add to it the well-beaten yolks of two eggs, a couple of spoonfuls of cream, with four of the broth the macaroni has been boiled in; butter a dish large enough to contain the whole, in which place the macaroni with the cheese custard poured over it, and bake in a quick oven.

Devilled Mushrooms.

Take fine dry mushrooms with red gills, peel off the outer skin, and see that they are perfectly free from sand or dirt; spread a little butter over the inside, and sprinkle plenty of black pounded pepper over them, with a little cayenne and salt; broil them on a gridiron over a clear fire. If the mushroom peels easily, you may almost be sure it is edible.

Bombay Pudding.

The yolk of an egg, one tablespoonful of sugar, and half a seer (one pint) of boiled milk, to be beat up and boiled together; when thick enough, lay it in a plate to cool, cut it in pieces, and fry them in a frying-pan; make a syrup of the white of the egg, with a little sugar and lime-juice.

Rice Pudding with Dry Currants.

Take a small basin of boiled dry rice, mix it with half a pound of currants, two tablespoonfuls of sugar, one of butter, and a beaten egg; boil it in a floured cloth or mould for nearly an hour.

Boiled Rice Pudding.

Wash and pick 4 ounces of rice very clean. Soak it in water half an hour, then tie it up in a cloth, with 8 ounces of picked currants or raisins; leave room for the rice to swell, and boil it nearly two hours. Serve with melted butter, sugar, and nutmeg.

Plantain Pudding.

Take some plantains, and have them fried in their skins; when done, you must peel and cut the fruit in slices; add sugar to the taste, the juice of two or three limes, the peel of one cut into small thin pieces, a glass of white wine, half a teaspoonful of pounded cloves, with a little butter. This is to be put into a paste, and boiled as an apple pudding. Cream, or lemon and sugar with butter, is a great improvement.

Plain Pancakes.

Light plain pancakes are made of a thin light batter of milk, eggs, and flour, with salt and sugar; rub the frying-pan with a buttered cloth; sift sugar over them as they are doubled or rolled and dished; serve with limes.

Pineapple Fritters.

Pare and core a pineapple, cut into slices, and stew them with a little water, sugar, and lemon-peel. When soft, add a little white wine and the juice of half a lime, with a bit of butter. When cold, make a batter with three spoonfuls of fine flour, two spoonfuls of cream, a glass of wine, some sugar, and four eggs. Beat it all together very well; put first butter or pure ghee in a frying-pan, throw the fruit into the batter, take it out in spoonfuls, and fry them one by one to a nice light brown; put them on a sieve before the fire to dry, and serve, with plenty of pounded sugar over them, on a white napkin.

Mango Fool.

Add cold milk and sugar to the pulp of green boiled mangoes in such quantity as the maker chooses; the milk must be added by a little at a time, stirring it well with the mangoes, otherwise the fool will not be smooth.

To Preserve Mangoes.

Take any quantity of the finest unripe mangoes, peel, and divide them in half, stones and all, removing the seeds; then weigh the mangoes; to each pound allow a pint of water and a pound and a quarter of sugar-candy; put the whole into a stewpan, and boil gently, removing all the scum as it rises. When the mangoes appear clear and sufficiently done, remove from the fire, and let it stand until cold; then put into bottles or jars for use or keeping.

Mango Jelly.

Peel and cut any quantity of unripe mangoes free from stone; put the slices into a preserving-pan, with a sufficient quantity of water to cover them, and boil gently till quite soft; strain the contents through a jelly-bag or cloth. To each pint of juice add a pound and a half of good sugar, pounded, and when it is dissolved, put it into a preserving-pan, set it on the fire, and boil gently, stirring and skimming it the whole time till no more scum rises and it is clear and fine; pour into pots while warm, and when cold cover it down close.

Milk Punch.

Put the rinds of thirty limes, pared fine, in a bottle of rum; let it stand twenty-four hours; then take three bottles of water, one bottle of lime-juice, 4 pounds of powdered sugar, two nutmegs grated, and six bottles of rum, arrack, or brandy; mix all together; add 2 quarts of milk boiling hot; let it stand two hours; then strain it through a flannel bag.

Fish Curry.

The native way is to cut 2 pounds of fish into slices, dip it in a little oil, and rub it with pounded raw grain; let it remain a short time, and wash it off; then partially fry it in ghee, with a sufficiency of salt, eight or ten dried chilies, and a pinch of fenugreek seed and nala zeera; then mix a few dried pounded chilies, some turmeric roasted, coriander-seed, fenugreek, and nala zeera, with some sliced onions and a clove of garlic pounded; cover this well over the fish, and place it again into the ghee with the fried chilies, adding sufficient water to dress it. An acidity may be given with tamarind-juice, green mangoes, vinegar, or lemon; vegetables may be added in the same way as directed for vegetable curries, putting in a layer of vegetables, and then a layer of fish, shaking the saucepan to prevent the fish from breaking and burning. The vegetables usually added to the fish curries are cauliflower, fennel-mother, mooringu pods and leaves.

Fowl Curry.

Take and cut the fowl by joints, and add to it some sliced green ginger, black pepper, salt, and coriander-seed, all ground well; hash the *nabool chunnali*, and boil it in a little water till it becomes tender, and put it to the fowl; strain the gravy into a saucepan, and mix the curry stuff well with it; give a *baghar* to it in ghee with cloves. Put the fowl into a stewpan with some ghee, and fry it; then pour the gravy over it; let it simmer for a short time, and serve it up. The right proportions of curry ingredients are as follows:

Ghee	½ lb.
Nabool chunnali ...	½ lb.
Onions	½ lb.
Coriander-seed	1 tolah.
Salt	2 tolahs.
Cinnamon	2 mashas.
Cloves	2 mashas.
Cardamoms	2 mashas.
Black pepper	1 masha.
Green ginger	1 tolah.

Fowl Pullow.

Put the mutton, cut in slices, with four whole onions into 6 quarts of water; boil all this together until reduced to one-third; take it off the fire, wash the meat in the liquor, strain through a towel, and set it aside. Take 8 ounces of rice, wash it well, and dry by squeezing firmly in a towel. Put half a pound of butter into a saucepan and melt it; fry in it a handful of onions sliced lengthways; when they have become of a brown colour, take them out and lay aside in the butter that remains. Fry slightly a fowl that has been previously boiled; take out the fowl, and in the same butter add the dry rice and fry it a little. As the butter evaporates, add the above broth to it, and boil the rice in it; then put with it the cloves, cardamoms, peppercorns and mace (be cautious not to put too much of the latter); add *narcy pank leaves* and salt with the green ginger; cut into thin slices. When the rice is sufficiently boiled, remove all but a little fire from underneath, and place some on the pan-cover; if the rice be at all hard, add some water to it and place the fowl in the centre to imbibe a flavour; cover it over with the rice, and serve up garnished with hard-boiled eggs, cut either in halves or quarters. The dressing is as follows:

Onions	5 or 6.
Eggs	3 or 4.
Mutton	1 lb.
Fowl	1 lb.
Rice	8 oz.
Butter	½ lb.
Black pepper	10 or 12 corns.
Mace	4 blades.
Cloves	10 or 12.
Green ginger	1 tolah.
Salt	1 dessertspoonful.
Narcy pank leaves	2 or 3.
Cardamoms	10 or 12.

Fish Kitcherie.

Take any cold fish, pick it carefully from the bones; mix with a teacupful of boiled rice 1 ounce of butter, a teaspoonful of mustard, two soft-boiled eggs, salt and cayenne to taste, and serve very hot. The quantities may be varied according to the amount of fish used.

CHUPATIES

Are made by mixing flour and water together with a little salt into a paste or dough, kneading it well; sometimes ghee is added. They may also be made with milk instead of water. They are flattened into thin cakes with the hand, smeared with a small quantity of ghee, and baked on an iron pan over the fire.

BREAKFAST DISHES.

Rice, if properly boiled and drained, will keep good for a few days. When required for use, all that is necessary is to pour boiling water over it, and to again drain it. A few slices of fried bacon cut up fine, a couple of eggs boiled only three minutes, pepper and salt mixed with the rice, will provide a palatable dish quickly prepared.

In travelling, when hurried, a meal can be quickly prepared by carrying with one cooked meats, but they are apt to go bad unless curried. Natives of India, by cutting meat into squares and saturating them with condiments, can preserve them even for a year.

Get some good mutton or veal free of bone and gristle, cut into cubes of about ¾ inch each face; get some good butter or ghee, melt it; add some good stock. When it has simmered for some time, add liberally a quantity of Barry's Madras curry-paste, about two and a half tablespoonfuls of the condiment to every pint of gravy used. Cover the ingredients up, and then let them simmer slowly for at least two hours, stirring gently. When the meat is thoroughly saturated, pour it into a jar with an air-tight screw top, and put it by. When required for use, take as much as is required, put it into a frying-pan, and place over a charcoal fire, if possible, until it is thoroughly heated, and then serve with rice, either freshly boiled or warmed up, and you will have a good meal ready in a quarter of an hour.

To preserve Fish.

In hot climates all fish should be split down the back and then laid open; they should then be salted, and should lie for a few hours to drain, after which they should be hung over the smoke of a dry wood fire. This treatment renders them delicious for immediate use, but if required to keep they must be smoked for a couple of days, and then be highly dried in the sun. If you have a bottle of pyroligneous acid, give the fish a couple of coatings with a soft brush. No flies will then settle upon the flesh, and the flavour will be improved.

To preserve Skins with the Hair on.

Soak the skin in water for one day; clean it well of fat; take alum 3 pounds, rock salt 4 ounces, and dissolve in as much water as will cover the skin in a tub or vessel; then boil the solution, and when lukewarm put in the skin and soak it for four days, working it well with the feet or hands several times; take it out and dry it in a warm place, but not in the sun. Boil up the water again, repeating the same process with the skin; wash it well, and beat it with a wooden mallet till quite soft, after which dry it in the shade, rubbing it between the hands at intervals. By this means it will be as soft and pliable as doeskin.

To take Rust out of Steel.

Cover the steel well with sweet oil and let it remain for a couple of days; then use unslacked lime finely powdered, and rub with it until all the dust disappears.

To destroy Ants, Red and Black.

After having discovered the aperture of their nests, surround it with soft clay formed into the shape of a funnel, and pour in boiling water. Where they are in the habit of infesting a floor or room, lay down thin slices of raw meat or liver, upon which the ants will soon congregate. Let a person go about with hot water in a basin, and throw in the meat as it is covered; then shake it dry and put it down to collect more.

To prevent ants getting on a table, bed, etc., tie round the lower end of each leg or post a thin slip of flannel dipped in castor-oil—they will not pass over this; or place the legs in pans of water.

WHITE ANTS.

To secure boxes from their depredations, the best plan is to place them on glass bottles laid lengthways, and if kept free from dust they cannot ascend. They have a great dislike to indigo, and will seldom touch cloth dyed in it or saturated in a solution of corrosive sublimate. The proportion of 1 pound to 4 gallons of water is sufficient. They also dislike salt, which may be mixed up with the mud or gober that is sometimes spread over the floor or wall. Though this is not an effectual remedy, it is as well occasionally to adopt it.

TO DESTROY BUGS.

Wash every part, crevice or corner where they can be secreted with a strong solution of alum-water boiling hot, of the strength of as much pounded alum as the water will dissolve; this is an effectual remedy. Or wash every part of the bedstead or furniture with a strong solution of corrosive sublimate; or dissolve the sublimate in spirits of turpentine, with the addition of water. It is almost impossible to prevent these insects from getting into your beds and furniture where there are native servants in attendance; the utmost cleanliness is requisite, by continually taking down the curtains, removing the bedsteads out in the sun, and pouring boiling water all over such parts as the insects can harbour in. If the bugs are in the walls of the house or anywhere else about, you may prevent them getting up the posts of the bedsteads by placing each leg in a vessel or tin saucer filled with wood ashes from the kitchen; they will not pass over this, and for children's cots nothing can be better. It is preferable to water, into which the clothes from the bed might fall; besides, domestic animals often lap the water, and servants forget to see that the pans are refilled. Never allow the *dhobies* to lay out the clothes on the bed when they bring them home from the wash, as they may have some of these insects amongst them.

Ticks on Dogs.

These vermin may be easily removed by rubbing the dog's ears, or wherever they have fixed themselves, with sweet or castor oil. Fleas will not remain on dogs or animals that have powdered butch rubbed over them, or if washed with an infusion of the same; rubbing them with train-oil is also an effectual remedy.

Eye-flies.

These little insects are very troublesome to persons reading, working, etc. Curled slips of paper or cotton thread suspended to the wall-shades will attract them, where, if undisturbed, they remain. It is said that they have a great aversion to the milk-hedge, also to the *ghee-gowan*, a small spotted green and white, aloe-looking plant which, if hung about the room, prevents the flies entering; this practice is adopted by the natives.

Tooth-powder.

No. 1.—Take common close-grained charcoal; pound it very fine, and sift through muslin. Add a little salt, or roast the betel-nut until it has become charcoal; then grind it up fine and add some salt. This is a great favourite with the natives.

No. 2.—Take powdered cascarilla bark 1 ounce, cream of tartar ½ ounce. Mix both well together, and use as any other dentifrice.

Bite of a Venomous Snake.

First apply a ligature, or bandage, tightly a few inches above the part bitten, and wind it round the limb till it is brought near the wound, when either suck the wound or apply a cupping-glass. Cut out the part with a knife, or burn it with a hot iron, or apply lunar caustic, or wash the parts bitten with eau-de-luce or spirits of hartshorn. At the same time give the patient a teaspoonful of spirits of sal volatile or half a teaspoonful of eau-de-luce in a claret-glass of water, or camphor and ammonia with cayenne pepper. If liquor arsenicalis is procurable or at hand, give 1 drachm with ten drops of tincture of opium, a tablespoonful of lemon-juice in sufficient peppermint, or strong brandy-and-water to fill a wineglass, and repeat this every half-hour until improvement takes place, when a purgative should be administered, the wound well fomented with warm water, and a poultice of mashed boiled carrots and onions applied to the part. A bottle of madeira may be taken in draughts at a few minutes' interval, or any equally large dose of spirituous and fermented liquor. Keep the patient walking about, and do not allow him to lie down to sleep. Should the wound exhibit numerous punctures in two parallel lines, it may be considered that the snake was harmless; but when there are only two small punctures, they have been inflicted most probably by a poisonous one.

NOTE.—Poisonous snakes have conical, tubular fangs, but only one row of teeth on each side of the upper jaw, whilst the harmless tribe have two. Also, in the former, the scales decrease in size as they approach the head, while the reverse is the case in the latter.

CURE FOR THE STING OF A SCORPION OR THE BITE OF A CENTIPEDE.

Apply a ligature above the part, if possible, making a strong pressure over it with a watchkey, or cut down on the spot and apply lime-juice and salt, or a warm poultice of ipecacuanha-powder, or the root of a thistle ground and rubbed into a paste and smeared over the wound, or lint dipped in hartshorn or eau-de-luce. If the pain continues, a glass of brandy taken occasionally will relieve it. A remedy lately recommended is to drop a little pounded burnt alum into the eye.

MOSQUITO-BITES.

To allay the itching in the first instance, wet the part either with eau-de-Cologne, sal volatile, lime-juice, salt and water, or a solution of opium and water; but if ulceration has taken place, a poultice may be necessary, or keep the sore bathed with Goulard's Extract, sufficiently diluted, in the proportion of a teaspoonful to a pint of water. Olive-oil is also a useful external application.

BURNS AND SCALDS.

Bladders arising from burns and scalds must never be cut or opened. In all accidents of this nature it is necessary to employ an immediate remedy, such as immersing in cold water, or surround the parts with fine cotton, and apply a bandage over the whole. Spirits of turpentine is also a useful remedy, the sore to be kept constantly wet by soaking lint or rag in it and applying to the part; this is an effectual remedy. Or take equal parts of lime-water, linseed, olive, or castor oil, and mix together; smear this over the burn or scald, applying the same frequently.

GUINEA-WORM.

While the tumour is in a hard state, apply a warm poultice twice a day, made of the pounded leaves of the prickly pear, until it breaks, and the head of the worm protrudes so far as to be laid hold of with ease, either by a piece of cotton rolled up like a quill, or by a thin bit of bamboo with a slit in it, so as to hold the end fast; this, as it advances, is to be daily twisted gently round until the whole is extracted, which will be greatly facilitated by pouring cold water above the part, whilst the worm is being twisted. No force is to be used when the worm can be drawn; do not apply the poultice again until the next attempt at removal is made.

CHOLERA MIXTURE WITH OPIUM.

Solution of ammonia	$9\frac{1}{2}$ drachms	
Essence of peppermint	5 ,,	Mixed.
Tincture of opium	19 ,,	
Brandy 19 ounces, and	$16\frac{1}{2}$,,	

N.B.—Of this mixture, 1 ounce contains 20 minims of the solution of ammonia, and 25 minims contain $1\frac{1}{4}$ minims of the solution.

When you can, eat the fruit that is in season. Mangoes are only procurable in India in May and June, but all the year round on the east coast of Africa, and at Lakoja on the Niger. Custard apples are ripe in September and October, and are delicious. Some people swear by the alligator pear (*Laurus Persea*), but I can't say that I like it. Apricots are grand in some parts of India, but the best come from Caubul. Some of the finest peaches I ever saw were grown in Assam. The *bhere*, or bear fruit, grows wild; when ripe it is not unpleasant. The *bilimbi* is an angled fruit, of which there are two kinds, sweet and acid. The blackberry is found in Mysore. The breadfruit grows to a large size in Bombay, and is occasionally found in the Deccan. Bullock's-heart, a species of custard apple, but very inferior to that fruit, grows everywhere in India.

The Cape gooseberry (*Physalis Peruviana*), better known as the *tipparie*, grows luxuriantly in a good soil, is self-planting, and soon spreads. I think it is the most delicious of all the fruits, whether for the table or for preserving. Vashen nut (*Anacardium occidentale*) grows almost in a wild state. Figs also are delicious and plentiful. Grapes only thrive in certain localities in India; those from Aurungabad equal the best hothouse grapes of Europe. There are two kinds of guava, red and white, more fitted for preserves than for the table.

The *jamoon* is a wild plum, with a rough, astringent flavour. The *leichie*, originally from China, grows in India, but does not equal that from its original habitat. Lemons and limes flourish everywhere, also sweet limes. Loquat thrives in the Deccan, and mangosteens have been introduced, but I have never seen the fruit in perfection. The *dorian* grows in Burma; it is much appreciated by the natives and by some Europeans, but the smell is most disagreeable, and the taste an acquired one.

There are many kinds of jack-fruit; the best are not bad eating if previously soaked in salt and water. Oranges grow in the hilly districts, but the most delicious are those from Burma and Assam. The *papoia* is also a favourite fruit of mine; I prefer it to the melon. The musk-melon and the water-melon are grown in the sandy beds of rivers, and are sometimes very good. The citron and the pumple-nose also thrive. Pineapples will do well if looked after; the fruit should be allowed to ripen on the plant. Pistachio nuts are grown, but the best come from the Persian Gulf. Plantains and bananas, of which there are many varieties, grow everywhere, but nowhere so well as in Burma, where there are some thirty-seven varieties. Pomegranates, of which there are two varieties, also abound. Soursop, a variety of the custard-apple, tastes something like black currants, and is not a favourite dish. Strawberries, apples, pears, etc., flourish on the hills, but do not thrive on the plains. The tamarind grows wild, but do not encamp under one, for the drippings from the tree will rot your tent. It is most wholesome to drink a decoction of tamarind daily; it keeps off fever, and is most refreshing.

THIRST-BALLS FOR TRAVELLERS.

Mix depurated nitre with an eighth part the quantity of transparent or Oriental sulphur, and make it into balls, one of which, being kept in the mouth when parched with thirst, will afford great relief.

THE END.

October, 1896.

MR. EDWARD ARNOLD'S

New Books and Announcements.

LONDON: 37 BEDFORD STREET.
NEW YORK: 70 FIFTH AVENUE.

THE ADVENTURES OF MY LIFE.

By HENRI ROCHEFORT.

The authorised English edition, revised and specially arranged by M. ROCHEFORT, and translated under his personal supervision by E. W. SMITH, editor of the *Daily Messenger* in Paris.

In two volumes, large crown 8vo., 25s.

In this work M. Henri Rochefort tells the amazing story of his adventurous life. Among the more important episodes are the author's personal narrative of the French Commune, his subsequent transportation to the penal settlement of New Caledonia, his marvellous escape, his numerous duels, his residence in England, and his deeply interesting journalistic ventures.

The work is appearing in five volumes in French, but M. Rochefort has decided to prepare a special and, in many respects, original version in English for sale in this country; he has reduced the bulk of the work to two handy volumes, by omitting much that is of purely local interest, and selecting only such of his adventures as will appeal to English-speaking readers. Apart from the value of the matter, the brilliance of M. Rochefort's style is notorious, and his strong personality penetrates every page of the work. The translation is being undertaken in Paris by Mr. E. W. Smith, editor of the *Daily Messenger*, in daily communication with the author.

THROUGH UNKNOWN AFRICAN COUNTRIES.

The First Expedition from Somaliland to Lake Rudolf and Lamu.

A Narrative of Scientific Exploration and Sporting Adventures.

By A. DONALDSON SMITH, M.D., F.R.G.S.,

Hon. Member of the Academy of Natural Sciences, Philadelphia.

With nearly 30 full-page Plates and a large number of smaller Illustrations, drawn from the author's Photographs and Sketches by A. D. McCORMICK, CHARLES WHYMPER, etc.

Large 8vo., One Guinea.

The body of the work is occupied by the narrative of the expedition, and its valuable scientific results are given in a series of Appendices to be contributed by such eminent specialists as Dr. Bowdler Sharpe, Dr. Günther, Dr. Gregory, Mr. Boulenger, Mr. Pocock, Dr. Holland, and others.

Dr. Donaldson Smith arrived at Berbera, on the coast of Somaliland, about Midsummer, 1894. During a previous expedition undertaken for sporting purposes in Somaliland, he had conceived the plan of penetrating into the unknown interior of the Dark Continent and forcing his way to Lake Rudolf. The present volume tells how he was enabled to achieve his object after just a year's march, beset by constant dangers and difficulties that would have proved fatal to a less hardy or persevering explorer. From Lake Rudolf Dr. Donaldson Smith made his way to the east coast at Lamu, by which time he had marched no less than four thousand miles.

Dr. Smith found it necessary to take with him the considerable force of eighty armed men, for self-defence in case of attack by the savage tribes of the interior, and on more than one occasion the force was called into action in a most exciting manner. The party experienced all kinds of hardships and perils, but nothing was allowed to interfere with the scientific objects of the expedition, although sport, both for its own sake and for purposes of food supply, filled an important place in the plans.

Valuable collections were made of plants, birds, insects, geological specimens, and ethnographical curiosities, by which the great museums of America and Europe have been sensibly enriched. Dr. Donaldson Smith discovered a town in which there were stone houses and beautiful shrines, in regions where only mud huts were supposed to exist. He came into prolonged contact with the warlike Abyssinians, and was even the recipient of an autograph letter from the Emperor Menelek. His journey took him through some of the loveliest scenery in the world.

IN AND BEYOND THE HIMALAYAS.
A Record of Sport and Travel in the Abode of Snow.

By S. J. STONE,

Late Deputy Inspector-General of Police, Western Circle North-West Provinces of India.

With 16 full-page Illustrations by CHARLES WHYMPER. Demy 8vo., 16s.

The author of this work has spent many years in India, and gives the record of several expeditions made for purposes of sport and exploration combined. He travelled through a great deal of practically unknown country in the Himalayas and borders of Tibet, and gives much valuable information about the scenes and people met with in the course of the journeys. The sporting incidents are exciting and graphically described, including the successful chase of nearly all the varieties of big game to be found in the regions traversed.

The book will be splendidly illustrated by Mr. Charles Whymper.

FIFTY YEARS' REMINISCENCES OF INDIA.

By LIEUT.-COLONEL W. POLLOK,

Late Madras Staff Corps,

Author of 'Sport in Burmah,' etc.

With 16 full-page Illustrations by A. C. CORBOULD. Demy 8vo., 16s.

Colonel Pollok's reminiscences go back as far as the old 'Company' days, when he first went out to India as a cadet. All through his long career he has had a succession of exciting adventures by flood and field, and has witnessed an immense variety of interesting and amusing episodes. He is a good hand at telling a good story, and the book fairly bristles with anecdotes. Considerable space is allotted to sporting recollections, and the author has had such hair-breadth escapes and such excellent luck in his pursuit of big game that he presents a record difficult to surpass.

THROUGH THE SUB-ARCTIC FOREST.

A Record of a Canoe Journey for 4,000 miles, from Fort Wrangel to the Pelly Lakes, and down the Yukon to the Behring Sea.

By WARBURTON PIKE,

Author of 'The Barren Grounds of Canada.'

With Illustrations by CHARLES WHYMPER, from Photographs taken by the Author, and a Map. Demy 8vo., 16s.

THROUGH THE SUB-ARCTIC FOREST—*Continued*.

Mr. Pike is well known as an explorer, and in the journey now described he traversed some completely unknown country round the Pelly Lakes. For many months he supported himself entirely by hunting and fishing, being absolutely cut off from any chance of obtaining supplies. Such a journey could not fail to be productive of many exciting episodes, and though the author treats them lightly, the hardships he went through form a fine test of the true explorer's spirit.

The Sportsman's Library.

Edited by Sir HERBERT MAXWELL, Bart., M.P.

This series will consist of a selection from the best works of past writers on sport, carefully chosen either on account of their literary merit, of the light thrown by them on the habits and resources of a bygone age, or of their permanent value as contributions to knowledge of the various subjects dealt with.

The volumes will be issued at the rate of two or three a year. They will contain in every instance an introductory chapter by the Editor, and such notes as may be necessary to explain or correct the author's statements.

Illustrations in the original works, when of sufficient merit or interest, will be reproduced in facsimile, supplemented with new ones by the modern artists best qualified to deal with the various subjects. Among the artists whose co-operation has already been secured are Messrs. G. E. Lodge, J. G. Millais, A. Thorburn, C. Whymper, G. H. Jalland, A. C. Corbould, P. Chenevix Trench, etc.

The size of the volumes will be a handsome 8vo., and special care will be bestowed upon every detail of paper, print, and binding. The following will be published this season:

THE LIFE OF A FOX.

By THOMAS SMITH,
Master of the Hambledon and Pytchley Hounds.

With Illustrations by the Author and SIX COLOURED PLATES by G. H. JALLAND.

Large 8vo., handsomely bound, 15s.

Also a limited Large-paper Edition, two guineas net.

This volume will contain both of Smith's published works—'The Life of a Fox' and 'The Diary of a Huntsman.' The author's reputation as a huntsman, as well as his gift of literary expression and his skill as a spirited draughtsman, made these books exceedingly popular in their day, and they have now become very rare.

The Sportsman's Library—Continued.

A SPORTING TOUR THROUGH THE NORTHERN PARTS OF ENGLAND, AND GREAT PART OF THE HIGHLANDS OF SCOTLAND.

By Colonel T. THORNTON, of Thornville Royal, in Yorkshire.

With a selection from the original illustrations by Garrard, portraits of the Author, and new plates by G. E. Lodge, F. C. Bennett, and others.

Large 8vo., handsomely bound, 15s.

Also a limited Large-paper Edition, two guineas net.

This work, published in 1804, and reviewed the next year by Sir Walter Scott in the *Edinburgh Review*, has never been reprinted. It is extremely interesting, not only on account of the graphic descriptions of shooting, hawking, and angling, but because of the author's shrewd observations on the state of society and manners, and his sympathetic description of scenery.

THE SPORTSMAN IN IRELAND.

By COSMOPOLITE.

With numerous illustrations and coloured plates by P. CHENEVIX TRENCH.

NEW AND CHEAPER EDITION.

A LITTLE TOUR IN IRELAND.

By 'OXONIAN'
(The Very Rev. S. REYNOLDS HOLE).

With nearly forty Illustrations by JOHN LEECH.

Large crown 8vo., 6s.

This famous book being now entirely out of print, a new edition, containing all the original plates, has been prepared, and will be issued at a popular price, in order that it may take its share in the good work of promoting a better acquaintance with the charms of the Emerald Isle. John Leech and his friend 'Oxonian' could not, it is true, foresee the birth of the Irish Tourist Association: but the inimitable pencil of the artist and the genial pen of the Dean of Rochester have helped in no small degree to familiarize the English public with the numberless attractions of Ireland and its laughter-loving people.

THE CHANCES OF DEATH;
AND OTHER STUDIES IN EVOLUTION.

By KARL PEARSON, F.R.S.,
Author of 'The Ethic of Free Thought,' etc.

With Illustrations and Diagrams. Demy 8vo., 16s.

This is the first substantial work published by Professor Pearson since his well-known 'Ethic of Free Thought' appeared some years ago. The volume contains several scientific essays dealing with Chance in various aspects, from the Chances of Death to so-called Games of Chance, and points out how far mathematical theory corresponds with actual results. Another series of papers discusses problems of deep interest in connection with Woman and Labour, while a third section deals with important problems of modern political progress.

HABIT AND INSTINCT.
A Study in Heredity.

By C. LLOYD MORGAN,
Author of 'Animal Life and Intelligence,' 'The Springs of Conduct,' etc.

Demy 8vo., 16s.

In the winter of 1895-96 Professor Lloyd Morgan delivered the series of 'Lowell Lectures' which form the basis of this work. The subject is one which has been the author's special study for many years, and in the present volume he has given the mature result of his researches.

SUMMARY OF CONTENTS.

I. Preliminary Definitions and Illustrations.—II., IV. Observations on Young Birds.—V. Observations on Young Mammals.—VI. On the Relation of Consciousness to Instinct and to Habit.—VII. On the Relation of Intelligence to the Acquisition of Habits.—VIII. On Imitation.—IX. On the Emotions in their Relation to Instinct.—X. On some Habits and Instincts of the Pairing Season.—XI. On the Instincts of Nest-building, Incubation, and Migration.—XII. On the Relation of Organic to Mental Evolution.—XIII. Are Acquired Habits inherited?—XIV. On Modification and Variation.—XV. Habit and Instinct in Man.

THE RELIGIONS OF INDIA.

By EDWARD WASHBURN HOPKINS, Ph.D. (Leipzig),
Professor of Sanskrit and Comparative Philology in Bryn Mawr College, U.S.A.

Over 600 pages, demy 8vo., 8s. 6d. net.

This is the first volume of an important series entitled 'Handbooks on the History of Religions.' Among the other volumes now in course of preparation are those dealing with the religions of (ii.) Babylonia and Persia, (iii.) the Ancient Teutons, (iv.) Persia, (vi.) Egypt, (vii.) Israel.

THE PLANT-LORE AND GARDEN-CRAFT OF SHAKESPEARE.

By HENRY N. ELLACOMBE, M.A., Vicar of Bitton,
Author of 'In a Gloucestershire Garden,' etc.

Fully illustrated by Major E. BENGOUGH RICKETTS.

Large crown 8vo., handsomely bound, 10s. 6d.

This is a new edition of a book originally issued for private circulation, which has now been long out of print. It was spoken of by the *Spectator* as 'a work which is entitled from its worth to a place in every Shakespearian library,' and efforts have been made in the present edition to give the text an adequate adornment.

The volume is a complete and standard work of reference on the plants mentioned by Shakespeare. Canon Ellacombe takes each plant separately, and gives interesting particulars of its life-history and its place in legend and poetry. The illustrations by Major Ricketts are very beautiful and characteristic of the work. The artist has made a special visit to Stratford-on-Avon to sketch the scenes of Shakespeare's Garden-Lore, and has also depicted many of the plants named with great skill.

A BOOK ABOUT ROSES.

By the Very Rev. S. REYNOLDS HOLE, Dean of Rochester,
Author of 'A Book about the Garden,' 'A Little Tour in Ireland,' etc.

Illustrated by H. G. MOON and G. ELGOOD.

The Presentation Edition, with coloured plates, etc., handsomely bound, 10s. 6d.; Popular Edition, with frontispiece, 3s. 6d.

The call for a fifteenth edition of this popular work has enabled Dean Hole to thoroughly revise and largely to rewrite the book, bringing the information in it well up to date. Advantage has also been taken of the opportunity to respond to the frequently-expressed wishes of many admirers of the book for a more handsome and illustrated edition; it has, therefore, been reprinted, and beautifully COLOURED PLATES have been drawn by Mr. H. G. Moon, while Mr. G. Elgood contributes charming black-and-white pictures. There is also a facsimile of a sketch by John Leech given to Dean Hole, and never before published.

The book will be issued in two forms: (1) with the coloured plates, etc., at half a guinea; and (2) with frontispiece, at 3s. 6d.

OLD ENGLISH GLASSES.

An Account of Glass Drinking-Vessels in England from Early Times to the end of the Eighteenth Century. With Introductory Notices of Continental Glasses during the same period, Original Documents, etc.

By ALBERT HARTSHORNE,
Fellow of the Society of Antiquaries.

Illustrated by upwards of 50 full-page Tinted Plates in the best style of Lithography, and several hundred outline Illustrations in the text. Super royal 4to., price Three Guineas net.

The plates and outline illustrations are prepared for reproduction by Mr. W. S. Weatherly and Mr. R. Paul respectively, from full-size or scale drawings by the author of the actual drinking-vessels in nearly every instance. The text will be printed in the finest style, and the lithographic work executed by Messrs. W. Griggs and Son. The volume is now in the press, and will, it is hoped, be ready for delivery before the end of the year. The First Edition will be limited to One Thousand Copies at Three Guineas net.

NOTE.—A full prospectus, giving a complete account of the principal contents of this elaborate and magnificent work, which treats of a subject never before comprehensively undertaken for England, can be had post free on application.

A TREASURY OF MINOR BRITISH POETRY.

Selected and arranged, with Notes, by J. CHURTON COLLINS.
Crown 8vo., 7s. 6d.

In compiling this volume Mr. Churton Collins has been influenced by a desire to form a collection of poetry containing many charming pieces hitherto ignored in similar works. It is believed that compilers of anthologies have confined themselves too much to a few standard authors, and that there are a number of less known writers who have composed one or two poems quite as fine as anything by the great masters. The present selection will reveal a mine of hitherto unsuspected treasures to many lovers of English Poetry.

EARLY ENGLISH FURNITURE.

An Account of the Famous English Cabinet-makers,
With numerous fine Illustrations of their Work.
By Mrs. WARREN CLOUSTON.
1 vol., crown 4to.

Mr. Edward Arnold's List.

THE CRUISE OF THE 'ANTARCTIC'

TO THE SOUTH POLAR REGIONS.

By H. J. BULL,

A Member of the Expedition.

With frontispiece by W. L. WYLLIE, A.R.A., and numerous full-page illustrations by W. G. BURN-MURDOCH.

Demy 8vo., 15s.

'The book is one of adventure in another besides the commercial sense, and as a record of Antarctic exploration one of the most attractive in print.'—*Daily News*.

'In reading his narrative we feel none of the *ennui* and worry of the voyage. The author's fun lightens up in a most welcome way a tale which has in it much that is intrinsically interesting.'—*Scotsman*.

PERSIA REVISITED.

With Remarks on H.I.M. Mozuffer-ed-Din Shah, and the Present Situation in Persia (1896).

By General Sir T. E. GORDON, K.C.I.E., C.B., C.S.I.,

Formerly Military Attaché and Oriental Secretary to the British Legation at Teheran,

Author of 'The Roof of the World,' etc.

Demy 8vo., with full-page illustrations, 10s. 6d.

'A book replete with first-hand knowledge, and one that must for the present be regarded as indispensable to an adequate acquaintance with the condition and prospects of Persia.'—*Aberdeen Free Press*.

THE EARLY CHARTERED COMPANIES,

A.D. 1296-1858.

By GEORGE CAWSTON, Barrister-at-Law,

AND

A. H. KEANE, F.R.G.S.

Large crown 8vo., with frontispiece, 10s. 6d.

'Mr. Cawston claims to have lighted on an almost unexplored field of research, and it must be conceded that his volume furnishes a great deal of interesting information which without its aid must for the most part have been sought for in sources not accessible to ordinary readers.'—*Daily News*.

THE EXPLORATION OF THE CAUCASUS.

By DOUGLAS W. FRESHFIELD,

Lately President of the Alpine Club, and Honorary Secretary of the Royal Geographical Society.

With Contributions by H. W. HOLDER, J. G. COCKIN, H. WOOLLEY, M. DE DÉCHY, and Prof. BONNEY, D.Sc., F.R.S.

Illustrated by 3 Panoramas, 74 Full-page Photogravures, about 140 Illustrations in the text, chiefly from Photographs by VITTORIO SELLA, and 4 Original Maps, including the first authentic map of the Caucasus specially prepared from unpublished sources by Mr. FRESHFIELD.

In two volumes, large 4to., 600 pages, Three Guineas net.

'We can only say, in a word, that a more interesting, more vivid, more conscientious, more exhaustive, and in parts more thrilling, account of a region as yet comparatively unknown has never come before us. No record of exploration has ever been published in this country in so splendid a material form, and, beyond contradiction, no pictures of mountains to illustrate the exploits of climbers have approached the very numerous photographs of Signor Sella.'—*Daily Chronicle.*

'Mr. Freshfield's work on the Caucasus is not merely the most important mountaineering book of the year, but probably the most important that has been published since the time of Tyndall and Ball. Every part of Mr. Freshfield's book is solid, and will remain permanently valuable. It brings within two volumes the record of everything that has been done and the substance of everything that has been learnt during the first twenty-eight years of Caucasian exploration by expert climbers.'—*Manchester Guardian.*

'Two superb volumes. No book of travel or exploration within our remembrance has disclosed such a wealth of illustration as the one now before us, in which are depicted every Caucasian range and mountain of any moment with perfect clearness and sharpness. There is not one blurred photograph or drawing in the whole collection. Nothing has been omitted that could impart completeness to this magnificent work.'—*Daily Telegraph.*

'What singles these magnificent volumes out on a very brief inspection from all climbing literature is that for once the illustrations are worthy of the text. If the publishers had done nothing beyond giving us these magnificent reproductions from the cameras which Signor Sella and others have carried upwards of 16,000 feet above the sea, they would still be entitled to our praise and gratitude. Mr. Freshfield has given us truly one of the most delightful and inspiring works upon the "everlasting hills" which any library can hold, and it is produced and illustrated with a sumptuousness which it is a pleasure to find so well bestowed.'—*Birmingham Post.*

'The two volumes are "great," not only from the prosaic standpoint of measurement and avoirdupois, but pre-eminently so in the more meritorious sense of representing infinite labour in the amassing of materials at first hand, and high literary and artistic skill in blending letterpress and photography in a way calculated to extort the admiration even of the most stoical reader.'—*Liverpool Post.*

'A princely example of British scholarship.'—*Glasgow Herald.*

'Enough, perhaps, has been said in recommendation of these volumes, which are instructive without being didactic, full of novel information without any suggestion of guide-book literature, which contain most graphic descriptions of the scenery, without ever descending to word-painting, and which contrive to impart freshness even to the well-worn theme of mountain and glacier expeditions. It would be difficult to praise too highly the map. Only a few in this country will be able to appreciate the geographical knowledge and the infinite labour that the construction of this map must have cost. For the first time the topography of this great mountain-chain from Elbruz to Kasbek is laid down in its entirety with accuracy, and the extent of the glacial system is clearly demonstrated on a scale of about 2½ miles to one inch.'—Mr. CLINTON DENT, in *The Daily News.*

FOURTH EDITION.

FIRE AND SWORD IN THE SUDAN.

A Personal Narrative of Fighting and Serving the Dervishes, 1879-1895.

By SLATIN PASHA, Colonel in the Egyptian Army, formerly Governor and Commandant of the Troops in Darfur.

Translated and Edited by Major F. R. WINGATE, R.A., D.S.O.,
Author of 'Mahdiism and the Egyptian Soudan,' etc.

Fully Illustrated by R. TALBOT KELLY.

Royal 8vo., One Guinea net.

'Whether Slatin's work is more important and attractive as a powerful exhortation on a subject of the greatest political importance and of special national significance from the noble English blood spilt in the Sudan, or as a chapter of human experience wherein truth far surpassed fiction in hair-breadth escapes and deeds of daring beyond what seemed possible, it would be difficult to decide; but the whole result is one that places this volume on a shelf of its own, not merely as the book of the day, but as the authority for all time on the great Mahommedan upheaval in the Sudan, which was accompanied by an amount of human slaughter and suffering that defies calculation.'—*Times.*

'It would be hard to name a fictitious narrative of more thrilling interest than this true story of Colonel Slatin Pasha's captivity in the Sudan and escape from the terrors which have marked the rule of the atrocious Khalifa Abdullahi.'—*Standard.*

'Here is a work on matters of contemporary fact, which for romance, colour, adventure, and complexity and intensity of human feeling, outdoes many a novel by the masters of the art of fiction.'—*St. James's Gazette.*

'Absolutely unique. Were we to try to extract, or even notice, all the striking things in this book, we should fill our paper.'—*Spectator.*

'Told with a vividness and vigour that will carry you away.'—*Truth.*

'The story told in this work is one of enthralling interest. In the whole modern literature of travel and adventure we cannot call to mind a work so absorbing as this.'—*Manchester Guardian.*

'An exceedingly fascinating and engaging book, which is not surpassed in interest by any other of the kind that has been published for many years. It is written with rare ability and force. The narrative throughout is vivid, graphic, and picturesque, abounding in dramatic incident and striking character.'—*Leeds Mercury.*

'One of the most interesting books of the year, or, indeed, of the past decade.'—*Daily Telegraph.*

'The story of the experiences of Slatin Pasha as a ruler, a soldier, and a captive in the Sudan is one of the most striking romances of modern times. The return of this distinguished officer, after a disappearance of eleven years and more, from what Father Ohrwalder with bitter recollections calls a "living grave," and the perilous incidents of his escape and flight, form in themselves an extraordinary tale. But the interest of the book is much increased by the importance which, in the minds of English people, attaches to the melancholy events in which he bore a part, and by the narrative in which this witness risen from the dead reopens the story of the great tragedy of Khartoum.'—*Speaker.*

WAGNER'S HEROINES.
BRUNNHILDA—SENTA—ISOLDA.
By CONSTANCE MAUD,
Author of 'Wagner's Heroes.'
Illustrated by J. W. MAUD. Crown 8vo., 5s.

SECOND EDITION.
WAGNER'S HEROES.
PARSIFAL—TANNHAUSER—LOHENGRIN—HANS SACHS.
By CONSTANCE MAUD.
Illustrated by GRANVILLE FELL. Crown 8vo., 5s.

'Miss Maud has done for the Shakespeare of music what Charles Lamb once did for the real Shakespeare.'—*Daily Telegraph.*

'Constance Maud has elected to convey into simple language the histories of "Wagner's Heroes," and has succeeded admirably.'—*Black and White.*

NEW AND POPULAR EDITION.
SEVENTY YEARS OF IRISH LIFE.
By the late W. R. LE FANU. Crown 8vo., 6s.

'It will delight all readers—English and Scotch no less than Irish, Nationalists no less than Unionists, Roman Catholics no less than Orangemen.'—*Times.*

FIFTY LUNCHES.
By COLONEL KENNEY HERBERT,
Author of 'Common-Sense Cookery,' etc.
Crown 8vo., cloth, 2s. 6d.

FANCY DRESSES DESCRIBED.
By ARDERN HOLT.
An Alphabetical Dictionary of Fancy Costumes.

With full accounts of the Dresses. About 60 Illustrations by LILLIAN YOUNG. Many of them coloured. One vol., demy 8vo.

A TEXT-BOOK OF NURSING FOR HOME AND HOSPITAL USE.
By C. WEEKS SHAW.

Revised and largely re-written by W. RADFORD, House Surgeon at the Poplar Hospital, under the supervision of Sir DYCE DUCKWORTH, M.D., F.R.C.P. Fully illustrated, crown 8vo.

NEW FICTION.

A RELUCTANT EVANGELIST,
AND OTHER STORIES.

By ALICE SPINNER,

Author of 'Lucilla,' 'A Study in Colour,' etc.

Crown 8vo., 6s.

INTERLUDES.

By MAUD OXENDEN.

Crown 8vo., 6s.

THE BAYONET THAT CAME HOME.

By N. WYNNE WILLIAMS,

Author of 'Tales of Modern Greece.'

Crown 8vo., 3s. 6d.

New Work by the Author of 'Into the Highways and Hedges.'

WORTH WHILE.

By F. F. MONTRÉSOR,

Author of 'Into the Highways and Hedges,' 'The One who looked on,' etc.

One vol., crown 8vo., cloth, 2s. 6d.

'Two most pathetic and beautiful stories make up this little volume. The writer is to be congratulated on the delicate beauty of her stories.'—*Liverpool Mercury.*

'Both the stories in this volume are of very superior quality. The characters are distinctly original, and the workmanship is admirable.'—*Glasgow Herald.*

RECENT WORKS OF FICTION.

(*See also p.* 23.)

A New Story by the Author of 'The Red Badge of Courage.'

GEORGE'S MOTHER.

By STEPHEN CRANE.

Author of 'The Red Badge of Courage,' etc.

Cloth, 2s.

'In his latest work Stephen Crane scores heavily. It is a swatch torn from the great web of city life, a picture in which every touch reveals the true literary workman. Its pathos grips the heart close; its characters are to the life, and here and there are caught gleams of humour that complete the symmetry of the pages. The already enviable reputation of the author of "The Red Badge of Courage" will be heightened by this small volume.'—*Aberdeen Free Press.*

HADJIRA.

A Turkish Love Story.

By 'ADALET.'

One vol., crown 8vo., cloth, 6s.

'Certainly one of the most interesting and valuable works of fiction issued from the press for a long time past. Even if we were to regard the book as an ordinary novel, we could commend it heartily; but its great value lies in the fact that it reveals to us a hidden world, and does so with manifest fidelity. But the reader must learn for himself the lesson which this remarkable and fascinating book teaches.'—*Speaker.*

'One of the best stories of the season.'—*Daily Chronicle.*

By the Author of 'The Apotheosis of Mr. Tyrawley.'

A MASK AND A MARTYR.

By E. LIVINGSTON PRESCOTT,

One vol., crown 8vo., cloth, 6s.

'A story which, once read, will never be forgotten.'—*Manchester Guardian.*

'This is an undeniably clever book. A picture of self-sacrifice so complete and so enduring is a rare picture in fiction, and has rarely been more ably or more finely drawn. This singular and pathetic story is told all through with remarkable restraint, and shows a strength and skill of execution which place its author high among the novel-writers of the day.'—*Westminster Gazette.*

THE BONDWOMAN.

A Story of the Northmen in Lakeland.

By W. G. COLLINGWOOD,

Author of 'Thorstein of the Mere,' 'The Life and Work of John Ruskin,' etc.

Cloth, 16mo., 3s. 6d.

'As for the thrilling details of the plot, and the other sterling charms of the little work, we must refer our readers to its pages, especially those of them who may be touring, or contemplating a tour, in Westmorland and Cumberland.'—*Leeds Mercury.*

NEW BOOKS FOR YOUNG PEOPLE.
(See also p. 26.)

HOW DICK AND MOLLY SAW ENGLAND.
By M. H. CORNWALL LEGH,
Author of 'How Dick and Molly went Round the World.'
With numerous full-page Illustrations.
Crown 4to., 5s.

TWO NEW BOOKS BY KIRK MUNROE.

SNOW-SHOES AND SLEDGES.
A Sequel to 'The Fur Seal's Tooth.'
By KIRK MUNROE.
Finely Illustrated, 5s.

RICK DALE.
By KIRK MUNROE.
Finely Illustrated, 5s.

TWO NEW VOLUMES OF THE CHILDREN'S HOUR SERIES.

THE PALACE ON THE MOOR.
By E. DAVENPORT ADAMS.
With full-page Illustrations, 2s. 6d.

TOBY'S PROMISE.
By A. M. HOPKINSON,
With full-page Illustrations, 2s. 6d.

Other Volumes in the Children's Hour Series.

MASTER MAGNUS.
By Mrs. E. M. FIELD.
With full-page Illustrations, 2s. 6d.

MY DOG PLATO.
By M. H. CORNWALL LEGH.
With full-page Illustrations, 2s. 6d.

TWO NEW VOLUMES OF THE CHILDREN'S FAVOURITE SERIES.

Each fully Illustrated, price 2s. ; gilt edges, 2s. 6d.

MY BOOK OF HEROISM.
MY BOOK OF INVENTIONS.

NEW AND CHEAPER EDITIONS.

GREAT PUBLIC SCHOOLS.

ETON.	HARROW.	WINCHESTER.
RUGBY.	WESTMINSTER.	MARLBOROUGH.
CHELTENHAM.	HAILEYBURY.	CLIFTON.
	CHARTERHOUSE.	

With nearly One Hundred fine Illustrations by the best artists.

Large imperial 16mo., cloth gilt, 3s. 6d.

'As to the suitability of the book for prize or present there can be no two opinions. We cordially recommend it to the notice of headmasters.'—*Educational Review.*

TALES FROM HANS ANDERSEN.

With over Thirty original Illustrations by E. A. LEMANN.

A beautiful volume, 4to., 3s. 6d.

'Miss Lemann has entered into the spirit of these most delightful of fairy tales, and makes the book specially attractive by its dainty and descriptive illustrations.'—*Saturday Review.*

'A very enchanting gift book for young people, Hans Andersen's delightful and ever-new stories being illustrated with rare grace and charm.'—*Lady's Pictorial.*

THE SNOW QUEEN,
And Other Tales from Hans Andersen.

With over Thirty original Illustrations by E. A. LEMANN.

Uniform with the above volume, 3s. 6d.

'The success which attended the publication, last year, of the first series of Hans Andersen's Fairy Tales, has led to an issue of a fresh series, illustrated by the same artist. So we have again a most exquisite book.'—*Spectator.*

THE BATTLES OF FREDERICK THE GREAT.

Extracted from Carlyle's History of Frederick the Great, and Edited by

CYRIL RANSOME, M.A.,

Professor of History at the Yorkshire College, Leeds.

With numerous Illustrations by ADOLPH MENZEL.

Square 8vo., 3s. 6d.

'Carlyle's battle-pieces are models of care and of picturesque writing, and it was a happy thought to disinter them from the bulk of the "History of Frederick." The illustrations are very spirited.'—*Journal of Education.*

TRAVEL, SPORT, AND EXPLORATION.

Balfour—TWELVE HUNDRED MILES IN A WAGGON. A Narrative of a Journey in Cape Colony, the Transvaal, and the Chartered Company's Territories. By ALICE BLANCHE BALFOUR. With nearly forty original Illustrations from Sketches by the Author, and a Map. Second edition. Demy 8vo., cloth, 16s.

'A charming record of a most interesting journey.'—*Spectator*.

Beynon—WITH KELLY TO CHITRAL. By Lieutenant W. G. L. BEYNON, D.S.O., 3rd Goorkha Rifles, Staff Officer to Colonel Kelly with the Relief Force. With Maps, Plans, and Illustrations. Second edition. Demy 8vo., 7s. 6d.

Bull—THE CRUISE OF THE ANTARCTIC. (*See page* 9.)

Colvile—THE LAND OF THE NILE SPRINGS. By Colonel Sir HENRY COLVILE, K.C.M.G., C.B., recently British Commissioner in Uganda. With Photogravure Frontispiece, 16 full-page Illustrations and 2 Maps. Demy 8vo., 16s.

'One of the most faithful and entertaining books of adventure that has appeared since Burton's days.'—*National Observer*.

Custance—RIDING RECOLLECTIONS AND TURF STORIES. By HENRY CUSTANCE, three times winner of the Derby. One vol., crown 8vo., cloth, 2s. 6d.

Freshfield—EXPLORATION OF THE CAUCASUS. (*See page* 10.)

Gordon—PERSIA REVISITED. (*See page* 9.)

Hole—A LITTLE TOUR IN AMERICA. By the Very Rev. S. REYNOLDS HOLE, Dean of Rochester, Author of 'The Memories of Dean Hole,' 'A Book about Roses,' etc. With numerous Illustrations. Demy 8vo., 16s.

Hole—A LITTLE TOUR IN IRELAND. (*See page* 5.)

Maxwell—THE SPORTSMAN'S LIBRARY. (*See page* 4.)

Pike—THROUGH THE SUB-ARCTIC FOREST. (*See page* 3.)

Pollok — FIFTY YEARS' REMINISCENCES OF INDIA. (*See page* 3.)

Portal—THE BRITISH MISSION TO UGANDA. By the late Sir GERALD PORTAL, K.C.M.G. Edited by RENNELL RODD, C.M.G. With an Introduction by the Right Honourable Lord CROMER, G.C.M.G. Illustrated from photos taken during the Expedition by Colonel RHODES. Demy 8vo., 21s.

Portal—MY MISSION TO ABYSSINIA. By the late Sir GERALD H. PORTAL, C.B. With Map and Illustrations. Demy 8vo., 15s.

Slatin—FIRE AND SWORD IN THE SUDAN. (*See page* 11.)

Smith—THROUGH UNKNOWN AFRICAN COUNTRIES. (*See page* 2.)

Stone—IN AND BEYOND THE HIMALAYAS. (*See page* 3.)

AMERICAN SPORT AND TRAVEL.

These books, selected from the Catalogue of MESSRS. RAND MCNALLY & CO., *the well-known publishers of Chicago, have been placed in* MR. EDWARD ARNOLD'S *hands under the impression that many British Travellers and Sportsmen may find them useful before starting on expeditions in the United States.*

Aldrich—ARCTIC ALASKA AND SIBERIA; or, Eight Months with the Arctic Whalemen. By HERBERT L. ALDRICH. Crown 8vo., cloth, 4s. 6d.

AMERICAN GAME FISHES. Their Habits, Habitat, and Peculiarities; How, When, and Where to Angle for them. By various Writers. Cloth, 10s. 6d.

Higgins—NEW GUIDE TO THE PACIFIC COAST. Santa Fé Route. By C. A. HIGGINS. Crown 8vo., cloth, 4s. 6d.

Leffingwell—THE ART OF WING-SHOOTING. A Practical Treatise on the Use of the Shot-gun. By W. B. LEFFINGWELL. With numerous Illustrations. Crown 8vo., cloth, 4s. 6d.

Shields—CAMPING AND CAMP OUTFITS. By G. O. SHIELDS ('Coquina'). Containing also Chapters on Camp Medicine, Cookery, and How to Load a Packhorse. Crown 8vo., cloth, 5s.

Shields—THE AMERICAN BOOK OF THE DOG. By various Writers. Edited by G. O. SHIELDS ('Coquina'). Cloth, 15s.

Thomas—SWEDEN AND THE SWEDES. By WILLIAM WIDGERY THOMAS, Jun., United States Minister to Sweden and Norway. With numerous Illustrations. Cloth, 16s.

HISTORY AND BIOGRAPHY.

Benson and Tatham—MEN OF MIGHT. Studies of Great Characters. By A. C. BENSON, M.A., and H. F. W. TATHAM, M.A., Assistant Masters at Eton College. Second Edition. Crown 8vo., cloth, 3s. 6d.

Boyle—THE RECOLLECTIONS OF THE DEAN OF SALISBURY. By the Very Rev. G. D. BOYLE, Dean of Salisbury. With Photogravure Portrait. 1 vol., demy 8vo., cloth, 16s.

Cawston and Keane—THE EARLY CHARTERED COMPANIES. (*See page 9.*)

Fowler—ECHOES OF OLD COUNTY LIFE. Recollections of Sport, Society, Politics, and Farming in the Good Old Times. By J. K. FOWLER, of Aylesbury. Second Edition, with numerous Illustrations, 8vo., 10s. 6d. Also a large-paper edition, of 200 copies only, 21s. net.

'A very entertaining volume of reminiscences, full of good stories.'—*Truth.*

Hare—MARIA EDGEWORTH: her Life and Letters. Edited by AUGUSTUS J. C. HARE, Author of 'The Story of Two Noble Lives,' etc. Two vols., crown 8vo., with Portraits, 16s. net.

'Mr. Hare has written more than one good book in his time, but he has never produced anything nearly so entertaining and valuable as his latest contribution to biography and literature.'—*Saturday Review.*

Hole—THE MEMORIES OF DEAN HOLE. By the Very Rev. S. REYNOLDS HOLE, Dean of Rochester. With the original Illustrations from sketches by LEECH and THACKERAY. New Edition, twelfth thousand, one vol., crown 8vo., 6s.

'One of the most delightful collections of reminiscences that this generation has seen.'—*Daily Chronicle.*

Hole—MORE MEMORIES: Being Thoughts about England Spoken in America. By the Very Rev. S. REYNOLDS HOLE, Dean of Rochester. With Frontispiece. Demy 8vo., 16s.

'Full alike of contagious fun and mature wisdom.'—*Daily Chronicle.*

Hopkins—THE RELIGIONS OF INDIA. (*See page* 6.)

Kay—OMARAH'S HISTORY OF YAMAN. The Arabic Text, edited, with a translation, by HENRY CASSELS KAY, Member of the Royal Asiatic Society. Demy 8vo., cloth, 17s. 6d. net.

Knight-Bruce—MEMORIES OF MASHONALAND By the Right Rev. Bishop KNIGHT BRUCE, formerly Bishop of Mashonaland. 8vo., 10s. 6d.

'To review this book fully is impossible, as there is not a single page devoid of interest, and all those who take an interest in South African affairs should not fail to read it. The concluding chapter of the Matabele War is quite as good as the previous ones.'—*Pall Mall Gazette.*

Lecky—THE POLITICAL VALUE OF HISTORY. By W. E. H. LECKY, D.C.L., LL.D. An Address delivered at the Midland Institute, reprinted with additions. Crown 8vo., cloth, 2s. 6d.

Le Fanu—SEVENTY YEARS OF IRISH LIFE. (*See page* 12.)

Macdonald—THE MEMOIRS OF THE LATE SIR JOHN A. MACDONALD, G.C.B., First Prime Minister of Canada. Edited by JOSEPH POPE, his Private Secretary. With Portraits. Two vols., demy 8vo., 32s.

Milner—ENGLAND IN EGYPT. By Sir ALFRED MILNER, K.C.B. Popular Edition, with Map, and full details of the British position and responsibilities, 7s. 6d.

Milner—ARNOLD TOYNBEE. A Reminiscence. By Sir ALFRED MILNER, K.C.B., Author of 'England in Egypt.' Crown 8vo., buckram, 2s. 6d.; paper, 1s.

Oman—A HISTORY OF ENGLAND. By CHARLES OMAN, Fellow of All Souls' College, and Lecturer in History at New College, Oxford; Author of 'Warwick the Kingmaker,' 'A History of Greece,' etc. Crown 8vo., cloth, 4s. 6d. net.

'This is the nearest approach to the ideal School History of England which has yet been written.'—*Guardian.*

Pilkington — IN AN ETON PLAYING FIELD. The Adventures of some old Public School Boys in East London. By E. M. S. PILKINGTON. Fcap. 8vo., handsomely bound, 2s. 6d.

Pulitzer — THE ROMANCE OF PRINCE EUGENE. An Idyll under Napoleon the First. By ALBERT PULITZER. With numerous Photogravure Illustrations. Two vols., demy 8vo., 21s.

Raleigh — ROBERT LOUIS STEVENSON. By WALTER RALEIGH, Professor of English Literature at Liverpool University College. Second edition, crown 8vo., cloth 2s. 6d.

Ransome — THE BATTLES OF FREDERICK THE GREAT. (See page 16.)

Rochefort — ADVENTURES OF MY LIFE. (See page 1.)

Santley — STUDENT AND SINGER. The Reminiscences of CHARLES SANTLEY. New Edition, crown 8vo., cloth, 6s.

Sherard — ALPHONSE DAUDET: a Biography and Critical Study. By R. H. SHERARD, Editor of 'The Memoirs of Baron Meneval,' etc. With Illustrations. Demy 8vo., 15s.

'An excellent piece of journalism, the kind of personal journalism which is both entertaining and useful.'—*Saturday Review.*

Tollemache — BENJAMIN JOWETT, Master of Balliol. A Personal Memoir. By the Hon. LIONEL TOLLEMACHE, Author of 'Safe Studies,' etc. Third Edition, with portrait, crown 8vo., cloth, 3s. 6d.

'A very remarkable success.'—*St. James's Gazette.*

Twining — RECOLLECTIONS OF LIFE AND WORK. Being the Autobiography of LOUISA TWINING. One vol., 8vo., cloth, 15s.

LITERATURE AND BELLES LETTRES.

Bell — DIANA'S LOOKING GLASS, and other Poems. By the Rev. CANON BELL, D.D., Rector of Cheltenham, and Hon. Canon of Carlisle. Crown 8vo., cloth, 5s. net.

Bell — POEMS OLD AND NEW. By the Rev. CANON BELL, D.D. Cloth, 7s. 6d.

Bell — THE NAME ABOVE EVERY NAME, and other Sermons. By the Rev. CANON BELL, D.D. Cloth, 5s.

Bell — KLEINES HAUSTHEATER. Fifteen Little Plays in German for Children. By Mrs. HUGH BELL. Crown 8vo., cloth, 2s.

Most of these little plays have been adapted from the author's 'Petit Théâtre,' the remainder from a little book of English plays by the same writer entitled 'Nursery Comedies.'

Butler — SELECT ESSAYS OF SAINTE BEUVE. Chiefly bearing on English Literature. Translated by A. J. BUTLER, Translator of 'The Memoirs of Baron Marbot.' One vol., 8vo., cloth, 5s. net.

Collingwood—THORSTEIN OF THE MERE: a Saga of the Northmen in Lakeland. By W. G. COLLINGWOOD, Author of 'Life of John Ruskin,' etc. With Illustrations. Price 10s. 6d.

Collingwood—THE BONDWOMAN. (*See page* 14.)

Collins—A TREASURY OF MINOR BRITISH POETRY. (*See p.* 8.)

Cook—THE DEFENSE OF POESY, otherwise known as An APOLOGY FOR POETRY. By Sir PHILIP SIDNEY. Edited by A. S. COOK, Professor of English Literature in Yale University. Crown 8vo., cloth, 4s. 6d.

Cook—A DEFENCE OF POETRY. By PERCY BYSSHE SHELLEY. Edited, with notes and introduction, by Professor A. S. COOK. Crown 8vo., cloth, 2s. 6d.

Davidson—A HANDBOOK TO DANTE. By GIOVANNI A. SCARTAZZINI. Translated from the Italian, with notes and additions, by THOMAS DAVIDSON, M.A. Crown 8vo., cloth, 6s.

Ellacombe—THE PLANT-LORE AND GARDEN-CRAFT OF SHAKESPEARE. (*See page* 7.)

Fleming—THE ART OF READING AND SPEAKING. By the Rev. Canon FLEMING, Vicar of St. Michael's, Chester Square. Second edition. Cloth, 3s. 6d.

Garnett—SELECTIONS IN ENGLISH PROSE FROM ELIZABETH TO VICTORIA. Chosen and arranged by JAMES M. GARNETT, M.A., LL.D. 700 pages, large crown 8vo., cloth, 7s. 6d.

Goschen—THE CULTIVATION AND USE OF IMAGINATION. By the Right Hon. GEORGE JOACHIM GOSCHEN. Crown 8vo., cloth, 2s. 6d.

GREAT PUBLIC SCHOOLS. (*See page* 16.)

Gummere—OLD ENGLISH BALLADS. Selected and Edited by FRANCIS B. GUMMERE, Professor of English in Haverford College, U.S.A. Crown 8vo., cloth, 5s. 6d.

Harrison—STUDIES IN EARLY VICTORIAN LITERATURE. By FREDERIC HARRISON, M.A., Author of 'The Choice of Books,' etc. Demy 8vo., cloth, 10s. 6d.

'Let us say at once that this is a charming book. One lays it down not only delighted by its literary excellence, but with something like affection for the person who wrote it.'—*Spectator*.

Hartshorne—OLD ENGLISH GLASSES. (*See page* 8.)

Hole—ADDRESSES TO WORKING MEN FROM PULPIT AND PLATFORM. By the Very Rev. S. REYNOLDS HOLE, Dean of Rochester. One vol., crown 8vo., 6s.

'A book of great interest and great excellence.'—*Scotsman*.

Hudson—THE LIFE, ART, AND CHARACTERS OF SHAKESPEARE. By HENRY N. HUDSON, LL.D., Editor of *The Harvard Shakespeare*, etc. 969 pages, in two vols., large crown 8vo., cloth, 21s.

Hudson.—**THE HARVARD EDITION OF SHAKESPEARE'S COMPLETE WORKS.** A fine Library Edition. By HENRY N. HUDSON, LL.D., Author of 'The Life, Art, and Characters of Shakespeare.' In twenty volumes, large crown 8vo., cloth, £6. Also in ten volumes, £5.

Hunt—Leigh Hunt's **'WHAT IS POETRY?'** An Answer to the Question, 'What is Poetry?' including Remarks on Versification. By LEIGH HUNT. Edited, with notes, by Professor A. S. COOK. Crown 8vo., cloth, 2s. 6d.

Lang—**LAMB'S ADVENTURES OF ULYSSES.** With an Introduction by ANDREW LANG. Square 8vo., cloth, 1s. 6d. Also the Prize Edition, gilt edges, 2s.

Maud—**WAGNER'S HEROES** and **WAGNER'S HEROINES.** (*See page* 12.)

Morrison—**LIFE'S PRESCRIPTION, In Seven Doses.** By D. MACLAREN MORRISON. Crown 8vo., parchment, 1s. 6d.

Pearson—**THE CHANCES OF DEATH.** (*See page* 6.)

Rodd—**FEDA, and other Poems, chiefly Lyrical.** By RENNELL RODD, C.M.G. With etched Frontispiece. Crown 8vo., cloth, 6s.

Rodd—**THE UNKNOWN MADONNA, and other Poems.** By RENNELL RODD, C.M.G. With Frontispiece by RICHMOND. Crown 8vo., cloth, 5s.

Rodd—**THE VIOLET CROWN, AND SONGS OF ENGLAND.** By RENNELL RODD, C.M.G. With Photogravure Frontispiece. Crown 8vo., cloth, 5s.

Rodd—**THE CUSTOMS AND LORE OF MODERN GREECE.** By RENNELL RODD, C.M.G. With 7 full-page Illustrations. 8vo., cloth, 8s. 6d.

Schelling—**A BOOK OF ELIZABETHAN LYRICS.** Selected and Edited by F. E. SCHELLING, Professor of English Literature in the University of Pennsylvania. Crown 8vo., cloth, 5s. 6d.

Schelling—**BEN JONSON'S TIMBER.** Edited by Professor F. E. SCHELLING. Crown 8vo., cloth, 4s.

Sichel—**THE STORY OF TWO SALONS.** Madame de Beaumont and the Suards. By EDITH SICHEL, Author of 'Worthington Junior.' With Illustrations. Large crown 8vo., cloth, 10s. 6d.

'A very good book indeed.'—*Saturday Review.*

Thayer—**THE BEST ELIZABETHAN PLAYS.** Edited, with an Introduction, by WILLIAM R. THAYER. 612 pages, large crown 8vo., cloth, 7s. 6d.

WINCHESTER COLLEGE. Illustrated by HERBERT MARSHALL. With Contributions in Prose and Verse by OLD WYKEHAMISTS. Demy 4to., cloth, 25s. net. A few copies of the first edition, limited to 1,000 copies, are still to be had.

FICTION.

SIX SHILLING NOVELS.

A RELUCTANT EVANGELIST. By ALICE SPINNER. (*See page* 13.)

INTERLUDES. By MAUD OXENDEN. (*See page* 13.)

A MASK AND A MARTYR. By E. LIVINGSTON PRESCOTT. (*See page* 14.)

HADJIRA. By ADULET. (*See page* 14.)

TOMMY ATKINS. A Tale of the Ranks. By ROBERT BLATCHFORD, Author of 'A Son of the Forge,' 'Merrie England,' etc. Second Edition. Crown 8vo., cloth, 6s.

ORMISDAL. A Novel. By the EARL OF DUNMORE, F.R.G.S., Author of 'The Pamirs.' One vol., crown 8vo., cloth, 6s.

THE TUTOR'S SECRET. (Le Secret du Précepteur.) Translated from the French of VICTOR CHERBULIEZ. One vol., crown 8vo., cloth, 6s.

THREE SHILLING AND SIXPENNY NOVELS.

THE BAYONET THAT CAME HOME. By N. WYNNE WILLIAMS. (*See page* 13.)

ON THE THRESHOLD. By ISABELLA O. FORD, Author of 'Miss Blake of Monkshalton.' One vol., crown 8vo., 3s. 6d.

THE MYSTERY OF THE RUE SOLY. Translated by Lady KNUTSFORD from the French of H. DE BALZAC. Crown 8vo., cloth, 3s. 6d.

DAVE'S SWEETHEART. By MARY GAUNT. One vol., 8vo., cloth, 3s. 6d.

MISTHER O'RYAN. An Incident in the History of a Nation. By EDWARD MCNULTY. Small 8vo., elegantly bound, 3s. 6d.

'An extremely well-written satire of the possibilities of blarney and brag.'—*Pall Mall Gazette.*

STEPHEN REMARX. The Story of a Venture in Ethics. By the Hon. and Rev. JAMES ADDERLEY, formerly Head of the Oxford House and Christ Church Mission, Bethnal Green. Twenty-Second Thousand. Small 8vo., elegantly bound, 3s. 6d. Also in paper cover, 1s.

'Let us express our thankfulness at encountering for once in a way an author who can amuse us.'—*Saturday Review.*

HALF-A-CROWN NOVELS.

WORTH WHILE. By F. F. MONTRÉSOR. (*See page* 13.)

LOVE-LETTERS OF A WORLDLY WOMAN. By Mrs. W. K. CLIFFORD, Author of 'Aunt Anne,' 'Mrs. Keith's Crime,' etc. One vol., crown 8vo., cloth, 2s. 6d.

'One of the cleverest books that ever a woman wrote.'—*Queen.*

FICTION—Continued.

THAT FIDDLER FELLOW : A Tale of St. Andrews. By HORACE G. HUTCHINSON, Author of 'My Wife's Politics,' 'Golf,' 'Creatures of Circumstance,' etc. Crown 8vo., cloth, 2s. 6d.

TWO SHILLINGS.

GEORGE'S MOTHER. By STEPHEN CRANE. (*See page* 14.)

COUNTRY HOUSE—PASTIMES.

Ellacombe—IN A GLOUCESTERSHIRE GARDEN. By the Rev. H. N. ELLACOMBE, Vicar of Bitton, and Honorary Canon of Bristol, Author of 'Plant Lore and Garden Craft of Shakespeare.' With new illustrations by Major E. B. RICKETTS. Second Edition. Crown 8vo., cloth, 6s.

Hole—A BOOK ABOUT THE GARDEN AND THE GARDENER. By the Very Rev. S. REYNOLDS HOLE, Dean of Rochester. Second edition. Crown 8vo., 6s.

Hole—A BOOK ABOUT ROSES. (*See page* 7.)

Brown—PLEASURABLE POULTRY-KEEPING. By E. BROWN, F.L.S. Fully illustrated. One vol., crown 8vo., cloth, 2s. 6d.

'Mr. Brown has established for himself a unique position in regard to this subject, and what he has to say is not only sound counsel, but is presented in a very readable form.'—*Nottingham Daily Guardian.*

Brown—POULTRY-KEEPING AS AN INDUSTRY FOR FARMERS AND COTTAGERS. By EDWARD BROWN. Fully illustrated. Second edition. Demy 4to., cloth, 6s.

Brown—INDUSTRIAL POULTRY-KEEPING. By EDWARD BROWN. Illustrated. Paper boards, 1s. A small handbook chiefly intended for cottagers and allotment-holders.

Brown—POULTRY FATTENING. By E. BROWN, F.L.S. Fully illustrated. New Edition. Crown 8vo., 1s. 6d.

White—PLEASURABLE BEE-KEEPING. By C. N. WHITE, Lecturer to the County Councils of Huntingdon, Cambridgeshire, etc. Fully illustrated. One vol., crown 8vo., cloth, 2s. 6d.

Gossip—THE CHESS POCKET MANUAL. By G. H. D. GOSSIP. A Pocket Guide, with numerous Specimen Games and Illustrations. Small 8vo., 2s. 6d.

Cunningham—THE DRAUGHTS POCKET MANUAL. By J. G. CUNNINGHAM. An Introduction to the Game in all its branches. Small 8vo., with numerous diagrams, 2s. 6d.

Kenney-Herbert—COMMON-SENSE COOKERY: based on Modern English and Continental Principles, Worked out in Detail. By Colonel A. KENNEY-HERBERT ('Wyvern'). Large crown 8vo., over 500 pp., 7s. 6d.

Kenney-Herbert—FIFTY BREAKFASTS: containing a great variety of New and Simple Recipes for Breakfast Dishes. By Colonel KENNEY-HERBERT ('Wyvern'). Small 8vo., 2s. 6d.

Kenney-Herbert—FIFTY DINNERS. By Colonel KENNEY-HERBERT. Small 8vo., cloth, 2s. 6d.

Kenney-Herbert—FIFTY LUNCHES. By Colonel KENNEY-HERBERT. Small 8vo., cloth, 2s. 6d. (*See page* 12.)

Shorland—CYCLING FOR HEALTH AND PLEASURE. By L. H. PORTER, Author of 'Wheels and Wheeling,' etc. Revised and edited by F. W. SHORLAND, Amateur Champion 1892-93-94. With numerous Illustrations, small 8vo., 2s. 6d.

SCIENCE, PHILOSOPHY, ETC.

Bryan—THE MARK IN EUROPE AND AMERICA. A Review of the Discussion on Early Land Tenure. By ENOCH A. BRYAN, A.M., President of Vincennes University, Indiana. Crown 8vo., cloth, 4s. 6d.

Burgess—POLITICAL SCIENCE AND COMPARATIVE CONSTITUTIONAL LAW. By JOHN W. BURGESS, Ph.D., LL.D., Dean of the University Faculty of Political Science in Columbia College, U.S.A. In two volumes. Demy 8vo., cloth, 25s.

Fawcett—THE RIDDLE OF THE UNIVERSE. Being an Attempt to determine the First Principles of Metaphysics considered as an Inquiry into the Conditions and Import of Consciousness. By EDWARD DOUGLAS FAWCETT. One vol., demy 8vo., 14s.

Hopkins—THE RELIGIONS OF INDIA. (*See page* 6.)

Ladd—LOTZE'S PHILOSOPHICAL OUTLINES. Dictated Portions of the Latest Lectures (at Göttingen and Berlin) of Hermann Lotze. Translated and edited by GEORGE T. LADD, Professor of Philosophy in Yale College. About 180 pages in each volume. Crown 8vo., cloth, 4s. each. Vol. I. Metaphysics. Vol. II. Philosophy of Religion. Vol. III. Practical Philosophy. Vol. IV. Psychology. Vol. V. Æsthetics. Vol. VI. Logic.

THE JOURNAL OF MORPHOLOGY. Edited by C. O. WHITMAN, Professor of Biology in Clark University, U.S.A. Three numbers in a volume of 100 to 150 large 4to. pages, with numerous plates. Single numbers, 17s. 6d.; subscription to the volume of three numbers, 45s. Volumes I. to X. can now be obtained, and the first number of Volume XI. is ready.

Morgan—ANIMAL LIFE AND INTELLIGENCE. By Professor C. LLOYD MORGAN, F.G.S., Principal of University College, Bristol. With 40 Illustrations and a Photo-etched Frontispiece. Second Edition. Demy 8vo., cloth, 16s.

Morgan—HABIT AND INSTINCT. (*See page* 6.)

Morgan—THE SPRINGS OF CONDUCT. By Professor C. LLOYD MORGAN, F.G.S. Cheaper Edition. Large crown 8vo., 3s. 6d.

Morgan—PSYCHOLOGY FOR TEACHERS. By Professor C. LLOYD MORGAN, F.G.S. With a Preface by J. G. FITCH, M.A., LL.D., late one of H.M. Chief Inspectors of Training Colleges. One vol., crown 8vo., cloth, 3s. 6d. net.

Young—A GENERAL ASTRONOMY. By CHARLES A. YOUNG, Professor of Astronomy in the College of New Jersey, Associate of the Royal Astronomical Society, Author of *The Sun*, etc. In one vol., 550 pages, with 250 Illustrations, and supplemented with the necessary tables. Royal 8vo., half morocco, 12s. 6d.

ILLUSTRATED GIFT BOOKS, ETC.

_{*} For further particulars of books under this heading see special Catalogue of Gift Books for Presents and Prizes.

WINCHESTER COLLEGE. Illustrated by HERBERT MARSHALL. With Contributions in Prose and Verse by OLD WYKEHAMISTS. Demy 4to., cloth, 25s. net. A few copies of the first edition, limited to 1,000 copies, are still to be had.

GREAT PUBLIC SCHOOLS. ETON — HARROW — WINCHESTER — RUGBY — WESTMINSTER — MARLBOROUGH — CHELTENHAM — HAILEYBURY — CLIFTON — CHARTERHOUSE. With nearly a Hundred Illustrations by the best artists. Cheaper edition. One vol., large imperial 16mo., handsomely bound, 3s. 6d.

A LITTLE TOUR IN IRELAND. By AN OXONIAN (the Very Rev. S. R. HOLE, Dean of Rochester). With nearly forty Illustrations by JOHN LEECH, including the famous steel Frontispiece of the 'Claddagh.' One vol., large crown 8vo., 6s.

WILD FLOWERS IN ART AND NATURE. By J. C. L. SPARKES, Principal of the National Art Training School, South Kensington, and F. W. BURBIDGE, Curator of the University Botanical Gardens, Dublin. With 21 Full-page Coloured Plates by H. G. MOON. Royal 4to., handsomely bound, gilt edges, 21s.

BOOKS FOR THE YOUNG.

SNOW-SHOES AND SLEDGES. By KIRK MUNROE. Fully illustrated. Crown 8vo., cloth, 5s.

RICK DALE. By KIRK MUNROE. Fully illustrated. Crown 8vo., cloth, 5s.

ERIC THE ARCHER. By MAURICE H. HERVEY. With numerous full-page Illustrations. Handsomely bound, crown 8vo., 5s.

THE FUR SEAL'S TOOTH. By KIRK MUNROE. Fully illustrated. Crown 8vo., cloth, 5s.

HOW DICK AND MOLLY WENT ROUND THE WORLD. By M. H. CORNWALL LEGH. With numerous Illustrations. Fcap. 4to., cloth, 5s.

HOW DICK AND MOLLY SAW ENGLAND. By M. H. CORNWALL LEGH. With numerous Illustrations. Foolscap 4to., 5s.

DR. GILBERT'S DAUGHTERS. By MARGARET HARRIET MATHEWS. Illustrated by CHRIS. HAMMOND. Crown 8vo., cloth, 5s.

THE REEF OF GOLD. By MAURICE H. HERVEY. With numerous full-page Illustrations, handsomely bound. Gilt edges, 5s.

BAREROCK; or, The Island of Pearls. By HENRY NASH. With numerous Illustrations by LANCELOT SPEED. Large crown 8vo., handsomely bound, gilt edges, 5s.

THREE SHILLINGS AND SIXPENCE EACH.

TALES FROM HANS ANDERSEN. With nearly 40 Original Illustrations by E. A. LEMANN. Small 4to., handsomely bound in cloth, 3s. 6d.

THE SNOW QUEEN, and other Tales. By HANS CHRISTIAN ANDERSEN. Beautifully illustrated by Miss E. A. LEMANN. Small 4to., handsomely bound, 3s. 6d.

HUNTERS THREE. By THOMAS W. KNOX, Author of 'The Boy Travellers,' etc. With numerous Illustrations. Crown 8vo., cloth, 3s. 6d.

THE SECRET OF THE DESERT. By E. D. FAWCETT. With numerous full-page Illustrations. Crown 8vo., cloth, 3s. 6d.

JOEL: A BOY OF GALILEE. By ANNIE FELLOWS JOHNSTON. With ten full-page Illustrations. Crown 8vo., cloth, 3s. 6d.

THE MUSHROOM CAVE. By EVELYN RAYMOND. With Illustrations. Crown 8vo., cloth, 3s. 6d.

THE DOUBLE EMPEROR. By W. LAIRD CLOWES, Author of 'The Great Peril,' etc. Illustrated. Crown 8vo., 3s. 6d.

SWALLOWED BY AN EARTHQUAKE. By E. D. FAWCETT. Illustrated. Crown 8vo., 3s. 6d.

HARTMANN THE ANARCHIST; or, The Doom of the Great City. By E. DOUGLAS FAWCETT. With sixteen full-page and numerous smaller Illustrations by F. T. JANE. Crown 8vo., cloth, 3s. 6d.

ANIMAL SKETCHES: a Popular Book of Natural History. By Professor C. LLOYD MORGAN, F.G.S. Crown 8vo., cloth, 3s. 6d.

TWO SHILLINGS AND SIXPENCE EACH.

THE CHILDREN'S HOUR SERIES. (*See page* 15.)

FRIENDS OF THE OLDEN TIME. By ALICE GARDNER, Lecturer in History at Newnham College, Cambridge. Second Edition. Illustrated. Square 8vo., 2s. 6d.

TWO SHILLINGS EACH.

THE CHILDREN'S FAVOURITE SERIES. A Charming Series of Juvenile Books, each plentifully Illustrated, and written in simple language to please young readers. Handsomely bound, and designed to form an attractive and entertaining series of gift-books for presents and prizes. The utmost care has been taken to maintain a thoroughly healthy tone throughout the Series, combined with entertaining and interesting reading. *Price 2s. each; or gilt edges, 2s. 6d.*

My Book of Wonders.
My Book of Travel Stories.
My Book of Adventures.
My Book of the Sea.
My Book of Fables.
Deeds of Gold.
My Book of Heroes.
My Book of Perils.
My Book of Fairy Tales.
My Book of History Tales.
My Story Book of Animals.
Rhymes for You and Me.
My Book of Great Inventions.

PICTURES OF BRITISH WILD ANIMALS.
For Decoration and Object Lessons. An entirely new and beautiful Series of Pictures in Water-Colours, specially painted by Mr. WILLIAM FOSTER.

The following is a list of the Series:

1. Hare.
2. Rabbit. Weasel.
3. Rat. Mouse. Bat.
4. Hedgehog. Snail. Slug. Spider. Worm.
5. Otter.
6. Dormouse and Adder.
7. Deer.
8. Snake and Mole.
9. Bees.
10. Water-rat. Frog. Toad. Newt.
11. Squirrel.
12. Fox.

The size of each plate is about 15½ by 10½ inches. The plates are supplied singly at the following prices: Unmounted, 9d.; mounted on boards, with metal edges, 15½ by 21 inches, 1s. 6d. net.; framed and mounted (unglazed), 3s. net.

PICTURES OF BRITISH FISHES.
For Decoration and Object Lessons. This is an entirely new and very beautiful series, designed by Mr. CHARLES WHYMPER, the well-known artist. Great care has been exercised in selecting representative types of the fish that are found in the rivers and seas of the British Isles, and it is confidently believed that such accurate and faithful pictures of them have never hitherto been exhibited.

The following is a list of the Series:

1. Herring. Sprat.
2. Cod.
3. Haddock. Mackerel.
4. Plaice. Lobster. Crab.
5. Salmon. Trout.
6. Pike. Stickleback. Minnow.
7. Eels.
8. Bream. Perch. Roach.

The size of each plate is about 15½ inches by 10½. The plates are supplied singly at the following prices: unmounted, 9d. net; mounted on boards with metal edges, about 15½ by 21 inches, 1s. 6d. net; framed and mounted (unglazed), 3s. net.

PICTURES OF BIRDS.
For the Decoration of Home and Schools.

List of Coloured Plates:

Blue Tit.
Thrush.
Chaffinch.
Bullfinch.
Swallow.
Yellowhammer.
Skylark.
Blackbird.
Sparrow.
Waterwagtail.
Starling.
Robin.

The Pictures can be supplied in the following styles: Unmounted, 6d. per Plate; Set of 12, in envelope, 6s. Mounted, Single Plates, mounted on boards, 12 by 15 inches, eyeletted and strung, 1s. each; Sets of 3 Plates, mounted together on boards, 34 by 15 inches, eyeletted and strung, 2s. 6d. each. Framed, Single Plates, mounted and framed, 2s. each; Sets of 3 Plates, mounted and framed together, 4s. 6d. each.

All the above prices are net.

WILD FLOWER PICTURES.
For the Decoration of Home and School. Twenty-one Beautifully-coloured Plates, issued in the same style and at the same prices as the 'Birds.'

Honeysuckle.
Forget-me-Not.
Convolvulus.
Hawthorn.
Lychnis.
Harebell.
Daisy.
Poppy.
Cornflower.
Iris.
Rose.
Buttercup.
Heather.
Water-Lily.
Foxglove.
Cowslip.
Bluebell.
Primrose.
Violet.
Daffodil.
Anemone.

THE INTERNATIONAL EDUCATION SERIES.

THE INTELLECTUAL AND MORAL DEVELOPMENT OF THE CHILD. By GABRIEL CAMPAYRE.
TEACHING THE LANGUAGE-ARTS. Speech, Reading, Composition. By B. A. HINSDALE, Ph.D., LL.D., University of Michigan. 4s. 6d.
THE PSYCHOLOGY OF THE NUMBER, AND ITS APPLICATION TO METHODS OF TEACHING ARITHMETIC. By JAMES A. MCLELLAN, A.M., and JOHN DEWEY, Ph.D. 6s.
THE SONGS AND MUSIC OF FROEBEL'S MOTHER PLAY. By SUSAN E. BLOW. 6s.
THE MOTTOES AND COMMENTARIES OF FROEBEL'S MOTHER PLAY. By SUSAN E. BLOW and H. R. ELIOT. 6s.
HOW TO STUDY AND TEACH HISTORY. By B. A. HINSDALE, Ph.D., LL.D. 6s.
FROEBEL'S PEDAGOGICS OF THE KINDERGARTEN; or, His Ideas concerning the Play and Playthings of the Child. Translated by J. JARVIS. Crown 8vo., cloth, 6s.
THE EDUCATION OF THE GREEK PEOPLE, AND ITS INFLUENCE ON CIVILIZATION. By THOMAS DAVIDSON. Crown 8vo., cloth, 6s.
SYSTEMATIC SCIENCE TEACHING. By EDWARD G. HOWE. Crown 8vo., cloth, 6s.
EVOLUTION OF THE PUBLIC SCHOOL SYSTEM IN MASSACHUSETTS. By GEORGE H. MARTIN. Crown 8vo., cloth, 6s.
THE INFANT MIND; or, Mental Development in the Child. Translated from the German of W. PREYER, Professor of Physiology in the University of Jena. Crown 8vo., cloth, 4s. 6d.
ENGLISH EDUCATION IN THE ELEMENTARY AND SECONDARY SCHOOLS. By ISAAC SHARPLESS, LL.D., President of Haverford College, U.S.A. Crown 8vo., cloth, 4s. 6d.
EMILE; or, A Treatise on Education. By JEAN JACQUES ROUSSEAU. Translated and Edited by W. H. PAYNE, Ph.D., LL.D., President of the Peabody Normal College, U.S.A. Crown 8vo., cloth, 6s.
EDUCATION FROM A NATIONAL STANDPOINT. Translated from the French of ALFRED FOUILLÉE by W. J. GREENSTREET, M.A., Head Master of the Marling School, Stroud. Crown 8vo., cloth, 7s. 6d.
THE MORAL INSTRUCTION OF CHILDREN. By FELIX ADLER, President of the Ethical Society of New York. Crown 8vo., cloth, 6s.
THE PHILOSOPHY OF EDUCATION. By JOHANN KARL ROSENKRANZ, Doctor of Theology and Professor of Philosophy at Königsberg. (Translated.) Crown 8vo., cloth, 6s.
A HISTORY OF EDUCATION. By Professor F. V. N. PAINTER. 6s.
THE VENTILATION AND WARMING OF SCHOOL BUILDINGS. With Plans and Diagrams. By GILBERT B. MORRISON. Crown 8vo., 4s. 6d.
FROEBEL'S 'EDUCATION OF MAN.' Translated by W. N. HAILMAN. Crown 8vo., 6s.
ELEMENTARY PSYCHOLOGY AND EDUCATION. By Dr. J. BALDWIN. Illustrated, crown 8vo., 6s.
THE SENSES AND THE WILL. Forming Part I. of 'The Mind of the Child.' By W. PREYER, Professor of Physiology in the University of Jena. (Translated.) Crown 8vo., 6s.
THE DEVELOPMENT OF THE INTELLECT. Forming Part II. of 'The Mind of the Child.' By Professor W. PREYER. (Translated.) Crown 8vo., 6s.
HOW TO STUDY GEOGRAPHY. By FRANCIS W. PARKER. 6s.
A HISTORY OF EDUCATION IN THE UNITED STATES. By RICHARD A. BOONE, Professor of Pedagogy in Indiana University. Crown 8vo., 6s.
EUROPEAN SCHOOLS; or, What I Saw in the Schools of Germany, France, Austria, and Switzerland. By L. R. KLEMM, Ph.D. With numerous Illustrations. Crown 8vo., 8s. 6d.
PRACTICAL HINTS FOR TEACHERS. By GEORGE HOWLAND, Superintendent of the Chicago Schools. Crown 8vo., 4s. 6d.
SCHOOL SUPERVISION. By J. L. PICKARD. 4s. 6d.
HIGHER EDUCATION OF WOMEN IN EUROPE. By HELENE LANGE. 4s. 6d.
HERBART'S TEXT-BOOK IN PSYCHOLOGY. By M. K. SMITH. 4s. 6d.
PSYCHOLOGY APPLIED TO THE ART OF TEACHING. By Dr. J. BALDWIN. 6s.

PERIODICALS.

THE NATIONAL REVIEW.

Edited by L. J. MAXSE.

Price Half-a-crown monthly.

THE PHILOSOPHICAL REVIEW.

Edited by J. G. SCHURMAN,
Professor of Philosophy in Cornell University, U.S.A.

Six Numbers a year. Single Numbers, 3s. 6d.; Annual Subscription, 14s. post free. The first number was issued in January, 1892.

The Review ranges over the whole field of Philosophy; the articles are signed, and the contributors include the names of the foremost philosophical teachers and writers of America, and many of those of England and the Continent of Europe.

THE JOURNAL OF MORPHOLOGY:

A Journal of Animal Morphology, devoted principally to Embryological, Anatomical, and Histological Subjects.

Edited by C. O. WHITMAN, Professor of Biology in Clark University, U.S.A.

Three numbers in a volume of 100 to 150 large 4to. pages, with numerous plates. Single numbers, 17s. 6d.; subscription to the volume of three numbers, 45s. Volumes I. to X. can now be obtained, and the first two numbers of Volume XI. are ready.

PUBLICATIONS OF THE INDIA OFFICE AND OF THE GOVERNMENT OF INDIA.

Mr. EDWARD ARNOLD, having been appointed Publisher to the Secretary of State for India in Council, has now on sale the above publications at 37 Bedford Street, Strand, and is prepared to supply full information concerning them on application.

INDIAN GOVERNMENT MAPS.

Any of the Maps in this magnificent series can now be obtained at the shortest notice from Mr. EDWARD ARNOLD, Publisher to the India Office.

Index to Authors.

	PAGE
ADAMS.—The Palace on the Moor	15
ADDERLEY.—Stephen Remarx	23
ALDRICH.—Arctic Alaska	18
AMERICAN GAME FISHES	13
ANIMAL PICTURES	28
BALFOUR.—Twelve Hundred Miles in a Waggon	17
BELL, MRS.—Kleines Haustheater	20
BELL (REV. CANON).—Sermons	20
,, Diana's Looking Glass	20
,, Poems Old and New	20
BENSON.—Men of Might	18
BEYNON.—With Kelly to Chitral	17
BIRD PICTURES	28
BLATCHFORD.—Tommy Atkins	23
BOYLE.—Recollections of the Dean of Salisbury	18
BROWN.—Works on Poultry Keeping	24
BRYAN.—Mark in Europe	25
BULL.—The Cruise of the 'Antarctic'	9
BURBIDGE.—Wild Flowers in Art	26
BURGESS.—Political Science	25
BUTLER.—Select Essays of Sainte Beuve	20
CAWSTON.—The Early Chartered Companies	9
CHERBULIEZ.—The Tutor's Secret	23
CHILDREN'S FAVOURITE SERIES	16-26
CHILDREN'S HOUR SERIES	15
CLIFFORD.—Love-Letters	23
CLOUSTON.—Early English Furniture	8
CLOWES.—Double Emperor	27
COLLINGWOOD.—Thorstein	21
,, The Bondwoman	14
COLLINS.—A Treasury of Minor British Poetry	8
COLVILE.—Land of the Nile Springs	17
COOK.—Sidney's Defense of Poesy	21
,, Shelley's Defence of Poetry	21
COSMOPOLITE.—Sportsman in Ireland	5
CRANE.—George's Mother	14
CUNNINGHAM.—Draughts Manual	24
CUSTANCE.—Riding Recollections	17
DAVIDSON.—Handbook to Dante	21
DUNMORE.—Ornisdal	23

	PAGE
ELLACOMBE. — In a Gloucestershire Garden	24
ELLACOMBE.—The Plant Lore of Shakespeare	7
FAWCETT.—Hartmann the Anarchist	27
FAWCETT.—Riddle of the Universe	25
FAWCETT.—Secret of the Desert	27
,, Swallowed by an Earthquake	27
FIELD.—Master Magnus	15
FISH PICTURES	28
FLEMING.—Art of Reading and Speaking	21
FORD.—On the Threshold	23
FOWLER.—Echoes of Old County Life	18
FRESHFIELD.—Exploration of the Caucasus	10
GARDNER.—Friends of Olden Time	27
GARNETT.—Selections in English Prose	21
GAUNT.—Dave's Sweetheart	23
GORDON.—Persia Revisited	9
GOSCHEN.—Cultivation and Use of the Imagination	21
GOSSIP.—Chess Pocket Manual	24
GREAT PUBLIC SCHOOLS	16, 26
GUMMERE.—Old English Ballads	21
HADJIRA	14
HANS ANDERSEN.—Snow Queen	16
,, Tales from	16
HARE.—Life and Letters of Maria Edgeworth	19
HARRISON.—Early Victorian Literature	21
HARTSHORNE.—Old English Glasses	8
HERVEY.—Eric the Archer	26
,, Reef of Gold	26
HIGGINS. — New Guide to the Pacific Coast	18
HOLE.—Addresses to Working Men	21
HOLE.—Book about Roses	7
,, Book about the Garden	24
,, Little Tour in America	17
,, Little Tour in Ireland	5
,, Memories	19
,, More Memories	19
HOLT.—Fancy Dresses Described	12
HOPKINSON.—Toby's Promise	15

	PAGE
HUDSON.—Life, Art, and Characters of Shakespeare	21
„ Harvard Shakespeare	22
HOPKINS.—Religions of India	6
HUNT.—What is Poetry?	22
HUTCHINSON.—That Fiddler Fellow	24
INDIA OFFICE PUBLICATIONS	30
INTERNATIONAL EDUCATION SERIES	29
JOHNSTON.—Joel; a Boy of Galilee	27
KAY.—Omarah's Yaman	19
KENNEY-HERBERT.—Fifty Breakfasts	24
„ „ Fifty Dinners	25
„ „ Fifty Lunches	12
„ „ Common-sense Cookery	24
KNIGHT-BRUCE.—Memories of Mashonaland	19
KNOX.—Hunters Three	27
KNUTSFORD.—Mystery of the Rue Soly	23
LANG.—Lamb's Adventures of Ulysses	22
LECKY.—Political Value of History	19
LE FANU.—Seventy Years of Irish Life	12
LEFFINGWELL.—Art of Wing-Shooting	18
LEGH.—How Dick and Molly went round the World	26
LEGH.—How Dick and Molly saw England	15, 26
LEGH.—My Dog Plato	15
LOTZE.—Philosophical Outlines	25
MATHEWS.—Dr. Gilbert's Daughters	26
MAUD.—Wagner's Heroes	12
„ Wagner's Heroines	12
MAXWELL.—The Sportsman's Library	4
McNULTY.—Misther O'Ryan	23
MILNER.—England in Egypt	19
„ Arnold Toynbee	19
MONTRESOR.—Worth While	13
MORGAN.—Animal Life	25
„ Animal Sketches	27
„ Habit and Instinct	6
„ Psychology for Teachers	25
„ Springs of Conduct	25
MORPHOLOGY, JOURNAL OF	25
MORRISON.—Life's Prescription	22
MUNROE.—Fur Seal's Tooth	26
„ Rick Dale	15, 26
„ Snow-shoes and Sledges	15, 26
NASH.—Barerock	26
NATIONAL REVIEW	30
OMAN.—History of England	19
OXENDEN.—Interludes	13
PEARSON.—The Chances of Death	6
PHILOSOPHICAL REVIEW	30
PIKE.—Through the Sub-Arctic Forest	3
PILKINGTON.—An Eton Playing-Field	20
POLLOK.—Fifty Years' Reminiscences of India	3
POPE.—Memoirs of Sir John Macdonald	19
PORTAL.—British Mission to Uganda	17
„ My Mission to Abyssinia	17
PRESCOTT.—A Mask and a Martyr	14
PULITZER.—Romance of Prince Eugene	20
RALEIGH.—Robert Louis Stevenson	20
RANSOME.—Battles of Frederick the Great	16
RAYMOND.—Mushroom Cave	27
ROCHEFORT.—The Adventures of My Life	1
RODD.—Works by Rennell Rodd	22
SANTLEY.—Student and Singer	20
SCHELLING.—Elizabethan Lyrics	22
„ Ben Jonson's Timber	22
SHAW.—A Text Book of Nursing	12
SHERARD.—Alphonse Daudet	20
SHIELDS.—Camping and Camp Outfits	18
SHIELDS.—American Book of the Dog	18
SHORLAND.—Cycling for Health and Pleasure	25
SICHEL.—The Story of Two Salons	22
SLATIN.—Fire and Sword in the Sudan	11
SMITH.—The Life of a fox	4
„ Through Unknown African Countries	2
SPINNER.—A Reluctant Evangelist	13
STONE.—In and Beyond the Himalayas	3
TATHAM.—Men of Might	18
THAYER.—Best Elizabethan Plays	22
THOMAS.—Sweden and the Swedes	18
THORNTON.—A Sporting Tour	5
TOLLEMACHE.—Benjamin Jowett	20
TWINING.—Recollections of Life and Work	20
WHITE.—Pleasurable Bee-Keeping	24
WILD FLOWERS IN ART AND NATURE	26
WILD FLOWER PICTURES	28
WILLIAMS.—The Bayonet that came Home	13
WINCHESTER COLLEGE	22, 26
YOUNG.—General Astronomy	25

www.ingramcontent.com/pod-product-compliance
Lightning Source LLC
Chambersburg PA
CBHW032009220426
43664CB00006B/191